A SHARK
NEVER SLEEPS

A **SHARK** NEVER SLEEPS

Wheeling and Dealing with
the NFL's Most Ruthless Agent

DREW ROSENHAUS

with **DON YAEGER** and **JASON ROSENHAUS**

POCKET BOOKS

New York   London   Toronto   Sydney   Tokyo   Singapore

POCKET BOOKS, a division of Simon & Schuster Inc.
1230 Avenue of the Americas, New York, NY 10020

ISBN: 0-671-01525-7

First Pocket Books hardcover printing November 1997

10 9 8 7 6 5 4 3 2 1

DEDICATION

This book was authored in large part by my brother, Jason. As always, Jason came through for me as my partner in helping to make this book something I am tremendously proud of. There are no two brothers who are closer or tougher to match up against. To my competitors who complain about there being a ruthless shark in this business, they're wrong—there are two of them. He has been the best brother and friend I could ever hope for. I am blessed for having a brother like him. Ever since we were infants he has always been right there with me. He has helped me, battled alongside me, and supported me. We have always stuck together through all the ups and downs. Jason is very unselfish and has allowed me to get the credit and fame. He is the unsung hero. We are best friends. We spend all of our time together. We have an uncanny bond. We look alike, dress alike, think alike, talk alike. He is strong in the areas that I am weak. We make an unbeatable team—the real modern-day Batman and Robin.

Every son thinks his mom is the best in the entire world, and I am here to tell you that my mom really is the best. She is one of a kind. There cannot be a more loving or beautiful person in the whole world. My mother, Jill, is the light of my life. She is nothing but pure love and goodness. She is my happiness. She has always put her children's happiness and future before her own. The kind, decent, and good-hearted side of me is the product of my mother's love, strength, and guidance. I would be the bad guy my competitors say I am if not for my mom. Ever since I was a child, my mom has been my world. I am, and always will be, a momma's boy. Every time I see or talk with my mom, she warms my heart and makes me feel like a little kid. No son is closer or loves his mom more. I see my mom almost every day. She has always taken care of me and still takes care of me. I love my mom more than life itself.

No one has a better heart than my father, Robert Rosenhaus. Like his parents, Ruth and Irv, did with him, he put his children's interests before his own. My dad sacrificed so that his sons could be everything he always wanted to be. He's a man's man who introduced me to football, karate, comics, women, etc. I love everything he loved. I thank my father for leading and teaching me about life. From him, I learned the all-important lesson to always, and without exception, do right by my clients. He is a great man of character, integrity, honesty, and kindness.

My sister, Dana, is one of a kind. I am very proud of her. She is a big part of my life. She is a great younger sister who I know will always be there for me whenever I need her. I know that as a law school graduate, she will become the Shark in her own legal waters. My sister is the most likeable and fun person on the planet. My girlfriends have always been fond of her. She has always been very supportive of me and I would do anything for her. No matter how old she gets, I will always look at her as my "little Dane." Although the last name won't be there for long, Dana will always be a Rosenhaus.

—DR

To Denise:
My wife, my love, my friend.
You complete me.

dwy

ACKNOWLEDGMENTS

Jason and I would like to thank the following individuals for making this book possible:

All of my clients. They have allowed me to live out my dreams.

Grandparents Irving and Ruth Rosenhaus and George and Beverly Jackman, cousins Jordan and Brett Rosenhaus, uncles Richard and Howard Rosenhaus and Warren Jackman, Gila Rosenhaus Weiner and Matthew Rosenhaus

Grand Master instructor Young Soo Do and his son, Ricky

Attorneys Glenn Waldman, Moura Sharon, Mark Feluren, Bruce Zimet

Allen Shaklan, Jim Berry, Yolanda Foster, Ed Filomia, Andy Rittor, Joe Zagacki, Pete McCoy and Mike Horvath of WFOR-TV 4 CBS

Friends Krissy Braun, Jim Mandich, Brad Kaplis and Gloria Martinez

Jay Mohr, Tom Cruise, and Cameron Crowe

Bob Kane, Robert E. Howard, Sylvester Stallone, and Bruce Lee, who created my childhood heroes: Batman, Conan the Barbarian, Rocky, and the Bruce Lee Legend

Capital Bank

University of Miami Professor David J. Graf and Dr. Frank Stringfellow, Duke Law School professor John Weistart

Jack Romanos, Emily Bestler, Tris Coburn, Jeff Theis, and Brett Freese of Pocket Books

Mark Levin, Tom DePaso, and Doug Allen of the NFLPA

Don Shula and all the great Miami Dolphin players I loved as a kid

Jim Finks

Sports Illustrated, ESPN, *The Miami Herald,* the Fort Lauderdale *Sun-Sentinel, USA Today, The Sporting News,* and the other media that has given me a forum for my views

All the players, coaches, executives, scouts, owners and media who have made the NFL so great

My English Bulldog, "Chubby," and Japanese Akita, "Ninja"

Don Yaeger and Basil Kane

My competitors

—DR

Our thanks to agent Basil Kane, whose constant encouragement made this possible. And to our editor, Tris Coburn, whose enthusiasm never wavered, even during the dog days that every writer experiences.

Thanks also to the writers and editors at *Sports Illustrated*—Bill Colson, Rob Fleder, Craig Neff, Sonja Steptoe, Mark Godich, and Michael Bamberger—who thought enough of Drew's controversial place in the agent business to put him on the magazine's cover in 1996. That story—and *Sports Illustrated*'s willingness to let me take the idea to book form—put this project in motion.

Finally, I want to thank Jason Rosenhaus, whose love of writing and intimate knowledge of his brother's life shaped—then reshaped—this book several times. You definitely have a novel in you.

—dwy

Foreword

A SHARK NEVER SLEEPS

There's something disarming about Drew Rosenhaus. He is everywhere. Literally and figuratively. Los Angeles, New York, Miami Beach. When in a room, he truly fills it. He demands to be noticed, although he doesn't need to, with matinee-idol good looks, fine-tailored suits, and a lightbulb smile. Drew looks like someone who should be *receiving* a million-dollar deal, not the one in the trenches *negotiating* it. Getting his hands dirty as he reads and rereads every word of every contract, going through the small print with a fine-toothed comb. Getting himself filthy so his clients can shine clean. While doing research for the role of Bob Sugar in *Jerry Maguire,* Cameron Crowe sent me a videotape of Drew Rosenhaus in action, labeled simply FOR YOUR ENJOYMENT. Say what you want about Drew and take him as you will, but know one thing—he's enjoying himself, laughing every day all the way to the bank, with his business cards in a holster located next to his handshake. You'd better be on guard, because this shark truly never sleeps.

—Jay Mohr
7/23/97
"Bob Sugar" of *Jerry Maguire*

1

Déjà vu

Y

OU'RE DREW ROSENHAUS, YATIL'S AGENT, RIGHT?" ONE OF THE
three guys said.

"Yeah, I am. What's up?"

My instincts told me these guys didn't exactly fit in with
the rest of Yatil Green's family and friends. They looked
more like former high school teammates of Yatil's, though
they didn't sound like they'd gone past the eleventh grade.

The guy talking had his initials engraved into one of his
four gold teeth. With all the jewelry he was wearing, he made
Mr. T look subtle. He wore expensive clothes, though they
were worn sloppily. His eyes were red, his baseball hat was
tilted to the side. It wouldn't take Sherlock Holmes to deduce
he and his two partners were shady characters.

He began again, "Yatil's very important to us around
here and . . ."

I held up my hand. I could tell he was about to get into
the same spiel I had heard all day long. He was getting to
the speech about doing a good job for his friend. I respect
that, I really do. But at that moment, I had more important
things to do for my client than spend the energy reassuring
these three that I am the best agent in the business.

1

"I understand where you're coming from. I'm going to do a good job for him," I said as I brushed these guys off.

I had more important things on my mind. Nothing personal, but this was Draft Day, the most important day of the year in any agent's and player's career. This is the day I have waited for—April 20, 1997.

"No, I don't think you understand. Let me explain it to you like this," he answered as I walked past him. Suddenly I heard two distinctive clicks. I knew that sound. I had heard it before.

I turned and saw that the guy had locked and loaded his nine-millimeter Glock pistol. Holding the gun at his side, he stepped toward me.

"Just so you know, I've heard all the stories about agents stealin' money and rippin' guys off. If you f—— him over, we'll bust a cap in your ass . . . quick."

At that point he definitely had my attention, and he knew it. He stared me down in an intimidating manner. He obviously had me at an advantage. My only weapons were my two Motorola star tac phones, my 800 pager, my Toshiba lap top computer, portable printer, palmtop Casio Boss computer, phone book, fax modem, and volumes of NFL contracts and statistics. I was there to do war with NFL executives, not these hoods. Therefore, I decided to take the friendly approach.

"Look, I'm going to bust my ass for Yatil," I said, trying not to look as shaken as I felt. "Save your cap for the poor bastard I'm going to negotiate against. After I'm through having him for lunch, he might want a bullet to put him out of his misery. And speaking of lunch, I brought in the best caterer from Miami for this party. Try the roast beef. It's excellent."

"You're a trip, man," the guy said, giving me a good look at those gold teeth. He and his partners all started laughing like I was their new best friend, a role I preferred to the alternative.

"Seriously, I will do right by Yatil," I said, my heartbeat slowing a little. "He is going to be a big success and make

Lake City proud." I shook their hand gangster-style—a trick learned years earlier in some sticky situations—and told them to let me go to work.

The long road of my nine-year career had led me here to Winfield Park, in Lake City, Florida. It was Yatil's Draft Day party. Hundreds of people from his neighborhood were here to celebrate. The tents were set up, the barbecue grills were lit, and the national media had gathered.

As it seems every year on Draft Day, my career appears to hang in the balance. In a few hours, my client would either be drafted high and be happy with me, or he would slip and blame me for not doing a better job. It is that way year after year. As my brother and partner Jason had put it the day before when he dropped me off at the airport, "The next time I see you, we'll either be big winners or big disappointments."

Jason was right. In the next few hours, Yatil would either go high to the right team, or low to the wrong team. Yatil will either be happy, or he won't. We will keep our client or he'll leave. There are millions of dollars at stake here. And I have little control over what will happen. It is exciting and excruciating at the same time.

This business, the glamorous life of an NFL agent, is that simple and that brutal. If things go well with Yatil, he'll recommend us to his University of Miami teammates next year. I have represented the top player out of UM the last several years, but this day that record could be shattered if things didn't go right. No rookie will sign with me if Yatil spreads the word I've done a bad job.

In this business, there is no second place. It is strictly pass or fail. And failing in the NFL—well, as former Atlanta Falcons Head Coach Jerry Glanville said, the NFL stands for "Not For Long." Someone else coined the phrase, "Not For Losers," which is just as apropos. Agents can have a great year and then practically be out of the business the next. This world is driven by the question: "What have you done for me lately?" And today would tell the tale for me.

After that wake-up call, the rest of the day had to get easier—didn't it? The tent where Yatil and his family would wait for THE CALL was already set. I checked the phone and heard the reassuring dial tone. I also made sure that calls to my home office in Miami Beach were being forwarded to my cell phone here in Lake City. I had all the technology working for me. I was plugged into the Internet to monitor late breaking news. I had a full-blown office right there in that tent. You see, I *am* the agent of the twenty-first century.

It seemed that everything was on track. In the fast and furious world I live in, there aren't many moments to reflect. But with everything seemingly ready, I had one of those moments. I pulled up a chair and relaxed, thinking about what this day could mean. I wonder if I will be happy as hell or heartbroken when the phone rings today. I stare at the phone and realize how much depends on that ring. A smile of irony crosses my face as I remember I've been here before.

FLASHBACK

It was April 21, 1991 and, just like I would be doing six years later, I was staring at a phone, begging, pleading for it to ring. On that day in 1991, it seemed like everything went into slow motion when it was announced the Miami Dolphins had fifteen minutes to make their selection. I had been waiting for this day all my life. It would be my dream come true to have my hometown team, the Miami Dolphins, draft my client, the local star from the University of Miami, Randal Hill, in the first round. Having the Dolphins' first round pick from the University of Miami would guarantee me future success in recruiting next year's Miami Hurricanes and recruiting this year's Miami Dolphins. This would be the ultimate. Ring, phone! . . . Please.

I looked around the private suite in Joe Robbie Stadium. My brother, Jason, and I were dressed in our best suits. It was a small room jammed with about twenty different television and newspaper reporters. We had all been in this room since noon waiting for the phone to ring and a coach to get on the line and say he was going to draft our client. That was five hours ago. As each name was called, I could see the look of disappointment on the faces of Randal's family members. I could hear their unasked questions, "Drew, what's going wrong? Can't you do anything?"

We were hoping Randal would be drafted by the fifteenth pick or so, but that pick had come and gone a few hours earlier. It had been the longest five hours of my life with the cameras glaring on us, and the microphones in my face. Each reporter wanted to know why Randal had not been picked, what the problem was, was there something going on, were there rumors or something we do not know about. Did Randal have some kind of injury concern?

A lot of the teams that we thought were going to draft Randal passed him up. The Cowboys took wide receiver Alvin Harper. The Falcons took wide receiver Mike Pritchard. Wide Receiver Herman Moore went to Detroit. All these receivers were being drafted, and we were wondering when it would be our turn to celebrate. I was burning up the phone lines, desperately trying to reach the next team on the draft board. I was literally begging NFL executives to draft Randal. It was embarrassing and I had to swallow my pride, but I would have done almost anything to get Randal drafted. I couldn't let my client down.

It is hard to reach the NFL executives on Draft Day. They only take calls from other teams to discuss trades. They are busy in meetings and selecting players. They have key decisions to make and they really don't want to hear from pleading agents. However, I kept trying. I called and called. Team executives kept telling me that they liked Randal but had decided to go in another direction.

Now the Dolphins were up with the twenty-third pick. Only five more choices were left in the first round if the Dolphins passed, and none of those five teams needed receivers. If Randal slipped into the second round, that would be devastating. This was it—either the Dolphins will call and make me and my client the happiest guys in the world, or they won't and we will be screwed. Ring, phone! Ring! My career felt like it was teetering. I felt like I was walking on a tightrope with no net below.

I have never been in so much pain. Each minute felt like an hour. The clock was ticking. ESPN was showing the draft clock as it wound down from fifteen to ten minutes for the Dolphins to make their selection. Randal's family was praying; we were all praying. I kept telling myself that I had to stay strong, that they were looking to me for a sign of strength.

As the Dolphins' brain trust conferred, I just kept saying, "They're going to take Randal, believe me they're going to take Randal." I believe in positive thinking and that you can will things into happening.

Thirteen minutes went by and the Dolphins still had not made their draft selection. There was a damn commercial on ESPN, which meant we wouldn't know if Coach Don Shula had already made their pick. I could hear the fans that had gathered at the stadium for a draft party. The fans were chanting "Randal, Randal, Randal!" I could also hear the local media on the TV and radio encouraging the Dolphins to make this pick. I was praying that the Dolphins would hear the fans and media clamoring for them to take Randal.

Only two minutes were left. The time was expiring and we hadn't heard from them yet. I looked at Jason—he wore an expression of consolation as if to say "we'll get em next time." When he saw me looking his way, though, his expression changed, and he said with confidence, "We still have two minutes left." Damn, it looked bad. We both knew it.

"Ring, ring, ring . . ." the phone cries out. I snatched up the phone before the first ring could finish. "Hello," I blurted. It was one of my friends calling to check in. I hung up without even saying good-bye. I was sick. I thought it was the Dolphins. I was just about ready to jump out of that box. I was nauseous. Then . . .

Suddenly, "Ring, ring, ring," the phone cried out again. As I picked up the receiver, my heart stopped, and I prayed to God that Coach Don Shula was on the other end. "Hello," I said.

When I heard the voice on the other end, my heart almost exploded with joy. It was Shula. He said "Drew . . . it's Coach Shula. How is Randal doing? Is he healthy? Has he been working out? Does he want to be a Dolphin? Would you put him on the phone."

I screamed "YES!" to all of his questions and blurted out to Randal, "It's for you . . . it's Don Shula—they are going to take you!!!"

In perhaps the most exhilarating moment of my life, Jason and I jumped up and down rejoicing like kids on a trampoline. I have never gone from pure despair to pure joy like that. The whole place went bonkers. In the stands below us, people were chanting "Randal, Randal, Randal" at the Dolphins draft party; the local radio stations were carrying the moment live.

"Yes!" I screamed again. I hugged Randal. Jason and I hugged each other. I reached out and started hugging reporters! At that moment in my life, I was the ultimate winner. My dream had come true. Not only did I have my FIRST first-round pick, but he was the Dolphins' first-round pick. I was the biggest Dolphin fan in the world as a kid, and without letting on, I still was at that time. My client, my friend, who gave me his trust and put his future in my hands, was going to play for Coach Don Shula on his hometown team, make millions, and catch balls from Dan Marino. I did right by Randal and I felt great. What could be better? Randal was at the Stadium he would playing in for the rest of his career. The draft party hit fever pitch. I was mobbed by the fans and the media. I was so euphoric I could hardly breathe.

That night, all across town the television stations were leading off the sports news with the footage of Jason and I going nuts. If I wasn't so happy, I would have been humiliated for making such a jackass of myself. Some of the video even made it to national TV. The next morning on the front page of the sports section, for everyone to see, was a big picture of me celebrating with Randal. My family and friends were thrilled. I was an overnight sensation. I had become a star in my own right. I loved the feeling. I had shown the entire world I was the man.

In the following months, I started to become a public figure among the circle of die-hard Dolphin fans in the area. I liked being a known man. I liked the respect that came with being on television and in the papers. And the television and papers seemed to like having me in the news because they never stopped calling. I was actually signing autographs for fans.

Now that Randal was drafted it was time to handle his contract negotiations, which became a big story. I wanted the Dolphins to sign Randal to a three-year deal. I wanted three years because I thought that once Randal won a starting job, in three years he could renegotiate and make millions. The Dolphins wanted a four-year deal, so that the fourth year he would be under his original contract, making about five hundred thousand instead of a renegotiated million.

The negotiation became a public standoff. Dolphin management publicly stated that Randal would not get a three-year offer. I publicly stated Randal was going to be a holdout and not play until after he got the three-year deal he wanted. It was a highly controversial negotiation that the public seemed infatuated with. At that early stage of my career, I believed that holding a player out of training camp was the only way to ensure that the team was giving you their best offer. It seemed to be logical at the time to push the team as far as you could. I also mistakenly believed at the time that involving the media in negotiations was a good way to put pressure on the team to sign your client. I thought the media was a valuable forum to state your case against the team.

Well, I was wrong. The only thing that happens when you use the media is that you piss the team off and embarrass them. By making the negotiations public, the team becomes tougher because they don't want to look bad in the public eye. Obviously, I have learned since that holding a player out and using the media in negotiations is not a good idea.

After Randal missed a couple of weeks, public opinion turned negative toward me. Suddenly it wasn't so much fun being in the spotlight. I was also holding my first Dolphin veteran client, J. B. Brown, out of training camp. J.B. was entering his third season in the NFL after being paid as a twelfth-round draft pick the previous two years. He was going to start for them and we believed he should be paid like a starter. Although the Dolphins had other players holding out who were not my clients, I was the point man for the fans' frustrations and I took the heat. I started to become public enemy number one. I became the scapegoat and the bad guy. It was painful for me and my family. I learned to grow thick skin at that time.

My mom took it particularly hard when the fans and media criticized me. They said I was a young punk holding these players out. But I was strong and took the shots. I adhered to this image they gave me—they called me a shark. I didn't mind being infamous, just as long as my clients and family knew the truth. In fact being infamous was kind of cool. I was like Batman, the Dark Knight.

Finally, after missing part of the preseason, the Dolphins offered Randal the three-year deal we needed and we took it. We won! Randal was ecstatic. I felt like a hero! I got Randal the three-year deal we wanted, he got his big signing bonus, and we were happy as could be. All the television and newspaper coverage regarding the negotiations was exactly as I wanted it to be. We had shown a lot of guts by holding out. After Randal missed three preseason games, the Dolphins just decided to cave in as it had become a war of attrition. By holding out, we had won the contract we battled for.

But the holdout had its price. Coach Shula was annoyed and became disenchanted with Randal. Three weeks later, after the first regular season game against the Buffalo Bills, Randal and I were driving toward my office. Randal had just closed on a beautiful country club condominium in North Miami Beach when my cellular phone began ringing.

Once again it was Don Shula on the line. I wasn't expecting his call, which told me that something must be wrong. He asked to speak to Randal. I handed Randal the phone.

"Randal, are you sitting down?"

"Yeah, coach, I'm just driving with Drew."

"Well, I have some tough news for you. You have been traded to the Phoenix Cardinals. Put Drew back on the line so that I can give him the details."

Stunned, Randal handed me the phone. I head Coach Shula's words, but I couldn't comprehend them. They couldn't have been real. This couldn't be happening. Don Shula doesn't make crazy trades like this. Don Shula doesn't trade a first-round pick at the start of his rookie year.

It turned out that the Dolphins still had receivers Mark Duper and Mark Clayton; they liked James Pruitt and the other rookie draft pick Scott Miller. They didn't really need a receiver, and Randal's holdout caused him to be behind the other guys in conditioning and learning the play book. He was not ready to start yet. Phoenix was a team that was going nowhere, so the pick they offered the Dolphins would almost assuredly be a high one. The Dolphins thought it was a good move.

The trade was devastating to Randal and his family. But he was very strong and took the news well under the circumstances. His attitude was that he wanted to play where he was wanted and that he was still going to make a nice salary.

Randal showed real character and maturity in dealing with the trade. I was so disappointed to lose Randal as a Dolphin that I swore I would make up for it by signing all the receivers he had been competing with: Duper, Clayton, Miller, Tony Martin—a feat I ultimately accomplished. I also vowed that someday I'd find a way to get Randal back to the Dolphins.

This had been a roller-coaster ride. First the ups and downs on Draft Day, then the contract negotiations, now the trade. For Randal's sake and my career's sake, I acted like I was happy about it. I painted a positive picture to the media and tried to persuade Randal as I got on the flight with him to Phoenix that this was going to be exciting and he would be better off.

I told myself that this was best for Randal, but I knew it

wasn't. I was crushed and humiliated. The public that chastised me for holding Randal out now rejoiced at my defeat and embarrassment. The media blamed me for Randal's trade. I was the scapegoat. Randal was the only guy outside of my family that seemed to be on my side. He knew that I worked day and night doing what I thought was right.

The Cardinals had called the Dolphins about Randal because they needed a speed receiver more than the Dolphins did. When the Cardinals offered a first-round pick, Shula let Randal go. Because of the holdout, Shula never developed any loyalty to Randal and didn't hesitate to trade him.

The day after the trade I was on the front page of the sports section again, except this time I wasn't celebrating with Randal. We were pictured getting on a plane to Arizona. Those two cover pictures told the story. We held out, got a great contract, but then Randal was traded. The flight to Arizona was the worst of my life. We left our ideal scenario of playing for the Dolphins behind and were on our way to a nondescript, average team.

Meanwhile, every agent had called Randal and his family to bad mouth me and demand that I be fired. In everyone's mind I was finished. I was dead and buried. My competition, despising me, basked in my defeat. A client of lesser character and loyalty probably would have fired me.

I gave it my best effort to seem positive and happy while I was with Randal, helping him get acclimated to life in Tempe, Arizona. But the minute I got on the plane coming home I had nothing left. I had won the battle over Randal's negotiations but lost the war. J.B. had a long holdout but he got paid in the end. That was the only thing I could point to as a success. The reality was my dream had been taken away from me and everyone knew it. It would have been easy to feel sorry for myself.

That first night back in Miami after taking Randal to Phoenix, I was watching TV late at night when some documentary on the great white shark came on. Exhausted, I fell asleep in the middle of it. As I nodded off, I heard the narrator say, "The only predator the great white shark has is sleep."

That stuck with me as I thought about it. The shark is the perfect predator—it moves fast, powerfully, stealthily, and ferociously. I guess it stuck with me because so many people during Randal's negotiations had referred to me as a shark.

Half asleep, I started dwelling on the analogy. It began to appeal to me and woke me up.

"Yeah . . ." I thought to myself, "there are other creatures of the deep that will get the best of the shark every so often; but the fierce and hungry battle-tested shark will win most of the time." Why? Because adversity makes the shark stronger and the tuna weaker. I saw the nature of my profession—the sports agent business. If I allow myself to fall asleep, I'll sink. As soon as that happens, I'll be devoured by another shark. Even though I keep swimming, I know more adversity will come. I know that this won't be the last time I get defeated and lose. But I also know that whether I am the shark who comes back to feast another day or the tuna who has its guts ripped apart, it is up to me. I knew which choice I would make. That's the mark of a shark. Never stops. Never gets satisfied. Never gets content. Always pushing himself. Always looking out for his clients.

Suddenly I wasn't sleepy anymore. My mourning period for Randal's trade was over. It was time to press on. I survived that adversity by realizing that what happened with Randal was in the past. I can't control that. What I can control is where I go next.

Where I went next was to become one of the most successful agents in the National Football League today. This is the story of what I had to do—and who I did it to—in order to get there!

2

A Young Fin Fanatic

IN 1966, I WAS BORN—TO BE AN AGENT. I WAS NURTURED TO dominate in this business from the day my parents brought me home from the hospital. That's because from my crib days, I was taught to love football more than life. My parents did an exceptional job of instilling in me the values of hard work, dedication, discipline, and the Dolphins. As a kid I grew up in a very close-knit family with my brother, Jason, who is about two years younger than me, and my sister, Dana, who is four years younger. I was so attached to my mom that she had to ride on the school bus with me and wait for me outside my kindergarten class every day or else I was too scared to go.

My dad saw what a mama's boy I was and wanted to make me into some kind of cool superhero. He introduced me to Tae Kwon Do karate, comics, and the Miami Dolphins. As I grew up, karate, Batman, and the Dolphins were my passions. Growing up, Jason and I read thousands of comics. My favorite was Batman. From the time I was three, I loved Batman. The reason I liked Batman so much was because he was a superhero who didn't have any super powers, yet he still got the job done. Batman was an ordinary man who was a superhero due to his training and dedication. I wanted to be like Batman, so I worked very hard in school and at karate. I also wanted to be like my dad. I always idolized him. He was the greatest father a kid could have. He sacrificed to give us everything he could so that we could have the best childhood imaginable. He always encouraged us to be thinkers and to plan ahead. So karate and school were my focus and the Dolphins were my fun.

The Dolphins and Miami became MY team and MY city thanks to my family. My father, who attended the University of Miami, fell in love with South Florida during his college days and moved us to Miami in 1969. In the early seventies, the Dolphins were unbeatable. They were also the only professional sports team in Miami at that time. Dad was a fanatic, he lived and died for the Dolphins. Needless to say, I grew up in an environment where everybody loved the Dolphins, and my surroundings molded me.

As early as the 1973–74 season, I was an immense Dolphin fan. My dad would take me to every game. He'd take me to the practices and then he made friends with the players— just became buddies with them and they started coming over to our house.

It all started when dad, Robert Rosenhaus, met a Dolphin player named Benny Malone. They were playing tennis at a local country club, the Jockey Club, when my dad struck up a conversation. Benny was a rookie at the time. He had no friends or family in South Florida and my dad was a fun-loving guy. Dad invited him over to the house to have something to eat. Then, Benny came over a number of times. He enjoyed spending time with my dad. We became his family away from home.

Soon we "adopted" lots of players and became friends with them. I grew up in a house where once a week a Dolphin player would come over. I was a little guy, six, seven, eight years old, and I was very comfortable with these guys— even at that age when most kids would be scared and run from them. I'd sit down and ask these guys football questions. I remember asking a wide receiver with the Dolphins at the time, Duriel Harris, about the New York Jet corner-

14

backs he was going up against, Johnny Lynn and Bobby Humphries. Impressed with my knowledge, he asked, "Drew, how do you know who all these guys are?"

How could I not? I was infatuated with the Dolphins. Like a lot of South Florida kids, the Dolphins were my LIFE. This was my version of heaven. These guys were sitting in my living room, comfortable talking football with a child. Here I was, this kid born in South Orange, New Jersey, who had started to learn the way that these professional players think and what they liked to talk about.

I asked about what they talked about in the huddles, what the tendencies of a particular opponent were, or what their times were in the forty-yard dash and they liked answering me. Soon I wasn't asking questions, I was offering answers. I knew every statistic about every player or team. I developed a photographic memory for anything pertaining to the NFL. At a young age, I studied stats and games like a pro scout so that I could impress these players with my knowledge of the NFL. I got tremendous satisfaction out of being able to talk football with them. I would wake up early in the morning and race to the newsstands to buy everything and anything having to do with the Dolphins and the NFL. As a youth, I was reading more magazines and newspapers than most adults.

People knew I loved the Dolphins because there wasn't a day that went by when I wasn't wearing some kind of Dolphin clothing or paraphernalia. Because I loved the Dolphins, I was a hard-core Draftnik when it came to the NFL draft. I ditched school to watch the draft the first time it was on ESPN by telling my mom I was sick. I'd come up with a new excuse every year. I remember when we first were wired for cable TV I skipped school for a week and pretended I had pneumonia so that I could watch ESPN. It was so novel, a twenty-four-hour network devoted exclusively to sports. As a kid I subscribed to the *Sporting News, Pro Football Weekly, The Football News, Dolphin Digest,* and *Sports Illustrated.* When everyone else was going out and playing sports and horsing around, I was reading football news and watching it on TV.

Football was so big in our house that I was the only kid

in the neighborhood who was able to watch Monday Night Football until one o'clock in the morning. If it was either eating or football, I'd choose football. I was such a football fanatic I loved just watching practice. The Dolphins trained at St. Thomas University, which was a small college in North Miami located about twenty minutes away from my house. St. Thomas was one of the worst facilities in the NFL. They had splintered bleachers, no concession stands, and no shade from the summer's sweltering heat, when temperatures would routinely rise above 100 degrees. I loved it. I enjoyed those conditions. I wanted the players to see me toughening out the thunder and lightning rainstorms when everyone else hid for cover. I wanted them to see my devotion by showing them I was the only one loyal enough (or crazy enough) to watch them in the rain.

I was fiercely loyal to the team. Jason and I must have gotten into at least a dozen fights with other fans who heck-led the players at practice. I would immediately defend the player that the fan was messing with. Sometimes this would lead to blows. I wanted the players to see me fight in their defense. One time the players cheered after I got into a fight with a real jerk. With all those players watching, believe me, I never lost a fight or an argument. These guys were my heroes and my friends. I would do anything for them.

I'll never forget one day when I was about thirteen, I had cut myself and split my arm open playing catch. My mom wanted to take me to get stitches. I told her, "No way, I don't want to go get stitches yet. I want to show all the Dolphin players how tough I am. I want to show them my wound." I put off going to the hospital and getting stitches so that I could go to the Dolphin camp and parade around with my cut. There I was, this thirteen-year-old kid walking around with this cut, just so I could show off to all the guys. "Hey, look at my cut, look at how tough I am." I'm not sure if they thought I was tough or just plain nuts.

I was also guilty when I was a youngster of keeping a souvenir or two. I remember one day during training camp, Dolphin quarterback David Woodley overthrew a pass that landed across from me by the fence. I couldn't help myself. I wanted that ball. I jumped over the fence, onto the practice field, grabbed the football, jumped back over the fence, and ran into the woods with several Dolphin ball boys trying to catch me. I was a fugitive with a football. They never did catch me, and to this day that football is in my office.

Jason and I still go to Dolphin training camp and watch practice. We often make the comment that we haven't changed that much over the last twenty years. Sometimes I can look at the little kids idolizing the players, and I can see myself as a youngster. To me, there was nothing like going to the football games. If they won, I was the happiest kid in the world. We would scream and yell for our Dolphins to win. Our neighbors all knew if the team did well.

As high as we were after Dolphin victories, the losses were cause for an even lower low. One year, the Dolphins lost a heartbreaker at the last second to the New York Jets. Jason went nuts. He ran out of the house, screaming and yelling all the way down the block. I had to go chase after him. Our neighbors were wondering what happened. One neighbor called and asked if someone in the family had died.

Another time, we were up in New Jersey visiting our grandparents. The Dolphins lost a close playoff game in overtime to the San Diego Chargers. It was a very memorable game. I cried for about four or five hours, and couldn't stop. The Dolphins had two chances in overtime to win the game and missed both field goals—I was sick.

The older I got, the more attached to the Dolphins I became. While some kids grow out of their fanaticism, my love for the Dolphins only grew. When I was in junior high school, if you had asked me, "What's the most important thing in your life?" it was still the Dolphins. I remember my girlfriend at the time used to hate the fact that I would put the Dolphins before her. On a Sunday, if she wanted to hang out, it could only be before or after the Dolphin game. It was me, Jason, my dad, my uncles, Howie and Richie, and my grandfather, Irv. No women allowed. Those were great days when the Dolphins won.

The Dolphins came first because to me, they were real-life superheroes, real-life Batmen. I loved heroes, toys, and comics. I looked up to the Dolphins. I respected them. And the players that I was friendly with liked and respected me as a smart kid. That gave me a feeling of importance. I started to like the way I felt when my heroes liked and respected me. I wanted to earn their respect more and more, and I did so by studying the game.

Most people might have a hard time understanding what it was like growing up as a Dolphin fan in South Florida during the seventies. The Dolphins were all we had. And the fact that they were good—remember they had the only undefeated season in NFL history—made them more than celebrities. They had godlike status. And because I was such a fanatic, I did a lot of things I shouldn't have done. I would sneak into their practices that were closed to the public and watch. When they shut it down after practice and all the players went in the dorms at training camp, I hid. I used to sit at this little pond with the players and fish with them. I remember hanging out right by the rooms and just walking up to guys. I wasn't a card collector, I didn't try to just get their autographs and sell them, which was very common. I got gratification from just being friendly with them and having them be cordial toward me.

One time I got caught, but got out of it, by using a ridiculous line about being punter Reggie Roby's nephew. I guess the guard wasn't all that familiar with the guys on the team and didn't know that Reggie Roby was black. It was just so much fun sneaking in to see those guys because they would bring me into the locker room or to eat with them in the dining room.

The players weren't the only people I cherished having a relationship with. I loved Don Shula. He was someone I looked up to as a winner with class and integrity. Although he had an intimidating look about him, I would still try to approach him and make conversation. He was courteous, but brief. I knew if I could approach Don Shula, I could approach anyone. Years later, when Drew the sports agent would sit across the table from Don Shula, my youth worked against me when I talked negotiations with him. It was very tough. Shula remembered me as a guy who was always around camp, a guy that was a great fan of his. I had an innate loyalty toward him, and I could feel it working against me as I dealt with him. Nevertheless, I never forgot who my loyalty belonged to, and that was to my clients. No matter how much I liked Shula, my absolute allegiance was to my clients. It was a great moment though, when I started dealing with Shula on a professional basis. As I sat in his office, I realized just how far I had traveled: from a star-struck fan, to a business associate and opponent.

But I didn't become Don Shula's adversary by watching football on TV. I became a top agent in a tough business by becoming hungry, disciplined, and focused. I didn't acquire these traits by hanging out with Dolphin players as a kid; I acquired these traits while training in a small Korean karate school. When I was twelve years old, I had a lot of friends in school. I was popular with the girls and the Dolphins were winning. It was a good time. At the time, those three things were all that pretty much mattered and I had them under control. I was a kid—innocent and happy.

But then one day, in a single defining moment, it was all over. There was a bully in my grade I will call Dominick. A girl that Dominick liked snubbed him in favor of me. Embarrassed, Dom told everyone he was going to beat me up after school. I thought I was tough like the Dolphin players and wasn't scared of him. After school, Dom and his friends were waiting for me and my friends. He looked big and mean. "You're mine, Rosenhaus. I'm going to kick your ass," Dom yelled, as he pushed me. I looked at my friends; they were scared and started backing into the circle with the rest of the crowd. I was betrayed. I was scared. I was on my own. Horrible anxiety seeped into my stomach. My hands couldn't quite form a strong fist. My legs felt heavy and movements felt slow, as if I was in a bad dream. I didn't want to get beaten up. I didn't know how to fight. I was also half the size of Dom, who beat kids up every week. I didn't want to be one of those kids. I didn't say anything or do anything. I was frozen with fear. Loving every second of it, Dom called me a coward again. I did nothing. I was still too scared to be angry enough to gain courage. He pushed me and mocked me again, knocking me down this time. I found myself staring at the ground. For some strange reason, despite all that was going on, my eyes focused on a four-leaf clover fighting for space among the thick blades of grass. I stared at it angrily because it wasn't bringing me any luck. I looked up at everyone around me encouraging me to fight. I wanted to be a hero like my Dolphins, but I was too afraid. I lowered my head, yanked that four-leaf clover out, got up amidst the chorus of taunts, and walked away. I went home and told my dad.

Screw John Wayne. Growing up, I always thought my dad was the toughest guy in the world. I idolized him because he got into so many fights in his youth and won them all. And now I had to go home and tell him I was too scared to fight. I broke my dad's heart. But he loved me and gave me encouragement. I was a sensitive kid and my dad made me feel a lot better and then a lot worse. I felt ashamed of not what my dad would think, or my friends or the girls, but of what I thought about myself. My heroes at the time were Rocky Balboa and Batman, two men who endured painful adversity by having heart, courage, and character. I had shown myself I had none. I was a disgrace as a son and a brother. How was my younger brother going to look up to me? When I saw my friends, who weren't friendly anymore; when I saw Dom, who smiled to mock me with satisfaction; and when I saw the girls who laughed at me, I knew that I had lost. I knew that they had beaten me and had gotten the best of me. I hated that self-realization more than I had ever hated anything in my life. I was very unhappy and thought about how young Bruce Wayne grew stronger from adversity to become Batman. I wanted to do the same.

Showing me the way, my dad took Jason and me to a karate school. As we drove up, I realized the school was much smaller, dirtier, and odorous than what I had expected. It was in a bad neighborhood, and every student in there was poor and looked mean. Jason and I were soft, rich kids. I walked in completely intimidated. "Boy!" I heard a man shout in a Korean accent, "Come here." I almost ran home when I saw the man who called me over. He was smiling at me with a smile that was scarier than any look I had ever seen. He had a long, black mane, a face toughened like hard leather, and dark eyes that made him appear immortal. He had my full attention!

"Smack!" A loud noise erupted from a collision between his hand and a dented steel frame in a concrete doorway. I watched in amazement as he smacked his hand into the concrete and steel. His eyes didn't wince and I could see he felt no pain. It was more as if he as hammering a spike into the wall. How could he do that and not break his hand, and why is he doing that, I wondered. My dad pushed Jason and me over to him, and asked Young Soo Do if he could make his sons tough. I suppose he saw that my dad was a good father who wanted his sons to be better than he was. Maybe he saw that he finally had some wealthy students to teach. I don't know. He had only been open for a couple of months and did not have many students. Maybe it was because my dad probably paid him a fortune. Maybe he saw that, although Jason and I were soft like sheep, deep down we had the ferocity of a lion. I don't know what he saw in us, but I know now that he liked us immediately. He extended his hand, looked me in the eyes, and asked in a strong accent, "You want to be tough, boy? You want to learn how to fight?"

"Yes," I answered, as I grabbed his hand.

"Yes sir! Boy," he corrected me in a military tone and bowed. "Then you will become tough and learn to fight."

"Yes sir," I answered affirmatively as I, too, bowed. I shook his hand and it did not feel real. The bottom of his hand was completely callused. His knuckles had bubbles of layered, hardened skin like I had never seen before. Only someone who spends years consistently pounding his hands and knuckles into concrete could develop calluses like that. My dad shook his hand and bowed.

Young Soo Do is an eighth-degree black belt in Tae Kwon

Do. He is from Korea, but for reasons of his own, he went to Vietnam to train American soldiers in hand-to-hand combat. To make extra money, he became a "Rock soldier," which is what the American soldiers called the Korean mercenaries who went out in patrols to kill the Vietcong for money. He was a natural warrior, trained to kill, and was good at it— you could see it in his smile. My dad knew right away that this guy was a one of a kind. Fate was good to us, as we were extremely lucky to find him.

"Make my boys tough," my dad said again with a smile. Having him as my *Sahbumnim* (Korean, for instructor or master) made me feel strong already. I could not wait to put on my uniform and learn how to be like him. Jason and I went almost every weekday we could. As soon as we started learning the basics and were as good as everyone else, *Sahbumnim* got tougher on us. He made us do more than everyone else. Whenever my dad would come to watch, he would make us fight two or three guys instead of just one. He would make us break bricks with our fists and feet. He would smack us with a billy club on the soft bottoms of our feet as we did push-ups on our knuckles. He would snap our necks to the side and make them crack—and he thoroughly enjoyed it. He would throw bone-smashing kicks and punches an inch away from my face—and I loved it. He would make us punch ourselves, and the harder we punched ourselves the more respect we earned from him.

The more punishment and discipline he gave—the more I wanted it. Earning his respect and friendship meant everything to me. The guy was a warrior and he would treat us like warriors. He took us in as mama's boys and made us like the Vietnam soldiers that he hung out with. We idolized him. We wanted to be tough like him. When I broke my foot kicking bricks, I finished class, fighting with the injury. I only wanted him to see that I was tough like he was.

Jason broke his fingers and toes regularly, and he didn't mind because it was another way to show *Sahbumnim* that we were like him. When he commanded me to punch a block of concrete for the first time, I was scared because that was what the real tough guys did. I was scared, but I did not want to allow fear to dictate my actions. I doubted that I had the strength to do it. Then I remembered that a man with Young Soo Do's dimensions could do the things he did. He saw the doubt in me and said, "Strong mind, strong body." Despite the heavy Korean accent and broken English, I knew instantly he was telling me that a man with a strong mind is a man with a strong body. He made me want to feel strong. I looked at the concrete and envisioned my fist smacking through it. I believed. Fear became my force of anger. I yelled like my life was on the line and thrust my fist cleanly through the center of the concrete block. I learned the all-important lesson that in your toughest times and lowest moments you are not supposed to feel sorry for yourself. Those moments of pain and defeat are to be seized and taken advantage of to turn the situation around and achieve your greatest victories.

I learned much more from Young Soo Do than just how to throw a mean jumping, roundhouse kick. One afternoon, while in the middle of a very difficult exercise, he asked in a military tone, "You done?"

"Yes sir. Only ten more to go." He smiled that scary smile again and walked up toward me. I knew I was going to be disciplined for lying. I was exhausted and had about thirty more to go. I did not think he would know the difference. But he knew that I had lied to him. And when I thought that he was mad at me for lying to him, and braced for him to rub his knuckles into my skull and crack my neck, he instead looked me in the eyes and simply said, "Not for me boy, for you." He walked away with a disappointed look. I realized that everything I was doing, I was not doing for him, but for myself. I then knew that to get away with throwing nine kicks instead of ten, to get away with anything and take shortcuts, was to cheat myself. Those six words taught me that anything less than my best effort is a failure in itself.

Throwing punches and kicks for two hours every day may not make me good enough to win a fight at the moment of truth. I pushed myself for two and a half or three hours—as long as I could—whatever my limit was, that is how far I went. And each day I pushed my limit just a little bit farther. All those hours of sweating, bleeding, bruising, and exhausting myself—with every punch, kick, and jump, I swore to myself over and over again that I was looking in the mirror at a winner. I took an oath that no matter what challenge I would face, I would face it with courage and never be a coward again. I accepted that you cannot control fear; but that it is unacceptable to let fear control you. The lessons I learned from studying Tae Kwon Do carried over into all aspects of my life. When everyone else studied just enough to get by, I studied longer and more intensely until I just couldn't do it anymore.

In college, I was the last person out of the library every night. When they shut the lights off on the upper floors, I continued to read with a flashlight and waited until they were about to lock the doors and close the bottom floor hours later. I realized that the brain is a lot like a muscle—the more you use it, the harder you push it, the more efficient and effective it will become. Studying thirteen hours a day in school to get only B pluses or A minuses was not good enough—it was unacceptable. If it meant studying fourteen hours to get As, then so be it—that was what I would do. Confidence and the hard-work ethic became embroiled in my personality. Yes, Young Soo Do made my father's boys tough in a fight, but he also made them tough in the real world, where brains overcome brawn.

The drive I had to be the best in karate and in school carried over into my professional aspirations. I realized I not only wanted to be around stars but I wanted to become a star. It was no longer good enough just to be with a Dolphin player. As I entered high school, I wanted to be someone who stood out so I started working extra hard in karate, in school, in every category of my life. I got very serious and became much more determined and aggressive. I loved the competition in karate: the matches, fights, and tournaments.

The brute force of man against man. I loved the combat and battle of wills. I loved to be a winner. I loved the compliments and adoration I received for my success. My ego was developing and I was hungry. I grew tougher and stronger every day. Karate gave me the confidence and will to take on guys who were much bigger than me or other students who were supposed to be much smarter than me. Through hard work, by the time I was sixteen, I was on top of the world again. Karate gave me the edge I needed to be a winner in all aspects of life. Looking back, I realize karate was one of the most valuable tools in my life. Through karate I had the discipline to be a great student, and I had the mental toughness to fear no one. My dad did a great thing when he took me to Young Soo Do. Then again, my dad was always doing great things for me. I've got to give our dad a lot of credit. He is a man's man, who knew exactly what he wanted for his boys: love football, love women, love your family, stay away from drugs, do karate, and get great grades. We've got to give him and mom a lot of credit. They were excellent parents, always there for us, leading us in the right direction and taking care of our needs so that we could focus and develop.

My first car was a Porsche 944, then I had a Delorean. I had cars like that in high school because my dad would sacrifice the world so that I could be THE MAN. Cars were the thing at that age. They identified you. So my dad, whatever it took, found a way to make me the man.

To me, being the man didn't mean driving a Porsche. It meant being like Young Soo Do. Jason and I looked up to the players that my dad brought around, but our first real role model, in addition to our dad, our uncles, and our grandfathers, was Young Soo Do. He was a great role model. He never smoked, he didn't drink, he had no vices. The man was a disciplined guy, a family guy who worked hard seven days a week. He was as tough as they get. He is a big reason why Jason and I have never worried about all the other agents who have threatened us. Why do you think not one agent has ever put his hands on me? They look at my eyes and know I'll kick the hell out of them and so will Jason. They're nothing compared with what we've gone up against. I have NO FEAR when it comes to this type of stuff. Tae

Kwon Do enabled us to become tough workers. We'll work seven days a week, twenty-four hours a day. Talk about endurance and stamina, we have it because we had to learn it in karate. We had to kick for two hours straight. We had to break ten, fifteen bricks a day with our hands and feet. It was like military training.

People want to know how Jason and I can work so hard, how we can work around the clock. Endless energy is all we know. How can we stay up all night working? How can we stay up all night recruiting? How can we travel from one place to another without getting tired? It's simple. It's called DISCIPLINE. Look at Jason. Look at me. What do you see? In the Rosenhaus brothers, you see THE BEST. You see focus, dedication, and training. We were born to be agents because of our background, with our dad teaching us to love football and winning; and Young Soo Do training us to succeed in whatever we do.

I'll match up, Jason will match up, with any team negotiator we know. We'll outwork anybody, we'll outlast them, we'll outperform them. We'll outsmart them, we'll outprepare them, we'll do whatever it takes. We were trained by the best. A simple Tae Kwon Do expert from South Korea made a gigantic impact on our lives. We made the time, we made the effort, and we believed in him. We bought into his program and our mentor taught us well. We are a reflection of that toughness, discipline, hard work, concentration, focus. NO FEAR. No fear of anything. We'll take anything and anybody on at any time.

It was this lack of fear that allowed me to do things no other agent had ever done before. It was this confidence and hard-work ethic that enabled a kid who grew up watching Mark Duper and Mark Clayton—I'm almost ten years younger than those guys—to one day become their agent. I grew up fast and hard in a short period of time from my days as a young fin fanatic to becoming the agent who represented the legendary Marks Brothers. They had seen me develop and recognized that I was born to be an agent, born to represent the best of the best in the National Football League.

3

Hurricane Drew

DON'T YOU EVER TAKE A BREAK?" SHE ASKED IN A PERturbed manner.

"Yeah," I said after spending almost fourteen hours studying in the UM library that Sunday, "when I get four hours of sleep."

She just shook her head and said out of frustration, "Later."

Good, anything to get rid of her. It's not that she was that bad. In fact, she was cute enough with a nice enough body, but I had an exam the next day and did not feel comfortable yet. She'd be back if I wanted her some other time, but she just wasn't worth an A minus instead of a perfect score. That's probably because she is a B minus chick. A perfect girl, on the other hand, would be somewhat tempting. And the only perfect girl I knew at UM was this Latin girl who I will call Cindy because she looked a lot like Cindy Crawford before I knew who Cindy Crawford was.

The only problem was that Cindy had some super-wealthy fraternity boyfriend named Dave I didn't see eye to eye with. He was the type that sarcastically joked around in class at other people's expense, cheated on exams to pass, and spent his time getting drunk, stoned, and high in no particular order. We had exchanged some words before; but when he

27

wasn't around his fraternity friends, his bark never had any bite. Besides, I had too much to lose to let him get the best of me by getting reprimanded by the school for fighting. On the other hand, he had nothing to lose.

Well, long after everyone else cleared out of the library on campus, I felt ready. I was eager, excited, and anxious to take on this history exam in the morning. I usually felt salty on Sunday nights as I looked forward to the exams on Mondays. Although I was carrying what felt like ten tons of books, I put my books in the car and stopped by the on-campus bar to see if any players were hanging out.

To my surprise, there were no players in the place, but there was Cindy standing alone in the bar. It was early in the semester of my junior year so I had not yet had the chance to make her acquaintance. She seemed agitated and in a bad mood. The perfect opportunity to introduce myself.

"Don't take it so hard," I said as I approached her.

She turned and looked me over, saying, "Maybe I like it that way, excuse me," and then walked away, smiling.

I tried to be cool, but she put a smile on my face. And then that girl from the library walked back in and started talking to me again. I didn't want to stand there alone like a dork so I pretended to be interested in what she had to say.

As I was talking to the girl from the library, I noticed Cindy would glance over at me from time to time while Dave was trying to talk things over. She was dumping him—I could tell, and she was about to trade up. She walked away from him and back over to the bar near where I was. She stood right next to me but had her back turned toward me. It was obvious she wanted me to initiate the conversation. Dave had seen me talking to her and he let his frat buddies know it. They seemed to be staring at me as if I should be intimidated or something.

"College kids," I sighed. I may have been their same age, but I was always older. There was going to be trouble I thought. And then I got another break.

The man himself walks in. Michael Irvin, larger than life, walks into the bar with some teammates and is mobbed. Everyone in the place circles around him. He scored the game's winning touchdown the day before and was an instant celebrity. A tall, muscular, handsome, intelligent, articulate athlete like Michael was born, destined, maybe even cursed, for stardom.

Dave and his friends surrounded Michael and tried to act like he and Michael were cool. And then Michael sees me standing by myself. He rudely walks away from Dave, embarrassing him, and comes over to give me his patented hug. The guy was the best. I had helped him study for a difficult exam last week and he did very well. This was his way of letting me know he appreciated it. And now I felt like a star too as I was kicking it with him and having fun. Cindy was impressed, especially when Michael and I came over to finish the conversation. Michael did nothing but sell me to this girl by telling her how cool and smart I was. This was no small favor and it did not go in vain—much to Dave's chagrin.

It was real cool being friends with these celebrities on campus. It made me the big man on campus. I liked that. I liked it so much that I didn't want my college years to be the peak of my life like so many other people. I wanted to be the big man in the real world, not just on campus for a few years. I wanted to sacrifice and work hard now, so that I would be able to enjoy things later. But the funny thing was that although I paid my dues by working harder than my peers, getting excellent grades, and laying a strong foundation for my future career, I still had a tremendous time doing it.

I went to college to find a career, not to have a good time. We all go to college hoping to find a career. I found mine early. I didn't just love the Dolphins, I was also a huge Hurricane fan. I had never had any doubt that Miami was where I was going to go to college. I wanted to stay close to my family and the teams. I finished high school as an A student and was ready for college.

I entered the University of Miami in 1984, right after the football team won the national Championship. The football program started getting good, and I loved the Hurricanes "Bad-Boy" image and rebel persona. The 'Canes were brash, brave, bold, and cocky. Just like me. I figured I would fit in well at UM.

Many of the Hurricane football players were wild and crazy guys from the hood, and all of them stuck together. They did not hang out much with the other students with whom they had so little in common. I was the exception.

The very first UM football friend I had was Alonzo Highsmith's cousin, Fred Highsmith. Alonzo was the star fullback and probably the most famous player on the team. Fred was a running back and was in my speech class, one of my best classes. The first day I gave a great speech, then I sat down next to this guy and said, "How you doing man? Nice to meet you. I'm Drew Rosenhaus."

He said, "I'm Fred Highsmith."

"Sure, I recognize you," I answered.

"Man, you gave a great speech," he said.

I told him I could help him any time he wanted. We hit it off right away. Then he said, "By the way, my cousin is Alonzo Highsmith. I'm friends with the guys on the team. I'll introduce you. Why don't you come out to practice?"

I went to all of the practices and scrimmages. At the time, I still lived at home with my parents. Fred came over to the house a lot and brought some of the guys with him. These Hurricane players and I started going on my cousin Brett's boat and hanging out at my house. I made an effort to become friendly with the players, and they responded, in part because I was an excellent student. I always spoke up in class and had my papers done on time. They saw me getting As on everything, finishing my test ten minutes early while everyone else was scrambling to get it done.

They also couldn't help but notice that I had the best looking girlfriends, sharp clothes, and stylish cars. I was the prototype UM student. I made good grades, worked out, scored with the women, and loved the football team. Within one month of being on campus, I was the favorite guy of the UM football team.

The players loved me. I was this cool kid who was always

there to help them with their school work, always there to have them over to my house and have a meal, watch a movie, hang out, just be there for them.

That was how it all started for me—I became friendly with one player who was a great friend to me. He introduced me to his friends and I became friendly with them. Because I had earned Fred's respect and friendship, the other guys gave me the same opportunity.

Some people are born to be football players, others entertainers or musicians. Me, I was born to be an agent. I first realized this one night sitting in my dad's house with Michael Irvin. Michael Irvin was THE MAN at the University of Miami. Here was a big, handsome, articulate superstar who the women loved and the NFL loved even more. I was helping Michael study for an exam he had the next day, when he said to me, "Drew, if you were older and had a little bit of experience, I'd hire you to be my agent." That was the ultimate compliment. Michael was a straight shooter and for him to say that meant a lot to me. He made me realize that I could do it. He convinced me that I had what it took. I owed Michael and was grateful to him.

At the time I was a sophomore doing well in college as a broadcast journalism major. I worked harder and got better grades than any other student I saw. I got more women than any of them, too, and I got along great with the players—the ultimate recipe for making a great agent. All this time, as I trained myself to be smarter and tougher than the next guy, I was training myself to be an agent. Like a superhero putting on his uniform for the first time and realizing his calling— that night as I talked with Michael Irvin, I realized my calling. I was born and trained my whole life to become this.

Suddenly everything became clear and made sense. I made up my mind—I was going to become an agent, and no one and nothing was going to stop me.

I had a vision and a strategy. In my second year of college, I realized I had better hurry up and get out of school so I could represent my buddies who said they wanted me to be their agent. I knew that I had to graduate from college before

I could represent them, so I increased my course load. I didn't want a career in broadcast journalism, but I stuck with it as my major so I wouldn't lose credits. I had a minor in history just to impress the law schools. I took summer courses and sometimes studied for eighteen hours a day. I became a regular at the study hall in the school library. It became my home away from home. I had a mission, and I was determined to make it happen no matter how hard I had to work. I loved the challenge and I responded to it with a monumental effort. I worked hard to get great grades and to finish school early. I got straight A's, made the President's Honor Roll, and graduated from college in just three years. I did this while still hanging closely with the players and keeping up with the Dolphins.

But let me tell you, it wasn't all work. Hanging out with the players was a lot of fun. These guys were wild. You can't imagine how much success these players had with women in college. The University of Miami was a nonstop party. The players were heroes on campus and they could have anything they wanted. There were no rules. They took what they wanted. The inmates definitely ran the asylum while I was at the UM in the mideighties. The football players owned the fraternities and sororities. It was out of control. I saw the wild and crazy sex parties with orgies and multiple sex partners. I saw girls have sex with ten different guys in a train. I saw fights and rumbles. I thought that the campus was going to explode in all the chaos. My college experience was memorable to say the least.

Before long, I became close friends with the big-name guys like Michael Irvin, the Blades Brothers, Brett Perriman, Jerome Brown, and more. These players were going to get into the NFL before I could become an agent. I talked to them about the draft and I talked to them about the NFL, and they started talking to me about agents. They would say things like, "Yeah, you know, I got to go see this agent tonight. I got a meeting with him. He better have a good rap."

I started reading up on agents, paying close attention to them in the newspapers, watching them on television. I became infatuated with it. I looked at these agents and saw that they were guys who got paid to do what I already was doing for the players, but just as their friend. These players came to me for advice on a lot of stuff. I was just a smart kid who was straightforward, who liked these guys. The players could look at me and say, "Now here's a guy who's real, he's not phony, he's not just trying to hang around us. He likes us, he's cool."

At the University of Miami, my identity on campus was as the smart, sharp-looking guy who was tight with all the players. Women were attracted to me in part because they wondered what made me so special that the players loved me. I guess the players liked me because I was just cool and natural with them. I cared about them, made them laugh, and helped them out. They trusted me. They believed in me. They respected me. I wasn't in a fraternity and I didn't have many nonathletic friends on campus. I'd go into the Student Union, which was the hangout spot, and I was the one guy in there, the one nonplayer with all those star athletes. They'd walk around campus and yell "Drew" when they saw me, or come over and give me a hug. Players were constantly trying to introduce me to women. I could be seen play-wrestling and joking with these guys every day. I was just accepted. I just had it. I had it naturally.

I would tutor them. I would prepare them for exams. I would help them write papers. I would show them how to write papers, but I wouldn't do homework for guys because that wasn't the answer. I never felt that that was really helping them. I've always felt that the idea is not to do something for somebody but rather to help them do it for themselves. That was my goal with those guys because I knew I wasn't always going to be there. If I did the work for them, it may help them get by one course, but the next class they were going to flunk. So I was a tutor. I did it on my own; I didn't get paid for it. The guys would come over to my house, and we'd have fun watching a movie, going out on the boat, and going to the country club to meet all my parents' friends. It was an identity thing for me. These were my guys, these were my buddies, these were my best friends.

Here I was, friends with all the Dolphins, then I went to UM and became friends with all the Hurricanes. So it was just a natural for me to become an agent. It was a natural extension of what I'd been doing my whole life. Jason and I are doing exactly what we've been doing our entire lives, except we get paid for it now. We read the papers, we study the contracts, we follow the players, we watch everything that has to do with football, we work at our own schedule, and we do what we want to do when we want to do it.

The University of Miami players were as outgoing, personable, colorful a group as you'll ever find. They were characters that were larger than life. They were not only just great football players, these guys had swagger. They had an attitude. I was hanging with the best and I loved it. There will never be another group of renegades and free-spirited souls like the Hurricane teams of the eighties.

I don't think I ever enjoyed hanging out with anyone as much as I enjoyed hanging out with Michael Irvin. This guy was the biggest ladies' man I had ever seen. The guy was legendary. And whenever we went out on the town, I always brought over the hottest women in the club to hang out with us. He was even better on campus. I would be walking on the other side of campus when I would hear him holler at me to come over and meet this girl he was working on for me. Believe me, I didn't need the help, but when Michael Irvin got involved, it was a slam dunk for me. People can say whatever they want about Michael, but no one, and I mean no one, was more fun to hang out with.

I was a guy who was with them for all the right reasons. I was a productive guy, didn't drink, didn't smoke. I was supportive and encouraged them to make the most of their abilities. To this day, I do not drink alcohol. I have never smoked a cigarette. I have never tried marijuana or any type of drug. I was the designated driver on a lot of occasions. I've always been the designated driver. Guys could count on me to be a sane, reliable guy. I'm very consistent. I think that's what those guys liked about me: no matter what day of the week it was, I was always in a good mood. I always had my stuff together. I was always organized and on top of things. I always had a plan and an explanation for things. I always had time for them. Whether it was rainy out or clear, if a guy needed a lift to a class, if a guy wanted to hang out, if a guy wanted to go talk about his paper, I was there for him. If a guy had a problem at home and he needed someone that he could talk to, if he got his girlfriend pregnant, I was there for him. I was stable, an anchor. I was the rock they could lean on.

I think one of the things these guys were really attracted to was the fact that I am positive. I am an optimist and always upbeat. I wasn't a coach, but I was a student of the game. I would even work out with these guys—throw them passes, try to cover them, even try to tackle them. It was always a mismatch, but they appreciated my sincerity and effort. I was even like that to the backups, and a lot of the backups eventually became superstars. Guys like Bernard Clark. He was a fourth string middle linebacker when I became friendly with him; he only got in one or two plays in a scrimmage. Still, I would say to him, "Hey great hit, you made a nice tackle." By the last game of his career in college, he was an MVP of his team. He was the MVP of the Orange Bowl the year the University of Miami won the National Championship. This guy became a superstar, a high pick in the NFL draft. Of course, I eventually became his agent. Bernard's nickname was Tiger. He was bald, mean looking, and weighed close to 260 pounds. He was a super guy and one of my best friends. From the first time we met, there was never any doubt that I was going to be his agent. Tiger isn't playing in the NFL anymore, but we will be friends for life. To this day, if he needs anything, I will be there for him.

Another key player was Jimmie Jones. When I became friendly with Jimmie, he had barely played any high school football. He was from a small country town in central Florida—Okeechobee. He was two hundred pounds, a skinny kid. After eating over my house a lot, he grew into a 285-pound defensive tackle superstar. He and I used to go to the beach. We worked out together. I watched him grow from a teenager into a man. I loved nothing more than to watch these guys mature into men and champions. Jimmie was an amazing story, because he had no background in football, was from a small town, and nobody had ever heard of him. Now he is a millionaire. What a story.

When I went to college at UM there were a lot of players who flunked out of school. Guys who were going to be superstars. Believe me, there are a lot more Bruce Smiths and Lawrence Taylors on the streets than there are on the football field. I remember a running back named Hilton Mobley who reminded me of Eric Dickerson. I thought that he was going to be one of the great stars, but it just wasn't important to him. He flunked out of the University of Miami. I don't know where he is now. I don't know what he's doing. That taught me a lesson and I always used him as an example to a lot of the guys who struggled academically or who would get into trouble off the field.

I'd say, "Do you remember Hilton Mobley? Hilton Mobley was one of the most talented guys I've ever seen. He should have been the best running back in the NFL. He could have been a Hall-of-Famer but he didn't stay focused. He let his grades get the best of him. He didn't care."

There were other guys who were arrested for doing drugs. I remember a really talented defensive tackle named Darius Frazier. Darius looked like he was going to be an NFL stud, but he got busted for dope and was kicked out of school. There was also a guy named Brian Smith that I thought was going to be a great player. I went to school with him, I liked him. He was kicked out of school after getting in trouble with the law. There are so many great players who are dead or in jail, or who just never could stay on the field.

Players like that used to break my heart. They were great guys with bright futures, but they couldn't keep their heads screwed on straight. I like to think I helped a lot of guys that I was friends with stay focused. I helped them keep their acts straight, not only academically but psychologically. That educated me on what a lot of these young guys go through. It was valuable for me as an agent. See, I had an edge. I grew up with these kids, unlike a lot of other agents who grew up in different generations. I knew the challenges that they had and the problems they had to overcome so I can relate to these guys, especially the Miami guys. When I was recruiting them and giving them my pitch, I knew what their challenges were, what their problems were, and what was important to them because I lived with them.

So I was having a fun time—big deal! So what if I was friends with a lot of guys on the team; plenty of other kids on campus are, too. I wanted to distinguish myself. I knew I wanted to become a sports agent so all I had to do was figure out how. I wanted to walk into a phone booth disguised as a mild-mannered broadcast journalism major and walk out as Super Agent. Many kids are friends with athletes, but almost none of them ever take it to the next level of becoming business partners with them. I wanted to take it to that next level. I knew I could do better than my competition simply because I wanted it more. I felt like I had the talent, the brains, and the heart. I knew I could make it in whatever I set my mind to. I refused to let it be otherwise. Now I just had to find a way to make it happen.

Because the university did not offer a major in sports agency and there weren't any books available or seminars on how to become a sports agent, it seemed to me that my only chance to break into this business would be to get a job working for a prominent sports agent. Being a student with no practical experience in negotiating NFL contracts, I knew I had to go to law school, become pretty damn smart, and create an impressive enough résumé to get a big time agent to hire me. Being an outstanding student was nothing more than a prerequisite. I had to walk in there and let that agent know that if he brought me on, he wouldn't regret it. I wanted to walk in that door and make it clear that I could deliver the best players at the University of Miami.

To do that, I would have to get real tight with these guys and prepare them for the future. It seemed like fate that I would be at the University of Miami in my junior year when that school was so rich in NFL talent. I knew that if I could stay tight with these guys I would get my chance. It is easy to look back now and say I was using these guys by acting like their friend while all along trying to become their agent down the road. But I didn't look at it that way. I genuinely liked and cared about these guys because they were my friends. That meant something to me. And what I liked about being an agent was that the harder you work for your client, the better he prospers under your counsel, the better you will do in your profession. The better job you do for your client, the happier he will be with you, and the more likely it will be that he will recommend your services to his teammates so that you can get more clients in the future.

I just couldn't understand then and still can't understand now why agents who have achieved a respectable level of success would steal money or wrong a client to get more money out of them. Forget about the friendship or the trust and honor of the relationship, just strictly in business terms it makes no sense to rip off a client today so that not only will you lose him, but also other potential clients as well. To me, the smart thing seemed to be to work hard, succeed for your client, and then, by following that path, being able to succeed for more clients. I had read the horror stories about agents ripping off their clients. I saw the reality that some agents just want to make money and then let the player go when he is no longer a valuable client.

I wanted to be different. I wanted to work as a team with these guys. I wanted to see them make money and be able to keep it down the road. I wanted to protect them from the wolves who would steal from them or con them out of their money. Because I had nothing but good-hearted intentions toward these guys, nothing I did seemed wrong to me. Because all I wanted was to fight side by side with these guys against the world and emerge victorious, I took a Machiavellian view that the ends justified the means. I never did anything I felt was morally wrong. Another agent in my position could have been less scrupulous and broken a lot of NCAA rules, getting himself, the players he was involved with, and the school in big trouble. That is why an agent should not have any contact with players until the season is over.

I know now that it is wrong for an aspiring agent to help student athletes with their school work. I also now know that it is wrong for an aspiring agent to hang out with student athletes in their dorm rooms, and it is wrong for an aspiring agent to invite student athletes to his parents' house for dinner. It is wrong, as well, for an aspiring agent to work out in the team gym with other student athletes.

But I didn't know all this ten years ago.

In the mideighties, life was very simple to me. All I had to do was get straight As, spend time with the players, go to karate, root for the Dolphins, and get women. Eventually it got more complicated.

Things started to change for me one fateful day on campus at the Hurricane gym. It was a hot Tuesday in the spring of 1986. I was nineteen. I was working out in the football gym when I saw Michael Irvin walk in and start working out.

There were certain unwritten rules in that gym. For instance, on Mondays, Wednesdays, and Fridays, rock and roll stations were played on the radio. On Tuesdays, Thursdays, and Saturdays, it would be more hip hop. The white guys liked listening to the rock and roll stations, and the black guys liked listening to the hip hop stations. Alternating days was the compromise.

Well, on that Tuesday, a bullish, tough linebacker decided he was going to listen to his music and the hell with anyone else. Now Michael Irvin is as jovial and likable as any guy I have ever met. He truly comes across as one of the friendliest guys you'll ever meet. But, make no mistake, Michael is from the mean streets of Fort Lauderdale, Florida. He was born a leader and a competitor. The Michael Irvin I knew was invincible because of the sheer force of his will to win.

So, when this linebacker I'll call "Joe" broke the truce by changing the station and intimidating everyone else, Michael remained undaunted. As Irvin finished his set on the bench press, I saw an anger come over him as if someone had stolen something away from him. Michael kept his composure though; he walked over to the radio and reselected the station he had been listening to.

"Joe, you know the rules. It's Tuesday," Michael said in a friendly manner as he walked back to his bench.

Joe's mannerisms seemed irrational and he acted enraged. He immediately got up, changed the station on the radio, and jumped right into Michael's face, cursing him out. His diction was not that of a well-mannered boy scout.

Joe bumped Michael with his chest and the two were separated immediately by the guys in the gym. Joe outweighed Michael by twenty-five pounds or so and was considered a tough guy.

I couldn't believe Michael had the guts to stand up to Joe. Joe seemed like one tough, crazy guy not to mess with. But Michael kept his cool, said he was okay, and the guys let him go. Bernard "Tiger" Clark, a middle linebacker, was there and was one of the only guys who Michael knew well and who was physically capable of holding Michael back. Tiger got everyone to back off and go back to where they were. But it struck me as odd that while everyone else walked away, Tiger stayed with Michael. Seeing these two guys come close to blows was dangerously exciting. Here are two powerful athletes who seem like they would break bones with a single punch.

Michael calmly walked back over to Joe to shake hands and be friends again. It looked like the show was over as the two shook hands. And then Michael's million-dollar smile left him as he pulled Joe toward him. Michael's face changed from that of a super-friendly guy to a stone-cold killer.

Boom, boom, and pop!

Before Joe could blink, or even think he was in trouble, Michael threw three of the fastest, cleanest jabs I have ever seen in my life. It was savage.

Blood was all over Joe's face as he lay on the floor knocked out. Tiger laughed in this high-pitched scream as he restrained Michael. Now it was over. Joe had fallen and wasn't getting up anytime soon. And when he had finally gotten up, Joe wanted no part of Michael. That hip-hop station blared that Tuesday and the rest of the Tuesdays in Michael's collegiate tenure.

Something other than Joe's blood hit me as I witnessed that spectacle. It dawned on me that there had been a lot of fights among the players. There was an intensity in the air. The atmosphere was one of confidence and success. Winning always seemed possible and losing was the only thing impossible. There was a tremendous urgency to win. I saw all of this in Michael. He was a winner in everything he did. He was going to win every competition big or small.

As the head coach of the team of the eighties in college football, Jimmy Johnson had fostered this unbeatable mentality in the minds of his players. Yet I could see that Michael was born with his.

Later on that day, the guys scrimmaged in a practice that was closed to the media and the public. Since I was personal friends with these guys and helped them study, I thought that those rules didn't apply to me. I didn't think any of the rules applied to me because I had nothing but the best intentions toward these guys. I figured my purity of heart was my pass to get on the field. Well, Jimmy Johnson didn't see it that way. As the team was in the middle of practicing, I saw Coach Johnson glancing over at me. He looked me over and then started jogging toward me.

As fearless as these guys were on the team, every one of them was afraid of this guy and now he was coming for me. I suppose I was too thrilled and excited to meet him to be scared.

"Son, you know this is a closed practice. You know you are not supposed to be out here," he said to me in a conversational tone with a slight Arkansas accent. I could see that he wasn't trying to intimidate me or scare me or be a disciplinarian at all. He wanted to know why I felt I could be there when no other students could. "I apologize for interrupting your practice, Coach. I just wanted to watch some of my friends play to see if they are going to win the starting job or not," I said.

I was very surprised at how personable he was. He seemed very friendly and easy to talk to. I couldn't believe that this was the guy every player was so scared of. "I see," he said. "Well, you are going to have to leave. You have to follow the rules." I looked at him and couldn't hide my enthusiasm in getting to speak with him personally. "I appreciate you coming over in person to tell me that, Coach. I will follow the rules. Thank you, Coach." He looked back at me and smiled as if he were about to chuckle. Practice resumed as I started to walk off of the field. I was honored that he came over to tell me himself. I respected that and in turn I wanted to respect his wishes. I never went to watch another closed practice again and I stopped working out in his gym. I had a strange feeling that we would be speaking again someday.

As I was walking, I heard the quarterback's "Hut," the pads crashing against each other, and the whistle blow. And then I heard the players yelling. A fight had broken out between two linemen and they were throwing some heavy blows. I couldn't believe my eyes when I saw Jimmy Johnson run in there like a mad man. He got in between those two guys, separated them like Moses parting the Red Sea, grabbed their face masks, and shook them like a bunch of rag dolls. He screamed at those guys like they had just cost the team the National Championship. I was scared for them and was thankful to be all the way on the other side of the field. This guy had no fear, just as if punches would merely bounce off of him. He reminded me of the military character played by Robert Duvall in Francis Ford Coppolla's *Apocalypse Now.* He had that quality of appearing indestructible and incapable of being defeated. Then he made those two guys run laps for the rest of practice. I suddenly realized why this guy is so respected. He's got as much guts as anyone on the field, he's more determined to win than his players, and he's smarter than anyone on that campus and I don't just mean in the athletic department. As one of the guys ran past me, I recognized one of them as a classmate that I had yet to meet. I said to him, "At least you got your licks in."

The player acknowledged my humor and kept going. As I

heard the wince of pain from the giant jogging past me, I
realized that things weren't just a game played for the fun of
it around here. Michael Irvin's bloody fists and Jimmy Johnson's fanatical screams summoned a clarity within me and
chased away my naivete. I had lost my innocence that day
and realized that football wasn't just a game or a business.
Football is these guys' livelihood. If they fail here, they may
very well end up as failures. Everything is on the line. Success is tremendous and failure is terrifying. If these guys get
into trouble for any improper conduct, it could ruin them.
And ruining them would do the same to me. What used to
be a childhood passion to me had now become business. I
saw my part and could see that I was no longer a spectator
rooting on the sideline. I could feel the threat of danger and
the fear of failure within me and I loved it. The game was
now afoot. It was up to me to see if I could figure out how
to win it. I tried to read everything I possibly could about
being an agent and the world of sports law. In my research
I found Professor John Weistart, who wrote a text book on
sports law and taught at Duke Law School. I thought it might
be a good idea to study under him. So I made a trip to North
Carolina to meet him. I said, "Professor, I want to be an
agent. I've been accepted at Georgetown. I can go to almost
any law school I want to. What should I do?"

I planned to go to Georgetown because I thought that being
based in Washington, D.C., with all the colleges and players
there, would be great for me, recruiting-wise. But then I went
and met Professor Weistart, and he impressed me with what
he had to say and how much he knew about the agent business. So I figured Duke was where I should go to law school.
It was also closer to home. Plus they called Duke "the Harvard of the South," and they had a good football team at the
time coached by Steve Spurrier.

Toward the end of my last year at UM, I knew I was going
to leave the campus and head off to Duke. I was concerned
that if I was away for three years, I would lose touch with
the University of Miami guys and thus lose my "in" to this
business. Well, my father, who has two brothers, has a say-

ing: "I trust my instincts and my brother!" I had to prepare my brother Jason, who was coming in to UM as a freshman, the same year I was heading off to Duke. So I brought Jason around the UM campus a lot with me. I loved having Jason around. I introduced him to the UM players and he became THE MAN as well. The players loved Jason. Maybe even more than they liked me! Where I am outgoing and loud, Jason is low-key and analytical. But in my absence, he picks up where I leave off. We complement each other well. We are Batman and Robin. Jason stepped right in and took over for me when I left UM. Jason has always been my partner since we were infants. I could never ask for a better brother. He is the most loyal and trustworthy person I have ever known. He is a great person with a super heart. When I left to go to Duke, my relationship with the players never missed a beat due to Jason. Jason was also an exceptional student and very knowledgeable about football. I thought the guys would miss me while I was in Duke. No way, not with Jason around. He didn't let me down. He spent more time with those guys than I did. Every time I would call one of the guys, it seemed like he was out with Jason. And the kid kept the discipline and got straight As. He kept the UM connection alive.

Knowing that everything in Miami was copacetic, I felt like a wild animal unleashed to study and succeed in the legal environment. I studied all day and all night. I studied longer and harder than any other student there.

During my days at Duke, I was the Miami guy, the guy from the University of Miami, Suntan U. I stood out like a sore thumb. I wore gold chains and tank tops, sport coats with silk shirts, shoes with no socks, mousse in my slicked-back hair. UM is fun, a place where there's a lot of parties going on and the lifestyle is fast and furious, with beautiful women all over the place. Casual sex was very common, particularly among the players there and the guys who run the show at UM. Duke was a serious step down, let me tell you, big time. So many of the women there were geeks. Going from the University of Miami to Duke was tough. I was miserable when I first got to Duke. At that time, I was a guy who was into weight lifting and having a suntan and walking around with almost no clothes, enjoying the beach and the warm weather in Miami, and suddenly I'm cruising around up there at Duke where it's much more conservative.

Worse than that, everyone at Duke was concentrating exclusively on basketball and studying. It was the first time I was really away from home, and thank God I had a lot of school work or I would have gone nuts. I hated to leave Miami. I had considered going to the University of Miami Law School where they offered me a scholarship to attend. They really recruited me to stay.

I also was miserable about leaving my family. I had still lived at home and was very homesick. I hated to leave my girlfriend and social life. And, of course, I didn't want to part from the Dolphins. But I knew that Duke was one of the top law schools in the nation, and it would be a great learning experience for me. Being a graduate of Duke Law School would give me an edge over the other agents. It was a painful decision, but I made the choice that was best for my future as an agent. I knew I would have to make sacrifices. By the way, I am still the only sports agent who has graduated from Duke Law. I don't believe there are any other big-time agents who have graduated from such a distinguished law school.

My first year at Duke was brutal. I was bored, cold, and waiting to pounce into action. I studied hard and learned sports law inside and out.

I never fit in at Duke. The other students called me "Miami Vice." They were conservative and dull. I was like a shark out of water, but I survived my first year by going home often and keeping up with the Dolphins and 'Canes. Jason was my eyes and ears for me back home. I spoke to him every day for at least an hour. While most law students were struggling to survive the first year of Duke Law, I was struggling to find my way to break into the agent business. I called Jason to get the word on what was going on there, and he told me Michael Irvin had signed with a local agent. I knew it was time to head back to Miami for a little while, time to make my move.

4

The Firm

As confident as I am—and always have been—in my abilities, I knew that to get started in the agent business, I needed some practical experience.

I had the talent, the connections, all I needed was experience. During my first year at Duke Law School, I started looking around for the right opportunity. I found it back home in Miami.

When I came home during Easter, Jason told me that my good friend Michael Irvin had signed with a local agent named Mel Levine. At the time, there were three prominent agents in Florida that represented the Miami Hurricanes. Robert Fraley out of Orlando represented defensive tackle Jerome Brown and running back Alonzo Highsmith. Jim Ferraro out of Miami represented wide receiver Eddie Brown and tight end Willie Smith. Mel Levine out of Fort Lauderdale signed wide receivers Michael Irvin, Brian Blades, Brett Perriman, and safety Bennie Blades.

I knew that as a law student far away in North Carolina, I had two main problems breaking into this business—time and age. I had to hurry up and become a qualified and competent agent in time to represent my remaining friends such as Bernard Clark and Jimmie Jones, as they were

46

going to be entering the draft by the time I was graduating law school.

I didn't plan on just showing up at their front door and saying, "Hey, I know we were friends in school and I helped you with some exams, so trust me with your once-in-a-life-time-opportunity." I didn't want to sign these guys because they were doing me a favor. I wanted to do THEM the favor. I wanted them to sign with an agent who would look out for them and do everything possible to succeed for them. I knew I would have to become as mentally disciplined as possible. I continued to study like a machine and push myself beyond what I thought were my limits. I knew that becoming the youngest agent ever to succeed in the NFL would be an ex-traordinary accomplishment and would require extraordi-nary effort.

I also knew that although my player friends were good-hearted guys, they were also smart. If I was going to be their contract advisor and handle their all-important financial af-fairs, it would be for professional and not sentimental rea-sons. To be the most qualified, I was going to need to get some real experience. To get experience, I would have to intern for an agent immediately following my first year of law school. The pressure was on. I needed to actually watch negotiations. I needed an introduction to the NFL team exec-utives. I needed access to the player contracts and statistics. I needed an introduction to the National Football League Players Association. I needed information on the agent regis-tration procedures. I wanted to see how an actual agent re-cruits players.

Since Mel Levine signed the guys I was most friendly with, I decided to TARGET him. He had several Miami Dolphin clients and represented all of the top prospects I was friends with that year. That was all I knew about him, but that was enough. Levine was the hot agent. He was coming off a year in which he signed Bennie Blades and Michael Irvin—two high first-round picks, and he also signed Brian Blades and Brett Perriman, two second-round picks. If I was going to intern for the summer and learn from an agent, it would have to be Mel Levine.

So I set out to get his attention. I called Mel every day, three times a day, for a month straight. It was spring, and I needed to land a job with him by the time I came home for the summer. I went to his office several times and was turned away. I wanted to show him my definition of persistence. I could see that my calls weren't getting me anywhere so I went to my ace in the hole.

I flew back to Miami for a weekend and drove over to the campus to find Michael Irvin. I asked him if he would recommend that his agent take me on. Michael went to bat for me and said he would call Levine. A few days later, Irvin told me he spoke with Levine and that I should call Levine back. I called Levine about two hundred more times before he finally took my call. Finally I got my opportunity to speak with him. He answered the phone by saying, "You're the kid who has called me a thousand times, right? Anyone as persistent as you deserves an interview. Meet me in my office next week."

I was ecstatic. I got the meeting I wanted. I felt that once he met me, I would get the job.

I knew Levine was a crafty guy. He had just beaten an NCAA investigation that claimed he had purchased cars for a number of his college recruits. This huge scandal in South Florida was called "Auto Gate." I didn't know whether Levine had cheated or not. All I knew at the time was that he was the top dog in South Florida, and I wanted to pick his brains. I didn't know anything about the way he did business. I had never met him before, never even seen a picture. But I called hundreds of times just to get a shot. I came down at the end of the school year hoping I could land a job with him for the summer, just an internship was all I wanted, just to learn a little bit so that the following year I could go out on my own. I wanted to stick with my UM buddies—Irvin and the others. I wanted to see them through this process. It was time for my first group of friends to get drafted.

For the next couple of days, I buried myself in the library

and studied Levine's clients, NFL personnel, and NFL sala-ries. I was already familiar with the information but I wanted to make sure I was ready to impress Mel. The morning of my interview, I put on my best suit, went to a barber shop, and got a warm shave. I had my hair slicked back, I had run and worked out in the morning—I felt ready. I had my brief-case with me. I was the picture of a young professional. I looked the part.

I knew I was the prototype agent: handsome, well-dressed, smooth-talker, polished, professional, well-educated, confi-dent, and cool as a cucumber. I was going to impress this guy. I would dominate him with my presence. I would force him to give me this job. I was ready for the interview that was going to shape my life. I knew if I got the job my life would be on course. If I didn't get the job, it would be a major setback. I wasn't sweating it, because I believed in myself and I was ready to rock and roll. I couldn't wait to meet this guy!

I got to Mel's office at 11:15 A.M.—forty-five minutes early, just to make sure I wasn't late. His office was on a houseboat. I like the water and I love boats, so I thought that was pretty cool. I figured the guy must be more casual than the typical attorney or certified public accountant since he wasn't in a stuffy office building. The name of his company was "Sport-Rep Inc."

After walking around for forty-five minutes, I stepped in-side at twelve on the dot. He made me wait another forty-five minutes while he was meeting with a Miami Dolphin offensive lineman, John Giesler. In the meantime, I saw sev-eral Miami Dolphins walking in and out of the office. I no-ticed former Dolphin players such as tight end Joe Rose, defensive end Kim Bokamper, and safety Mike Kozlowski walking in and out of the office. Then finally his secretary appeared and said that Mel was swamped and that he would have to reschedule our meeting. I said "No way!" I had to meet with this guy. I wasn't going to let this opportunity slip out of my hands. I barged right past his secretary, went up-stairs to his office. Then I knocked on the door and went in.

Interrupting him was a gamble. I didn't want to offend him, but I wanted him to see how much this meeting meant to me. You have to go for it in life.

I was not surprised to see he was in a short-sleeved shirt and a pair of jeans—no suit. He was short and chunky. He wore glasses and had a mustache. The guy looked like a geek. The minute I saw him I said to myself, "This is Mel Levine, the top agent?" I knew at that instant that I would dominate the business. This little dork and his fellow agents couldn't compete with a shark like myself. I almost laughed.

He saw me walk into his office, and he said, "I know you have been waiting to see me, but I have to see another client. I can't see you today." He told his secretary to schedule an appointment for me later in the week, and he and Giesler, a huge offensive lineman, started to walk past me. I went to shake his hand as a way to stop him, held his hand, looked him in the eyes, and said,"Mr. Levine, I am only asking for two minutes of your time, just two minutes is all I need. You have to meet with me now. I guarantee you won't regret it."

He smiled and seemed shocked by my aggressive approach. He then said, "Okay kid, here's your two minutes. You better be good."

As I always do, I looked him right in the eyes with a fiery intensity and said with a passion, "I'll dominate for you. I've got the greatest connections with the players. I can sign anybody you want. The players love me. I was born to be an agent. I'm hungry. I'm eager to learn. I'll run errands for you. I'll work day and night. I'll work weekends. I'll work for free. I'll be an awesome recruiter. I'll do all the research. I'm a Duke law student. I can talk to players up in North Carolina. I will travel across the country. I'm an animal. I'm a shark. You need me. I will make you even stronger."

At this point I was raising my voice, waving my hands, pounding my fists together, being as loud and dynamic as I could be. This was my one chance to command his attention so that he would be overwhelmed by my energy and desire. I put on a show. It was my most powerful presentation to date.

"I can hand deliver all these guys to you," I said. "I will

make this job a lot easier for you. Just give me the chance. I will go after guys in the North Carolina area and guys with ties to South Florida. I will help you expand your operations to become the biggest and best in Florida and ultimately in the country." I named the top prospects in the upcoming college season. I told him which I guys I would go after. I was bowling him over. It was a hell of a sales job. He was looking at a young, aggressive, polished, educated monster!

I told him all about his own clients—their strengths and weaknesses. I knew when their contracts were going to be up for renegotiation. I told him what the best players in the league were making and what his clients should make in comparison. I told him almost every statistic in the book. I just kept talking and talking, hoping to get him to hire me by submission. I was a walking dictionary when it came to the NFL. I was spitting out information like a computer. I could see the excitement in his eyes as I was talking to him. He was amazed. I could read his mind. It looked as if he was asking, "Who the hell is this kid? Where did he come from?"

I answered the question for him. "I was born to be an agent. Hire me and I will take Sport-Rep to the top."

Two minutes turned into thirty minutes. Levine looked exhausted. He interrupted in midsentence and said, "All right, I'll give you a shot. You've got the job. I'll pay your expenses, a two hundred fifty dollar per week salary and I'll give you twenty-five percent of my fee for every player you refer to me. Now, I think your two minutes were up a half hour ago. You will start in May when your semester is over. Call me then."

I was THRILLED! I jumped for joy. I hugged the man. A total stranger. He must have thought I was insane. It was one of the happiest days of my life, and I can still remember how good that moment felt. At first there was no chance this guy was going to hire me, and I won him over. If I could win an agent over, I knew I would win the players over. This was the break I needed and now it was going to become official. Now I was REALLY going to work hard. I thanked him, looked him in the eyes again, and said, "You will remember this day for the rest of your life."

He remembered it all right. He had let the shark into the fish pond. It was a day Mel would never forget. I walked out of Mel's office determined to take Sport-Rep to the top. As I walked to the car, I started to plot my strategy. By the time I got into the car and started driving, I knew it was just a matter of time before I took over. Within fifteen minutes of getting the job, I wanted to make ME the top guy. All in good time, I thought. For now, it was time to start walking the walk. And I took off with a running start.

Mel already had another young agent working for him, Rich DeLuca. DeLuca was a nice kid with a great personality. But he couldn't keep up with me. Levine also had a bunch of former Dolphins working for him at that time. Joe Rose was one of them. Rose was one of my father's friends. He remembered me well. Rose said to me, "This is perfect. I knew when I met you as a kid that someday you were going to be an agent. I know you are going to do great."

Levine loved me right from the start because I worked like a dog. I worked seven days a week. I was the first person at the office by 8:00 A.M. and I didn't leave until after 10:00 P.M. I immediately became a registered sports agent with the state of Florida and a certified contract advisor with the NFLPA in the summer of 1988. I now had access to all the teams. I called and introduced myself to most of the NFL executives. Mel gave me a few free agents to try and sign in the Canadian League. I said forget the CFL, I'll get these guys into the NFL. I called the NFL teams round-the-clock and made them sign these players. Would you believe that during the first few days on the job I was already getting players signed to NFL teams! I immediately made a name for myself with the NFL clubs.

I also went to the NFLPA offices in Washington, D.C. I introduced myself in person to all the key personnel at the Union. I spent hours and hours reading contracts and learning about negotiations. I met with people such as Mike Duberstein and Mark Levin who taught me about the Collective

Bargaining Agreement. I realized that there were hundreds of registered sports agents. I knew I had to find a way to separate myself from the pack. Little did I know at that time, when I was just one of many agents, that less than a decade later I would be the only agent ever to grace the cover of *Sports Illustrated!* I never dreamed that I would also be in a movie with Tom Cruise.

I was the point man on the research for the contract negotiations. I studied contract after contract, stat after stat. I told Mel what strategies I would use in the negotiations. I had unbelievable input with him. I did everything except actually negotiate the contracts for the Blades Brothers, Perriman, and Irvin. I watched and learned how Levine dealt with his clients: both the rookies and the veterans. I remember how hard he tried to persuade Irvin to sign the contract he negotiated for him. I told Irvin I thought the deal could be better. Irvin listened to me and called the Cowboys himself. After speaking directly to them and saying he wasn't going to sign until he got more money, the Cowboys gave him an extra $25,000.

The players never really trusted Levine. But they did trust me and they often came to me for advice. I knew Levine wasn't going to be able to keep these guys for long. He just didn't have their respect or any rapport with them. I never did spend much time with Mel either. He was a very secretive and private man.

I kept busy from day one. I spent a lot of time with our clients. I helped them with everything from shipping their cars, to setting up their new apartments, to driving them places. I was a jack of all trades. I learned a lot from Levine at the beginning. He was both a lawyer and a CPA. But very soon after I started working for him, I started teaching him about the agent business. The student had become the teacher.

Levine was impressed with my knowledge on the NFL and the colleges. I could tell him everything about the players and the recruits and who the top guys were. I had a feel for it—an instinct—and then I started telling him how to recruit. They wanted to reach Deion Sanders from Florida State, who was a great prospect at the time. But they didn't know how. What they saw as a problem, I saw as an opportunity— and I took it. Within one hour, I came back into Levine's office with every single phone number they needed on Deion. He was shocked and impressed. I told him I got the numbers by calling up the school directories and telling the operator that the student had checked out a book from the library in my name, or that I was the guy's tutor or assistant professor, anything I could think of to get a player's phone number. I showed Levine I could be creative and resourceful. Now I wanted to show him I had the talent to succeed in this business. I grabbed his phone and dialed the number of the best player on the list—Deion Sanders.

One of the most important parts of the business is cold calling athletes and creating a rapport over the phone. This is not easy as every guy you call has already talked to twenty other agents and is aggravated by the constant intrusion. That is why you have to love this part. If you do not love it, if you do not make yourself love it and be good at it, then you are never going to get anywhere. By loving and being good at it, you can win these guys over and put yourself in a position to set up a meeting. This was my first time to cold call guys.

As I dialed the digits, I remembered the first time I ever made an important call. I was about ten years old. I called a girl named Missy Linksman to ask her out on a date. Well, I got a little nervous when she answered, "Hello."

I said, "Uh . . . Hi, Missy this is Drew . . . My mom wants to talk to you . . ." I was nervous and handed my mom the phone. I was no Casanova.

I said to my mom, "Mom, would you ask her for me?"

My mom asked her for me. Missy said yes and my mom drove us to the movies that day. Who would have known that one day the same kid would grow up to be the Shark.

Things have changed since. Deion answered the phone, and since my mom wasn't there to talk to him for me, I introduced myself and the firm. He was polite and responsive. By the end of the brief conversation, he told me to keep in touch so that we could meet at the end of the year. I could tell my phone call wasn't the first he had received, but he was a gentleman and I didn't look bad in front of Levine. I can tell in the first conversation I have with a guy if I am going to get him as a client. Even back then I could tell— and Deion wasn't going to be one of them. I knew enough to focus in on the guys I could get for Levine.

I never had a problem tracking guys down and getting their address or phone numbers. I was resourceful and felt like a combination of an actor and a private detective. Often I had to put on an acting job to get a number. Sometimes it was just a matter of checking the student directory or local information. Occasionally I would find out the player's hometown and call information to get the number. Then I would call the family and get the player's number. In those days it was all right to call a player while he was in college. Now the rules in Florida state that you can't call a player or his family until his eligibility has expired. The business has certainly changed since I got started.

Let me go back to my first day on the job with Levine. While the rest of the office was out eating lunch, I wanted to stay to see what more I could do. Just after they left, I noticed something very interesting. I was looking over the list of all of the other rookies and their agents on the Seattle Seahawks' roster because Levine's client (now my client), wide receiver Brian Blades, was their second-round draft pick. I wanted to see who the other agents were because I did not want an incompetent agent to set the trend of accepting below-market contracts. I noticed that their third-round pick, Tommy Kane, a wide receiver out of Syracuse, did not have an agent listed.

I raced out the door to tell Levine the news; he thought it was good work on my behalf. He said he would get in touch with Kane. When I asked him at the end of the day what the development was with Tommy Kane, he said that he wasn't able to get his phone number. "Leave it to me," I said. "I'll be back in ten minutes."

I got on the phone with the school's athletic department

and told them I was Kane's tutor trying to help him study for an exam. I said I had lost his number and needed to call him to set up a study session. I got the number and then called Kane. I told Kane we represented Brian and that we would have great leverage in dealing with the Seahawks if we had both the second- and third-round picks. I implored Kane to meet with us. I promised him a good time on Miami Beach. I told him about the beautiful girls and hot nightclubs. I used my best sales pitch to entice him into coming to visit us. Within ten minutes, I was back in Levine's office with Tommy Kane's phone number and an airline reservation bringing him into Ft. Lauderdale.

Levine looked at me and said, "Drew, you are a natural at this business." He was impressed. I had accomplished in one day what they didn't know how to do. I taught them with my instincts. Here I was on my very first day and I was making things happen. I had scored big, or so I thought.

I felt like a million bucks when I spoke to Tommy Kane and he said he was coming. I went to the airport looking forward to meeting him. I was ready to sign him up at the gate. He was my first recruit. Slowly but surely every passenger got off the plane. There was no sign of Tommy. I waited at the airport for two hours. I was crushed. I didn't want to leave empty-handed. I went back to the office having learned a lesson the hard way: *this business ain't easy.* These are college kids; many are unpredictable. I was embarrassed to tell Mel what had happened. Yet to my surprise he wasn't moved by the news. He told me that in the agent business you must expect disappointment and that you will fail in recruiting many more times than you will succeed. He made a comparison to a baseball player's batting average. He explained that three out of ten hits is excellent. The same applied to recruiting. This was a tough lesson for me to learn, because I wanted to sign every player I recruited. Unfortunately, I learned it doesn't work that way. You are a great success in recruiting if you can sign 20 percent of the players you recruit. I hate to lose. But as an agent you have to learn to deal with it so that it doesn't eat you up inside.

I really enjoyed my first summer as an agent. I got a lot accomplished. I developed a great rapport with the clients. I made inroads with both the NFL teams and the NFLPA. I became an accomplished recruiter. I learned how to access NFL stats and contracts. I became a solid contract negotiator. In short, I knew the business well and felt that I was ready to go to the next level.

When my summer job was over, Levine wanted me to stay on working full time during my second year at Duke, and I jumped at the chance. I was now a full-time agent, not just an intern. I was given the title of Director of Player Personnel for Sport-Rep. My job was to go out and make things happen.

Back at Duke, I was faced with a whole new challenge. I wasn't at the University of Miami just trying to hang out with the guys. It was tough to leave Miami and go back to school that fall. I couldn't befriend guys by hanging out with them and helping them study for exams. Now I was cold calling guys and meeting with them as an agent. And, unlike my pals at UM, these guys didn't know me. They didn't know I was a good guy trying to do right by them. They didn't know I was different. They didn't know I believed in them, that I wanted to help them. To them, I was just one of several hundred agents calling to get their business.

In college, I had the luxury of approaching players casually, taking my time and coming across as a fellow student and football fan. Now I had been stripped naked with nothing but the hard truth to defend myself with—and that's the way I wanted it to be. No more, "One day I want to be your agent when I am good enough." Finally, I WAS good enough. I went to one of the best law schools in the country, competed against the brightest young minds in the nation, and smacked them like they were schoolyard punks.

I had to get used to the traveling, because now I would be traveling from one campus to another meeting with recruits. The traveling was tough and demanding. All the while I had to maintain my status in school.

What I lacked in experience I would make up ten times over with HUNGER, HEART, and ENTHUSIASM. My preparation was second to none. It was time to kick down the door, run into the burning building, shoot the bad guys, and come out with the freed hostages.

One of the toughest parts of being a successful agent is figuring which players to recruit. It is always a gamble deciding on which players to recruit, because you can't go after everyone. When I first got started in this business and I was working for Mel, there was little out there to help people identify the top prospects. The only way to determine who the top prospects were was to watch the game, talk to NFL scouts, college coaches, other players, as well as by reading the draftniks like Mel Kiper Jr. and Joel Buchsbaum. With no other information available, I would go off searching for kids Kiper and Buchsbaum identified, setting up visits to go and meet these guys. I'll never forget, I met with a guy who at one point was projected to be the second pick of the draft and a couple of weeks later they didn't even think he was going to be picked. I think guys like Kiper and Buchsbaum are great, but as time went on, I developed key sources within the league and my own network of guys who gave me an advantage over other agents who were CLUELESS. These agents were signing players that they thought were going to be first-round picks, and they didn't even get drafted. That's how you get buried in this business.

During the season, I read every source of information possible to try and find out who the best players in the country were. I watched the films of games and formed my own conclusions about the top players. I compared my notes with Buchsbaum's and Kiper's opinions and was able to get a pretty good grasp of who I thought were going to be the good players. I read the *Sporting News, Pro Football Weekly, Sports Illustrated, Dolphin Digest, Don Peterson's College Football, Street & Smith's College Football Weekly, etc.* If it was out there, I read it. And I not only read it, I learned it and spoke it fluently. I knew about every senior who was likely to get drafted and every junior who was good enough to come out early.

5

Kid Agent

ONCE THE SEASON ENDED, I WASTED NO TIME. I LEFT THE South Florida recruiting to Levine. I targeted the guys in the region where I went to law school in North Carolina. The number one guy I wanted was Robert Massey. Robert was the perfect candidate. He went to North Carolina Central University and was an excellent cornerback in a Division I-AA school. He was fast and physical, and I liked his style of play. After his last game, I arranged to set up a meeting with him at his dorm room. I was dressed in a gray Italian sport coat with a black pair of slacks, a black vee-neck shirt, and black dress shoes with no socks. Of course, my hair was slicked back. I had my own style, straight from my roots in Miami Beach. I was wearing my father's special-made Korean gold chain like it was a trophy. I was not dressed like your conventional baby boomer agent. Nor am I.

NC Central was a historically black college. I was the only Jewish kid on campus that night. But that didn't intimidate me. Ever since I was a kid, I was always comfortable in that environment. The people on campus definitely took note of my strange appearance. It wasn't every day that a slick-looking agent comes to the NC Central dorms. The dorms were old and worn down. The athletic dorms were next to a large garbage bin. This definitely was not the University of Miami.

I showed up at Massey's room, and some guy answered the door and looked at me in shock, like I must have had the wrong room. He recovered, looked at my attire, and burst into laughter saying, "Yo, there's a white dude dressed like Don Johnson at the door. It's Miami Vice."

I looked inside the small, cramped room and saw seven or eight big football players. There was no room for me to come inside and sit down so I stood my ground at the entrance. I said hello and introduced myself as an agent. They all laughed again, making other jokes at my expense, saying I looked like I was with the Mafia. I went on to say I was at Duke Law School. At the time I didn't realize that guys from NCCU generally looked at guys from Duke as being snobby and soft, and they didn't like them. I was definitely in front of a tough crowd. These were big, mean-looking dudes, who I could tell were jealous that I was there to see Massey and not them, so they belittled and tried to berate me. I was NOT welcome and they let me know it.

Massey was the only guy in the room who was not offensive and who was paying close attention to me. I recognized his face and said, "You must be Robert."

"You don't look much like an agent," he responded.

"He looks more like the pizza delivery guy. Hey, you're late, man. You ain't gettin' no tip!" one of the other guys shouted in my face.

"Go back to Duke, you fag!" one guy shouted.

I almost got angry but instead I laughed and joked, "What, am I not welcome here?" I could only smile while looking Robert in the eyes. He looked back; I wanted him to see that these guys and what they had to say couldn't make a dent in my armor. I wouldn't let him see how uncomfortable I was.

"What, are you here to suck all of us off?" another guy asked as he started to unzip his pants.

The smile had left my face. I looked Robert in the eyes, not breaking the stare, and responded, "If your friend sucks me off first, then I'll take his request into consideration and go get some of my freaks to come up here and take care of you guys."

I was smiling and only joking when I made the comeback remark, but Massey's insulted teammate jumped up toward me and was a fraction of a second away from taking a punch, when Robert stepped in between us and stopped him. Here was Robert, a hundred eighty-pound cornerback, intimidating a mean, tough, sloppy three-hundred-pound offensive guard—and I was scared for the guard. Robert looked like some rough warrior from the old school of true tough guys.

Robert started laughing at my joke. I could see he was the boss around there and had everyone's complete respect. Those guys may have been a lot bigger than Robert, but I could tell that he could take all those guys on and hurt them badly.

Robert said, turning to me. "You're all right, Drew. You're young, but you've got balls." I loved this guy right away. He was smart. He was tough. He looked me in the eyes and he was a thinker. He was no immature little kid. This was a very smart young man who had been toughened by adversity and learned a great deal from it. He and I, despite our drastically different backgrounds, had much in common. I knew all of this in an instant.

"Give me five minutes of your time. Just hear me out. Let's do this meeting like we had agreed." He paused, thought it over, and nodded his head saying, "Okay Drew, Mr. Movie Star agent, let's see what you got."

"You're right, Robert. I am young. And that's a tremendous advantage because I'll work my fingers to the bone for you. I live just five minutes away and will be here every single day. That's right, every single day I will come over here and personally take care of you. Whatever you want handled, I will handle myself. No secretaries, no middleman, just me. I will get you the best deals on a car, the best endorsements possible, the best deal on a house or condo, the best mortgage rate, and, of course, the best contract.

"With me and Mel Levine you get the best of both worlds. Last year our firm negotiated first-round contracts for Michael

Irvin of the Dallas Cowboys and Bennie Blades of the Detroit Lions. Our firm also negotiated second-round contracts for Brett Perriman of the New Orleans Saints and Brian Blades of the Seattle Seahawks. And they were all awesome contracts. You won't find another agent with the experience and track record combined that we have who will also work with you and meet with you every single day until the team drafts you. I will be there to help you train with a trainer. I will be there to wake you up in the morning to go work out. I will be there to give you a ride whenever and wherever you need it. I will be there to set up local card shows to give you some pocket change. I will be there to help you with your school work. I will be there to help you with your family and friends. The bottom line is I will be there for you. No one else is going to work that hard for you. And that's because no one wants to work for you like I want to. No one wants your business like I do. I want it bad. I was born for this. You are going to be my first client. You are going to be the guy who gets me into this business. Next year I am going to tell every premier college player in the country that I represent Robert Massey and look at the great job I did for him. You are going to be the standard for all recruits. And by giving me this opportunity, by giving me my first shot, I will be forever grateful and loyal to you. I will break my back for you.

"Talk is cheap. I want to prove it to you right now. Tell me to come back tomorrow at four o'clock in the morning and I will be here with orange juice and doughnuts. I will work with you every day to market you to the NFL teams.

"And that is critical with you playing for North Carolina Central University. Coming from a small school where you did not get any television exposure, it is absolutely imperative that you have an agent who will pound the pavement, knock on every door, and force-feed videotape of Robert Massey. I will have a videotape made up of your best plays and games and I will call the teams day and night to make sure that they have not only seen your video but know it by heart. They will see more of you than they will a guy from the University of Miami.

"Although you are not known right now, you are going to come on like gangbusters. I am going to arrange for autograph sessions and get tons of hype for you. Every weekend between now and the draft, I will have some type of paid appearance lined up for you, and the hype that I am going to get for you locally will ensure that. You are going to be a household name by the end of your rookie season. I will not rest until you are successful.

"I am going to be here so much you are going to have to throw me out the door to stop working for you."

"I can see that. I am about to throw you out now," he playfully interrupted with a smile, but I dazzled him with how hard and fast I could bring my game to him.

"Robert, I can tell you are already comfortable with me. A lot of that has to do with the fact that we are the same age. You can sign with an agent who is more like a father figure, who can't relate to you, who can't appreciate and understand your circumstances while still thinking he can tell you what to do. Or you can have an agent like me who will listen to you, work with you, respect your opinions, and accommodate you. Make no mistake. I am not going to tell you what you want to hear. I will never bullshit you. I am always, without exception, going to tell it to you straight. But I will be able to understand your viewpoint and communicate with you so that you and I are on the same page.

"Communication is the key. With good communication between you and me, you will see what I see, and you will learn the business aspect of being a professional in the National Football League. The NFL isn't just about football. It's about being a professional. It's about conducting yourself with maturity and acting responsibly. Say and do the right things and you will be rewarded. Make mistakes, and you will pay for them—sooner or later. It's that simple.

"This is your one shot in the NFL to make millions. I will do everything within my power to succeed for you. I promise you that on Draft Day you will be watching that TV and saying to yourself 'I know that I worked as hard as I could to get here. I know that I sacrificed and paid the price.'

"Whichever way it goes, you will have peace of mind because you will have done everything you could to go as high as you could possibly go. I will not let you blow this opportunity. With me as your agent you will have no choice but to succeed. I will not let you down. It will be you and me standing together. If you fail I fail. And I am not going to let that happen. I will work day and night to see to it that it doesn't."

"You'll talk day and night. I can see that!" Robert interrupted. He then went on to ask me a lot of personal questions about my family, my education, my background, my experience or lack thereof. I could see that my youth and hunger were what he wanted in an agent. He knew he needed an agent who would go out and canvas the teams since he was from such a small school and lacked exposure. After we talked for a while, he said, "Okay Drew, Mr. Movie Star agent, be here tomorrow at four o'clock in the morning."

I smiled, looked him in the eyes, shook his hand, and said, "Thanks for the opportunity."

"I said just meet me here. I didn't say bring the contract."

"I know," I added, "but you will." I walked out of there knowing that it went well. I knew I would get him.

I knew I was going to like this profession. I knew I was going to succeed. I also knew that I didn't need Mel Levine. The fact that I worked with Levine meant nothing to Robert. All it did was give me credentials over the phone to set up the initial meeting. Once I already had a client, especially a client the caliber of Robert Massey, I knew I wouldn't need to work for anyone else anymore. I always wanted to be my own man, not work for someone else. It was my destiny to be the number one agent in the world, not someone's partner or associate.

I planned on doing things my way. I also knew that if I was going to be successful, I was going to need someone to watch my back. I was going to need someone to work with me when I made my move to go solo. I called my brother Jason that night. It was late, but Jason was all fired up about taking an exam first thing in the morning. He knew he was ready and couldn't wait to set the curve.

Jason had that soldier mentality. When he was an incoming freshman, I used to tell him that school is like a warrior's rock. Conan the Barbarian sharpened his sword by scraping the edge of the steel blade against the rock's hard surface. The friction of stone against steel sharpens the weapon as the rock scrapes away the dull edges and leaves only the strongest, sharpest, truest edge of the blade. I told him that our weapons were our minds and that we sharpen and shape them with the friction of exams. I remembered the feeling well, but now it seemed very distant to me.

Getting straight As no longer did anything for me. But it was still important for Jason, who at the time was a sophomore at the University of Miami.

"Jason, I am going to be making my move soon and I am going to need you to be ready," I told him.

"What do you want to do?" he asked.

"The best way you can help me as my partner is to become a certified public accountant and an attorney. I want you to be extremely educated and qualified. I want you to have an extremely impressive background. No top agent is both a CPA and an attorney. I want you to be a crack tax man, a real ace. You have to be very impressive."

"Now you tell me," he said rhetorically. "I just spent the past two semesters studying premed classes to become a plastic surgeon. I have a biology exam tomorrow."

"Switch majors to accounting. You don't have to like it. You just have to ace it. And get some outstanding achievement and academic awards while you're at it."

He was silent and said, "Okay, Drew. I am with you. You better be THE MAN in this business by the time I am ready. I better not be studying taxes for nothing!"

I knew he would switch majors from biology to accounting. I knew he would forego taking the classes he enjoyed like history and literature for business classes such as taxes and finance. To Jason school was nothing more than a challenge on the way to something greater. If it meant studying subjects that were boring and difficult, he would find excitement in the challenge of excelling in those difficult circumstances. And that he did. My brother knew me better than anyone, well enough to know that I would make it, and so he switched majors and careers, gambling on my success. Smart move.

I told him about Massey's 4:00 A.M. meeting and he said he'd call me at 3:00 A.M. to make sure I was up. I was already gone by the time he called. I barely slept that night and made sure that I was there on time.

When I knocked on the door, it took him a while to answer. He opened the door and said, "No juice and doughnuts?" I pulled them from behind my back and smiled. Massey then said, "Go home! And don't call me until the afternoon."

I could see he was asleep and was just testing me to see if I would show up. I had done what I said I would do, and that was good enough for us both.

After meeting with him every day here and there for almost two weeks, he finally said to me, "All right, Drew, I have the contract you gave me to look over right here and I've got this pen. I will sign with you on two conditions."

"You name it," I said, completely gung ho.

"First you have to take me in wrestling," he said.

I looked him in the eyes to see if he was serious or not. He had a poker face on so I couldn't tell. Now Robert was only twenty pounds heavier than me and I had an inch or two of height on him so on paper it didn't seem so tough. In reality, Robert was one of the toughest street kids I have ever come across and could pin me in five seconds flat. He had these very hard and heavy hands with knuckles that always seemed to find a way to bruise your exposed bone. I knew he wasn't serious, because it would be too absurd and I knew that he liked me enough not to hurt me. I trusted him not to mess me up.

There was no point in saying anything. If I was going to make a good showing here, I would have to surprise him by immediately trying to grab him and go for the neck. And that is exactly what I did—sort of.

I jumped on him but I didn't make it to the neck. He was surprised and laughed hysterically as he bounced me off of him. Getting up off the floor, I poised myself to try again.

"Close enough, Drew," he said as he waved me off.

I asked myself, "Is anything ever easy?" I knew anything worthwhile never is. And then I realized that's how I liked it. If everyone else was talented, determined, and smart enough to do it, then there would be nothing special or gratifying about it. Then I asked him, "What's the second condition?"

"That you don't call me or talk to me for at least one week!"

"No way! We have too much work to do," I said with a huge smile on my face.

"All right, you're a tough negotiator," he conceded.

"Don't forget that. We'll fly in to Fort Lauderdale to see Levine tomorrow and sign," I told him as I shook his hand and then grabbed him from behind in a bear hug screaming like a lunatic. He couldn't help but laugh at my enthusiasm.

He signed the deal the next day. I felt like a million bucks. And then I felt like I had work to do. I had successfully recruited a client for another agent. In the coming weeks of the spring of 1989, I signed several other players for Levine— D. J. Johnson and Ivy Joe Hunter out of Kentucky University, Naz Worthen out of North Carolina State University, and David Braxton out of Wake Forest University. I got Levine his top players that year. Sure, I got them in part by selling Levine's track record instead of my own, but I felt that was a very small part of the overall picture. What it came down to was that these guys signed with me for one reason and one reason only—they felt comfortable putting their future in my hands because they knew me well. They saw how hard I worked for them despite the fact that I was going to Duke Law School. They saw how I was up at four in the morning with them knowing that I had to walk into a classroom with a law professor just waiting for me to show up unprepared, so that he could make an example of me. They saw how devoted and dedicated I was to becoming a success. They believed in me—not Levine's background. They would have signed with any legitimate, experienced agent I worked for.

The problem was the only agent I trusted to do right by my guys was me. I did not want to take my guys to an agent who would screw them over. To protect the guys who showed their loyalty to me, I would ultimately have to become their agent. I spent a lot of time with Robert. I went to his daily workouts and I hung out with him at nightclubs. I got my ear pierced and put a big diamond stud in my ear. I bought a couple of big flashy rings and gold bracelets. If I looked like a Miami Vice character before, I looked like I was one of Tony Montana's crew from *Scarface* now. The more I fit in with Robert and his friends, the more I stood out among my Duke Law school classmates. I became the big man on campus with students constantly congratulating me and asking how I pulled it off while still in school. Law professors started singling me out in class and debating with me. Because of Robert, I had become what I wanted to be, and I worked harder and harder for him.

We transcended the agent-client relationship and became partners. Robert had given me the green light to be the man, and I was making it happen on my own. I saw that I didn't need to work for anyone else to succeed. More importantly I started to get some power as several huge articles were written about some twenty-two-year-old Duke Law student who had signed several local football players. There was a big article on the front page of the sports section with three pictures of me. I loved it. It seemed like everyone around the campus came up to me and congratulated me on the recent articles.

I felt like somebody—a contender—and I liked it. Girls were calling me constantly, wanting to meet me and sending me modeling pictures in the mail. My law professors showed me respect in the classroom. And my clients could see that I was getting a lot of publicity both for me and them.

I was getting so much local recognition that I felt it appropriate to walk up to Duke Head Coach Steve Spurrier and introduce myself.

Before I could finish giving him my story he said, "Yeah, I know who you are. I've been reading about you a lot in the paper. You've been getting more hype than me." He was extremely cordial and asked me if I was going to start representing Duke football players. Like with Jimmy Johnson, I could see a guy who absolutely, without a doubt, will win—period. I knew he wouldn't be at Duke for long. I also knew that I wasn't going to be at Duke for long either and I had a tough decision to make. The easy thing was not to rock the boat and stay with Levine. I had a job as an agent recruiting for one of the most successful agents in the country, and he was talking about paying me very handsomely in reward for my performance. Working for Levine with his track record and my hard-core recruiting, I was guaranteed success without any financial pressure. I would have it made, and I was only twenty-two years old and in my second year of Law School.

If I was going to go out on my own, if I was going to have the guts to be my own man, I would need a track record. I would need Robert Massey as my client. And even if I could pull that off I would have a whole new set of problems. I would be starting from scratch. I would have no office. No money coming in to finance my recruiting. I would still have to manage to graduate from law school. And with all this against me, I would still have to go out and convince players that I am the best agent for them. To make things worse, I would have to compete head to head with Levine for University of Miami players, and he had all the selling points in his favor by representing Irvin, the Blades brothers, and Brett Perriman. I told myself that I would have to be crazy to do it.

I called Jason and we talked about it. He knew what I was going to do, and he also knew that I needed to explain it to him as a way to convince myself. It's funny how talking to Jason is a lot like talking to myself.

When we were growing up, he always knew what I was

thinking and what I was going to do, and nothing has changed since. I told him that all the heroes that we admired when we were kids, every single one of them took a chance, risked it all, and bet on themselves to come up a big winner. Here was my opportunity, and like Rocky Balboa, I wanted to take my shot at the title.

I had one chance of pulling it off and his name was Robert Massey.

Robert was my guy from day one. I was as close with Robert as I was with any friend other than family that I ever had, and he trusted me because he believed in me as an agent. About a month before the 1989 NFL Draft in April, I knew I had to make my move.

Robert was coming over to my apartment in Durham, North Carolina on a Tuesday night. I think I managed to say two or three sentences about being my man and personally overseeing that things go right for him when he interrupted me and said, "Drew, if you want to be my agent and be on your own it's cool with me."

It was that easy and I couldn't believe it. That twenty-two-year-old man gave this twenty-two-year-old man the biggest break of his life. I will never forget it and will always be loyal to Robert. Clients like Robert—ones you can trust and communicate and bond with—are hard to come by. Agents are always complaining behind closed doors that too often their clients are arrogant, inconsiderate, selfish, immature, and have no loyalty or appreciation for your hard work over the years. You won't catch me saying that about Robert Massey behind any doors. It meant a lot to Robert to do that kind of a favor for me. It made him happy to help me out with my career as I was helping him out with his career. If ever a player and an agent were ever truly a team—it was Robert Massey and Drew Rosenhaus.

Robert was the only guy I approached because I did not want to damage Levine any more than necessary. I liked Levine and was appreciative of the opportunity he gave me. It was never personal, just business. I did what I had to do to him, nothing less, nothing more.

Now that I had Robert Massey on board, it was time to prepare for the holiest day of the year—the 1989 NFL Draft.

I quickly developed a reputation among the other agents as a man to be feared and respected. While working with Levine, I signed about a dozen players. I really did it on my own because I was the guy who met the players, gave them the presentation, and got them to sign. In fact, I was never impressed with Mel's sales pitch. It infuriated me when I would get top prospects to meet with him, and he did little to excite them. It didn't matter because I was there to get the job done. In my first season of recruiting players, I had a knock-out year with Massey, Danny Peebles, Naz Worthen, David Braxton, David Johnson, Ivy Joe Hunter, Michael Brooks, Tim James, Deon Booker, Rod Carter, Donnie Ellis, and Willie Culpepper. The other agents were scared of me because I was different. I was young. I had a great rapport with the players.

I will never forget my first Indianapolis Scouting Combine where all the draftable players attend and it becomes an agent convention. Every agent goes to the combine to protect the players they have signed and to recruit others. I loved being around my competition. It made me work harder. I was the first guy waiting to see the players and the last guy to leave them. The other agents ran to their clients when they saw me coming. I was ahead of my competitors from day one due to my nonstop work ethic and hustle. I was one of the first agents in 1989 to use a cellular phone. In fact, I was so aggressive at the combine, that a year or two later they stopped letting agents come to the players' hotel. Hah! That couldn't stop me.

I was also unstoppable at the All-Star games such as the Blue-Gray Game, the Senior Bowl, the Hula Bowl, and the East-West Shrine Game. The Hula Bowl was a long trip from Miami out to Honolulu. The flight is the pits and the time change is tough to adjust to, particularly when you have to keep up with the players on the East Coast at the same time. Because Hawaii is an expensive trip, most agents don't at-tend. It is a great opportunity for probably twenty or so agents to clean up. On the other hand, the Senior Bowl in Mobile, Alabama, is a mob scene. Every agent, NFL scout, executive, and coach is there. It is a madhouse.

After only one year in the business, I was already a known man. Other agents would shudder when they heard my name. They knew the agent business would never be the same. And in the ensuing years, I did, in fact, revolutionize the industry. The other agents may have all been sharks. But they would soon learn that I was "Jaws"—the biggest and baddest Great White of them all!

6

David Versus Goliath

At the age of twenty-two, I became the youngest agent ever to break into this business. I had gone where no twenty-two-year-old had gone before. The Durham media warmed up to me as I always had a brash, outlandish remark that made for good print. I made several live television appearances and wanted to do more. Instead of being nervous that I would look bad or give a poor showing, I was eager and hungry to get my face on TV for all of next year's recruits to see.

I was a natural for TV; it made me look good and I loved it. I liked and resembled the look of the Charlie Sheen character from the movie *Wall Street.* I was able to get Robert Massey a lot of TV time as well. Robert was a guy on the bubble, he had a chance to go in the first round but was more likely to go in the second. No one had ever heard of Robert before I signed him, now almost everyone in North Carolina knew of him.

I knew Draft Day would be a big day media wise. I wanted to capitalize on that as best as I could. I told the local media that I would have several local football players who were going to be drafted over to my apartment for the draft. I sold the local media on the idea of sending some camerapersons to film it. They jumped at the chance. It seemed easy. I couldn't understand why more agents didn't do this themselves. It's good for the player and the agent to get this type of exposure for marketing.

I figured if it was this easy to convince the local media to spend the day with us, maybe I could reach the national media, too. It couldn't hurt to take a shot I thought. I immediately called ESPN and started selling them about Massey and myself. I told them how Robert was a guy on the bubble who could go in the first or second round. I told them how I was going to have other guys over who were going to be third or fourth rounders. I told them about myself, how I was, at twenty-two, the youngest agent in the history of the NFL and that these guys were my clients.

I never mentioned Levine. This was my chance to hype myself as my own man and I went for it. I felt that I deserved the publicity since I was the one who signed these players, not Levine. ESPN liked the drama of Massey being on the bubble and me being such a young agent. They decided to send a cameraman out to my apartment and televise us live on Draft Day. After talking some more with me, they liked the idea so much that they sent ESPN reporter Jimmy Roberts to interview us. They aired the piece before the draft, and it was tremendous. Jimmy Roberts did right by us. He could have taken a skeptical approach that I was too young and Robert was making a big mistake. He could have done a hatchet job on me. Instead he pumped me up and made me look like a real up and comer.

Then Draft Day finally arrived. In my apartment were Robert Massey and some of his family, along with Naz Worthen of North Carolina State, David Braxton of Wake Forest, and Michael Brooks of North Carolina State. These were my guys, all local players I signed from within the state of North Carolina. ESPN and the local media were there. Jason and my father Robert were back at the house in North Miami. There was a satellite truck that pulled up, and my neighbors and fellow law students were coming out and asking, "Wow, Drew, what's going on?" They couldn't believe that the satellite trucks were going to beam the NFL draft from my apartment.

Guys still in school at UM and guys I went to school with were calling me. This was my second year in law school and people could not believe it. They kept calling me, asking, "Drew what are you doing on the draft? Is that really you from your house?"

Friends that knew I was working for Levine were calling, saying, "Drew, what the hell are you doing telling these guys that they're your clients, that you're the agent?" I just smiled and didn't say a word.

Being on national television was awesome. Remember, every player in America—especially underclassmen and future NFL prospects—watches the draft. Other than the Super Bowl, it's the most watched event by the prospects because that could be them next year or a few seasons down the road. Even the veterans all watch because they are concerned that someone might be drafted to take their job.

During the draft, all the agents and NFL teams were saying, "Who the hell is this kid? He's got ESPN broadcasting from his house and he doesn't even have an NFL client list."

All the agents had to ask themselves, and I am sure their clients asked them as well, "Why is some twenty-two-year-old rookie agent on the draft instead of you. Why aren't you on the draft? More importantly, how is it that he got his clients national television hype and you did nothing for me?" I made every other agent in the business look bad and I loved it. Bring 'em on! Bring 'em all on! One by one or all at once—I don't care! I am honest and straightforward about it. I don't like other agents because they are my competition. If I had a friend in the business, it would cloud my judgment and make the competition more difficult; therefore, I have no friends in the business. It is nothing personal—just business. However, they make me sick at agent seminars when they all gather and act like they are friends. They are hypocrites lacking self-respect as they smile to each other's faces and then talk trash about them behind each other's backs. I don't smile, and it's not my style to talk behind another agent's back, I'll let them be the weasels. I don't need to resort to that to succeed.

I don't play their games and they lose clients to me. For this I am considered immoral and a bad guy. As long as my clients know that I am the hardest worker in this business and that I will go all out all the time for them, that is all I care about. Every good agent loses clients. It is a part of the business you have to overcome. Just like with any other tough business, it is a constant challenge where you have to hunt to survive; grow fat or get tired and you will not last. It didn't take me long to realize this.

I once made an effort to develop a rapport with one of the top agents in the business—Marvin Demoff. I was at the 1989 East-West Shrine game with Robert Massey in January prior to the draft. I introduced myself to Demoff and told him that I was going to dominate this business and be a top agent like himself one day. He was very friendly and I thought I had learned a few things from our conversation. I learned all right. I learned as I walked into Robert's room and saw him hang up the phone in an agitated mood. It turns out that the instant I turned my back, Demoff called Massey and told him that I said I wanted to be like him and that Robert should go with the real deal and not some young agent wanna-be. Now here was the class of the business, one of the most respected agents in the business, and he had stabbed me in the back.

So when I had made it to the big time on ESPN, I knew it had killed my competitors that some twenty-two-year-old kid in just his first year was already featured on ESPN although many of these agents remain anonymous their entire careers.

Throughout the draft, Massey was as mentally tough as could be. He knew he did everything he could to go as high as possible and whatever was meant to be would happen. We waited a couple of hours and were on ESPN the entire day. I had prepared him for the fact that he was most likely going to go in the second round. He knew that I had manufactured the likelihood of him being a first-round pick to the media to create the drama necessary to garner publicity. Robert knew the truth and did not get lost in the hype.

The phone call came as expected in the second round. It was the New Orleans Saints calling to draft him. When I thought about the New Orleans Saints, one thing came to mind—Jim Finks. The general manager of the Saints was an icon in the NFL as the prototype old-guard general manager. He was known for being a very tough negotiator that agents feared.

I love a good fight. But a fight is much easier if the playing field is level. My first time out of the box as an agent, it looked like I had stumbled into the unkindest of all fights, the most one-sided agent/management negotiation in the history of football.

My opponent was Finks, the favorite to succeed Pete Rozelle as the next NFL commissioner. Finks was a former player who did all the right things to make himself arguably the most respected executive in the NFL. His reputation was that of a straight-shooting, hard-line, tough negotiator. He was sixty-two years old at the time—old enough to be my grandfather. He was going to be the head of the NFL's Competition Committee, and he was—in the minds of many—the most powerful executive in the League.

On the other hand, I was as young and inexperienced as an agent could get. But I was a fearless and hungry hired gun looking to make a name for myself. This was truly David versus Goliath. Other agents called Massey and warned him that he needed to hire them and not some child who was in over his head. They told Robert that I was a student about to learn a real lesson, and it was going to be at Robert's expense.

But for some reason, I wasn't intimidated. I was thrilled by the challenge and my adrenaline was pumping. I was excited by the opportunity to show the world that I could match-up against the best NFL executive. I never had a doubt that I would hold my own against Finks. I certainly didn't lack confidence.

Neither did Robert. He knew I would go to war for him, and he knew that as a second-round pick, he was going to get more money than he had ever seen. It was a great situation for him as he was going to start right away for the cornerback-starved Saints. He had become nationally known among avid football fans as he received national television exposure. Robert was happy. But I was unhappy. I wanted more for Robert. I wanted him to be a first-round pick. Then again, I always want more for my clients.

On that Draft Day, a day that will live in infamy to my competitors, I served notice to the National Football League that Drew Rosenhaus hath cometh. The next day I had also served notice to Levine that I was going on my own. That meeting was one of the toughest meetings I ever had in my life, but I wanted to tell him face to face what I was going to do. I liked Mel and I had hurt him. He watched Draft Day, too, and was shocked to see me with Massey and his other clients representing myself, and not Mel, as their agent.

Mel was furious. He said I spent a lot of his money recruiting these guys, and now I was leaving him. He complained that I had only worked for him for a few months, and I was already taking away his top rookie client. He thought I stabbed him in the heart. The bottom line is I did what I thought was in my best interest. It was never my intent to hurt Mel. It was just the natural evolution of my career. It was my destiny.

Mel knew that my leaving the firm meant I was going to compete with him head to head for the University of Miami recruits. I assured him that Massey was the only client I was taking with me and that he didn't have to worry about the rest of his clients. He was bitter and I couldn't blame him. I thought Mel was a nice enough guy, but business was business. I had outgrown him in a short period of time. He called me the "Natural" my first day, and he knew I was going to be top dog one day. I was a shark on a rampage and he couldn't keep me caged in. I never wished Mel any ill will, but I taught him more about being an agent the very first day than he could ever teach me. No other agent, including Levine, has my passion for the business, the sport, and the guys.

It was simply a matter of time until I would leave and pass him on the agent totem pole.

I walked out of Mel's office knowing I had done something that could not be undone. He told me I had made a big mistake. If he was right, it was one I could not correct. I had already pulled the trigger and there was no bringing this bullet back. Now I could only hope that I had hit my mark.

But I never had any doubts. I knew I made the right decision and was excited about my future. It was going to be Rosenhaus Sports: me and my brother. It felt good to be in business with Jason. We were Batman and Robin, just like the old days. Except now everything we did counted and we were in the game for real.

I came home that summer with no money. I had no office, no secretary, no apartment. I took out a $40,000 credit line from the bank and lived at home for the summer with my family. Jason and I worked out of my mom's interior designer office, and we were eager to take on the New Orleans Saints. I had Jason print out every type of statistical graph analysis pertaining to rookie contract negotiations on his computer. I worked day and night, preparing for this contract.

The media was ready for us. They loved the story of this negotiation. *USA Today* called Massey's selection by the Saints the most interesting pick of the draft. The *Miami Herald* and the *Fort Lauderdale Sun-Sentinel* wrote several articles about the local kid who made good. Jim Berry, a prominent sportscaster in South Florida, came over to the house and interviewed me and Massey for TV. It was great. Just about every south Florida newspaper and radio and TV station did feature stories on me. Not only was I famous at my law school, but now I was famous in my own hometown.

I suddenly had become the star. Instead of me being the guy next to the star, I became a celebrity in my own right. But I wanted more. Like a shark smelling blood, I went into a media frenzy. So once again, I did something no one else had ever done. With Jim Finks's consent, I took ESPN's camera crew with me behind closed doors to film the actual negotiations between me and the icon. Jim Finks was making a push for commissioner, and I can only assume that the reason he allowed me to bring an ESPN camera crew into his office was to score some points with the public by handing me my lunch. I think he didn't shy away from the ESPN piece because he was so confident that he would overwhelm me in the negotiations.

You see, this just isn't done in the NFL. Never before had an NFL negotiation been filmed. I was the first to do it, and no one has done it since.

Everyone thought I was insane. Jim Finks is reputed to be one of the toughest negotiators in the business. I had never negotiated an NFL contract before. And I was going to bring in ESPN to televise the actual negotiations?

That took intestinal fortitude. I don't think Jim Finks wanted to be embarrassed by turning down the challenge of negotiating with a kid on ESPN, and I think he genuinely was nice to me. He used to compare me to his son. I wasn't crazy about that, being called a son. I was supposed to be his counterpart, his competitor, a worthy adversary, not his son. So, I used that pity or fondness for me to my advantage.

The other agents loved it and said I was like the lamb being led to the slaughter for all to see. Everyone thought it was a big mistake; everyone but Massey and Jason, that is. Jason thought it was a stroke of marketing genius. Dan Patrick, ESPN's reporter and anchorman, handled the feature. The pressure was on. If I dropped the ball on these negotiations, ESPN was going to show it on national television. This was going to make me or break me. I was fired up. I knew all my arguments and anticipated all of his.

Like a prize-fighter pacing back and forth in the ring, I couldn't wait to get at it. I walked in Finks's office and was directed to the conference room where Finks and the camera crew were waiting. I started to feel a little claustrophobic. I didn't like the atmosphere. So I took control. There was no small talk, no chitchat about the family or his background, I just went at him. The ESPN cameras came on and I hit him with a flurry of blows. I talked and talked. I thought if I didn't let him talk, I couldn't look bad, so all I did was talk,

talk, talk, talk. I would say that I talked about 90 percent of the time and he got no air time.

I just started rambling: "Robert should have been a first-round pick . . . and he should get a contract reflecting first-round money . . . Robert is going to start for you and should get a contract reflecting that . . . I don't like what your second-round pick got last year . . . I want a much bigger raise for my client than what other second-round picks are getting . . . Robert participated in your minicamp to act in good faith and show you he can play in this league . . . We will not sign for anything less than that . . . We will hold out if necessary."

I talked for ten minutes straight, looking right into his eyes. He didn't say anything. He just watched me like he was watching a theatrical performance. I think he wanted to see what I had. I could have kept going for another ten minutes on my monologue, and when he saw that, he finally interrupted me and said, "Robert was a second-round pick. He could have very easily been a third-round pick. He is going to get a contract commensurate with what other second-round picks are getting . . . Drew, you know, every agent says his player should have been drafted higher. Your player was a second-round pick and he's going to get paid like a second-round pick. We're not going to pay him any less than a second-round pick or any more than a second-round pick. We're going to give him a fair contract."

We went back and forth exchanging opinions. I was very loud and animated while he was precise and composed. We left things at a stalemate which is what always happens that time of year. We both knew we weren't going to get the deal done for at least another month, but we met to size each other up anyway.

After the meeting, Finks said to ESPN, "Drew doesn't lack enthusiasm . . . (and) he's a pretty smooth operator." It is very rare for a general manager to ever compliment an agent on the other side of the table, especially a man of Jim Finks's caliber. I took it as an indication of what I had become. I was no longer a kid in school telling people that one day I was going to be an agent. I was no longer just a dreamer. This was for real. I was for real. I had arrived in the NFL.

After the meeting, with ESPN still focusing the camera on me, I walked on to Head Coach Jim Mora's practice field and introduced myself. He was friendly and we shook hands. Robert's teammates, wide receiver Brett Perriman in particular, couldn't believe I walked onto the practice field. Nobody walked onto Jim Mora's practice field, especially not an agent. After battling with Jim Finks, nothing could intimidate me. Mora, who was strict and disciplined, looked shocked to see me, but he was apparently impressed by my bravado.

I also met Robert's new defensive back coach, Dom Capers. Capers was extremely impressive. He looked you in the eyes and could communicate with you. He had a great presence about him, and I knew it wouldn't be long before he became a successful head coach. It was no surprise to me that a few years later, Capers went on to become the defensive coordinator for the Pittsburgh Steelers and then was named the coach of the year for the Carolina Panthers in 1997. It is great meeting the future legends of the game while they are in their up-and-coming stages. I had a special feel for guys that I knew would become head coaches. I had similar experiences with Jeff Fisher, the head coach of the Houston Oilers, and Pete Carroll, the head coach of the New England Patriots.

Shortly after I returned home, ESPN televised its production of the negotiations. I was happy to get the national recognition of matching up against Jim Finks, but I wasn't thrilled with what they showed. They showed a few lines from me demanding that Robert get first-round money and several lines from Jim Finks saying Robert wasn't going to get that. They slanted the negotiations in Jim Finks's favor, in my opinion. I obviously wanted a lot more footage of me making my points. Overall, I wasn't satisfied. I was embarrassed that ESPN, in my opinion, campaigned for Finks and made him look good. I was pissed because the other agents loved the way the piece turned out. I wasn't going to let up on ESPN after this. They ripped me off.

So I got right on the phone with the producers and demanded that they air a new piece that would be more accurate. After a short while, ESPN aired a new piece that made me look great and focused on my relationship with Massey as well as the negotiations. I had turned a negative into a positive and got double the hype. This was a valuable lesson, if the media screws you, make sure you get them to make it up to you in the future. Normally, they will make it up to you and then some.

ESPN continued to follow Massey's negotiations and waited for him to sign the contract. Finks and I were at a stalemate. I wanted to get the impossible—I wanted a huge contract, better than what anyone else got in the second round. This was my first and quite possibly my last contract if I did not succeed for Robert. Everything was on the line for us.

As for Jim Finks, he was considered a top candidate to become the next NFL Commissioner, and he wanted to make an impressive showing among his peers. He would have looked like a fool if he gave me one cent more than what everyone else got. Both of us were pinned between a rock and a hard place. I wanted first-round money and wasn't going to get it. He wanted second-round money, and I wasn't going to give in to his demands. Stuck in the stalemate, I had no choice but recommend to Robert that he hold out. The New Orleans media was all over us. The Saints' management and coaches started to get upset with Robert. The one guy who maintained a positive relationship with Robert was Coach Capers.

Things were not going like I wanted them to. This was my career on the line and Robert's future, and I was watching them fall apart. I felt like Captain James T. Kirk in one of those *Star Trek* episodes where the *U.S.S. Enterprise* was about to be captured by the Romulans, and there was no escape. I love *Star Trek*. The point I liked about the show was that Captain Kirk always found a way to turn a negative situation into a positive one. He would always find a way to win.

I knew that was exactly what I needed to do. I asked myself over and over again where the compromise was. Finks wanted a standard three-year deal and I wanted an extraordinary four-year deal. At the time, all second-round picks would sign either a three- or four-year deal. Like Captain Kirk, I rewrote the rules and passed the test that could not be passed. My solution was to do a two-year deal. The downside was that if we did a two-year deal, Robert would get less money up front in the form of a signing bonus. If Robert got hurt or was a disappointment after his second year, then he would not get the chance to make that money back.

The upside was that Robert still got a signing bonus in line with what other second-round picks got. Had he signed a four-year deal, his third year and fourth year would only be a small increase over what he got in the year before. However, if Robert could start for those two years and then renegotiate, he would get a much bigger raise, and he would make up the lost signing bonus money and then some.

It was a gamble. If Robert were to have a productive two years, we would win. If Robert were to have a substandard two years, we would lose. This is the approach today taken by many agents when they have a client who they feel will be forced by the system to take less money up front on a contract than is satisfactory. The idea is to get the client into camp so that he can be productive. Then do a short-term deal allowing for a quick renegotiation for the mega signing bonus. If you can get it, take it.

If you can't get what you need up front, then you take this short-term approach and load up with numerous incentives, and try to set it up for the next deal. For years since, other agents have followed my model with Massey. It was a creative solution for a player who didn't belong where he was drafted.

Other teams did not want to give in and do two-year deals, and there haven't been many two-year contracts in the second round since Massey. The teams have been very reluctant to give two-year contracts. At least I left my mark on the NFL with my very first contract. Robert had the confidence in himself to be a starter and I believed in him. Since the brief nine-day holdout had been creating some negative publicity for the team and was a distraction, I knew the deal would appeal to them. We came to an agreement on a two-year deal totaling $560,000.

Robert and I were happy. We felt like we got what we wanted. We won and the beauty of the deal is that the Saints got what they wanted. They did not have to pay first-round money to a second-round pick. All that they had to do was break from convention and give us a short-term, two-year deal. The next day, Jason and I were reviewing all the various contracts that had come in from the second round. When Jason finished his analysis, he congratulated me. "Drew, you did it. You won. We're going to be able to hang our hats on Robert's contract. We're going to be able to show everyone in the world what a great job you did."

Robert was so appreciative of the efforts I gave him that he did something I have never seen any other player do— instead of paying me 2 percent, he more than doubled my fee and paid me 5 percent. That was the ultimate compliment and I take a great deal of pride in that. A year or two later, when I started to become more established, I refused to accept it and did not receive anything more than what we originally agreed upon.

It's funny how things work out. It's a blessing that I was at Duke because I was able to meet Robert Massey, who was right down the road at a small school, North Carolina Central. Massey was so loyal to me, and that's all I needed was one guy, one loyal guy, and then a lot of other guys followed. Massey put me on the map. He had the bravery and the courage to give me a shot. Can you imagine being a young kid like Massey, having a once-in-a-lifetime opportunity to play in the NFL, and you put your confidence in a kid agent? I love Robert Massey for that. Robert did more for me than I did for him.

Since those early days, everything has worked out great for Robert and for me. With a good contract under my belt and a client who would bend over backward to see me succeed, I declared war on the NFL.

7

Second Place Sucks

Aᴼᴿᴱ SIGNING Mᴀssᴇʏ wɪᴛʜ ᴛʜᴇ Sᴀɪɴᴛs, ᴛʜᴇ ɴᴀᴛɪᴏɴᴀʟ, the South Florida, and the Raleigh-Durham media were great to me. I was on the cover of sports pages with big articles about the young, fearless agent ready to take on the NFL. The reports in the North Carolina area proclaimed Duke Law School as one of the toughest schools in the country. Most students struggle to keep their heads above water in their second year, and here I was already starting my career.

The most popular question reporters would ask was, "Drew, how are you able to do it? Wasn't it extremely difficult to become an agent while still being a student in law school? It had to be tough."

No, it wasn't that tough for me. I breezed right through it. Spoken like a true agent. No challenge is too tough, whether that's the truth or not. Yeah, I painted a positive picture to cover up some of the dark days, but that is necessary. As an agent, it is critical always, without exception, to be positive. You will be tested, time and time again, and you must always keep your head high. Why? Because your client and their family depend on you. They can get down. They can get depressed. They can fail. They can get their feelings hurt. They can drop the ball. But never the agent. Because if the agent drops the ball, then the player is in trouble. When the agent folds, the player gets hurt.

A good agent will always be there to pick the client up off of the ground and get him on his feet. When a team makes a disappointing offer, I always ready myself and my client to bounce back with our counteroffer. When a player gets into trouble on the field, the agent has to encourage him to work harder, improve, and play his way out of it. When a player gets into trouble off the field, the agent has to be there to help him correct that mistake and make amends. When a player has a personal problem, the agent must be there to offer him friendly advice and encourage him to stay positive.

The agent is the last line of defense. My clients know that they can count on me whenever they have any type of problem. I give them that confidence that things are going to work out as long as they continue to do the right thing. This is what separates me from my competition. My players don't deal with a secretary or a large corporation. They talk to me or my brother. They know us well and have spent a lot of time with us. They don't talk to a different guy each time they call.

When my clients call, they don't just talk to an agent, they talk to a friend. I will help a client with any problem—big or small, and they know this from firsthand experience. I am always there because I am always working. *Sports Illustrated* labeled me on its cover, "The Most Hated Man in Pro Football." I may be the most hated man by my competitors, but I am also the most liked by my clients, and I have a productive rapport with every top executive in the NFL. I take a lot of pride in all three.

My competition hates me because I walked all over them and crushed them on my way to the top. They're scared because they know it's just a matter of time before the so-called "Boogey Man" of the NFL strikes again. They're going down and can do nothing but watch my meteoric rise to the top.

The worthiest competitor I ever had was Duke—the law school. If I was going to declare war on the NFL, the first line of defense I had to get past was law school. I wasn't going to be able to pick up any new clients if other agents could go around telling my recruits that I had flunked out of school. The only problem was that I didn't have time to go to class that much or study for exams. In the fall, I spent a lot of time visiting Massey and scouting recruits. In the spring, I spent a lot of time out of town with recruits.

My professors, who were at first delighted to have a local sports celebrity in their class, soon became insulted by my lack of attendance. And when I did show up, I was always on my cellular phone walking into and out of class or my pager would go off. And although I was known for giving Duke's sports law program a lot of recognition, I think many other professors disliked the fact that I was working so hard as an agent.

Duke's law school is one of the toughest in the nation, where the brightest minds in the country have to work their butts off just to pass. I guess I made law school look easy. But it wasn't. Some professors felt I was making a mockery of the school by merely moonlighting as a law student. I went to class with Ivy Leaguers from Harvard, Princeton, and Yale. Me, I was a Miami guy, a brash Hurricane. If the Miami Hurricanes were considered the Oakland Raiders of the NFL, than I was the Al Davis of law students. They wore glasses with neatly combed hair and nice suits; I wore a diamond stud earring, dark sunglasses, and slicked my hair back with mousse. I went to class in Nike sweat suits and wore more gold than King Tut.

I took a lot of pride in the fact that I came in to the law school with all these other so-called geniuses, and I finished as one of the students who really distinguished himself. If my confidence and ego were big coming into Duke, they were higher than Mt. Everest by my final semester in the spring of 1990. That was when I needed it the most. This was the time when the 1989 college football season was over. This was the time I was going to be either a one-hit wonder or a Stevie Wonder in this business.

I was on my own at the ripe age of twenty-three. I didn't want my first year in this business to be the pinnacle of my career. Aside from law school, I had to deal with competition from Levine. He was the King who represented Michael Irvin, Brett Perriman, and the Blades Brothers. I was the newcomer hoping to take his crown away from him. I wanted the title.

I bared down getting ready for fierce competition with Levine—and then it happened. Almost over night, Levine was out of the business. The claim was Levine stole money from his clients. I was shocked. Levine was charged with certain white collar crimes and ultimately he went to jail on a tax charge. The suspicion that Levine was another one of those agents who stole money from his clients spread like a brush-fire. He lost his clients. Money got lost—and when that happens, bad things follow.

Brett Perriman, a former Miami Hurricane and New Orleans Saint receiver, who saw my work with Massey, called me up and said he wanted to meet with me about representing him. I met with Brett and I signed him. This was a very significant signing for me. He was the first of many NFL veterans I picked up.

By signing Brett, I realized that there was, for me at least, an entirely untouched market of NFL veterans who are in the process of firing one agent and hiring another. I realized that I could pick up a lot of new clients. And veterans were a pleasure. They were smart guys who had been around the block. They weren't going to sign with the agent who gave them the most money as an allowance; they would sign with an agent who got them the most money from the NFL and that's the bottom line. Most veterans appreciate hard work whereas sometimes rookies don't know any better.

After signing Brett, I was like a rogue shark getting its first taste of blood. I liked it and came back for more. I wanted more veterans. I signed the guys that I recruited while working for Mel. I signed D. J. Johnson of the Pittsburgh Steelers, Ivy Joe Hunter of the Indianapolis Colts, Naz Worthen of the Kansas City Chiefs, and David Braxton of the Minnesota Vikings. With Robert and Brett, I now had six clients. Like a speeding snowball gaining size and momentum, I was on a roll.

Now it was time to get some rookies. I had two groups of recruits to go after. The University of Miami players and the North Carolina players. At the University of Miami, I had targeted defensive tackles Cortez Kennedy and Jimmie Jones, and linebacker Bernard "Tiger" Clark. At North Carolina State University, I targeted defensive tackle Ray Agnew and linebacker Bobby Houston. I also went after the huge tight end from nearby Liberty College—Eric Green.

I was good friends with Tiger and Jimmie dating back to the University of Miami college days. When I went off to Durham, they were entering their redshirt sophomore years. And now, as they were graduating college, I was graduating from Duke. Before I left for Duke, I told them I was going to be ready for them, and I had made good on my word!

I had experience in representing a second-round pick and negotiating a good contract. I also had the respect and confidence of their former teammate Brett Perriman, a new client. They were impressed with what I had accomplished in just the three years since I graduated from UM. They had seen me on ESPN during the draft and the ESPN segment on the negotiations with Jim Finks. There had been a lot of articles in the South Florida newspapers and plenty of TV features about my exploits. I came back to Miami as a known man.

My competition knew I was coming to town, too. Other agents knew I was going to come after the Miami Hurricanes—and they weren't the only ones. One day, I went with Jason on campus and walked right into the Hurricane gym looking for Tiger and Jimmie. By now, Jimmy Johnson and his coaching staff had left for Dallas and the Dennis Erickson regime had begun. As Jason and I were talking and joking with all of the guys in the gym, one of the other players, who was jealous that we were not talking to him, told an assistant coach that Jason and I were agents. The coach kicked us out of the locker room.

I was shocked. This was my turf. I was at home at the University of Miami. This was my alma mater and this newcomer coach kicked me out. To the coach's dismay, the players looked at him with disrespect and followed me outside.

When we got outside, I continued to relate stories about my sexual adventures at Duke and how these guys better watch their girlfriends now that I was back in town.

We looked up and the assistant coach had followed us out. The players, who I hadn't seen in a while, kept saying, "Fuck him. He's just some pee-on assistant coach. If we want to kick it with you, we will." Although the coach was not a gentleman about it, I knew an agent shouldn't be hanging out like this. I may have been a good guy with good intentions, but there are plenty of others who, if they were in my shoes, could have done a lot of damage to the university. I understood his reasons and respected them.

What was my haven, where all my friends were, was now a place I was no longer welcome. The University of Miami soon developed rules requiring that agents notify the school whenever they come on campus. I was required to follow rules and regulations. I was now like all of the other agents and had to restrict my contact with players.

It was a big adjustment for me to go from being a good guy to a bad guy who couldn't have any contact with players until after the season. I had lost my big edge of being able to go on that campus to recruit. On the other hand, Jason was still a student and was on campus every day. Jason went to the University of Miami for a total of eight years to become a certified public accountant and an attorney. There was a Rosenhaus presence on that campus for eight years after I had left. He did exactly as we planned he would do—and much more.

With all the agents going after UM players, I had plenty of competition. My competition's main point of persuasion was that my youth and inexperience were too much of a risk to take. My competitors figured that if they said I was too young and inexperienced often enough it would start to sink in.

My competitors underestimated me. What they thought was my weakness was actually my strength. Because I was the same age as Tiger and Jimmie, they were able to see my evolution from student to agent. The fact that they had known me for several years was a big factor and made them feel comfortable with me. Sure, I was younger and less experienced than the other agents, but these guys knew me. They knew my work ethic, they knew my hunger for success, and they knew I wanted them to succeed. They didn't know anyone else like they knew me.

The way I saw it, everyone else was an unknown factor—they were the risk. With the once-in-a-lifetime opportunity before them, these players could not afford to take any unnecessary risks. Besides, I would outwork and outthink any competition I came across. These players knew this. The other guys didn't stand a chance. Despite the other agents, Tiger and Jimmie signed with me right off of the bat. They were a pleasure to deal with.

The other player I really went after, Cortez Kennedy, was the highest-rated player I recruited. Cortez had transferred to the University of Miami from a junior college after I had left. I never went to school with Cortez, so to him I was in the same boat as the other agents.

Having Jimmie and Tiger under my belt, I also zeroed in on Ray Agnew. Mel Kiper and Joel Buchsbaum had Agnew, a defensive tackle from North Carolina State, rated as a first-round pick. Tiger and Jimmie were expected to go anywhere from the second to the fifth round. I wanted to improve upon my previous year of having a second-round pick by getting that first-rounder. Ray Agnew was that first-rounder and I felt he was mine.

I needed to get a first-round pick to vault myself into the top echelon of the up and coming agents. I felt Ray was it. I felt we had gotten pretty close. He was real tight with his former teammate Naz Worthen who I had recently picked up as a client. I drove to visit Ray's family and they liked me. I took him out to some nightclubs and helped him meet plenty of pretty girls. Naz had even called one night to tell me that Ray said he was going to sign with me. Shortly thereafter, I arranged to bring Ray down to Miami to sign the contract.

It was a done deal. Or so I thought. Jason was pretty good friends with Cortez. I would call Jason after the Hurricane games to get his scouting report, and often he would be on the phone with Cortez when I called. Cortez was one of the highest rated players in the draft. I thought maybe if he saw me sign Ray, it would impress him enough to want to sign with me. When Ray and I were in town that weekend, Cortez wanted to get together as well. So Jason, Ray, Cortez, and I all went out. Ray wanted to go to Club Rollexx—a nationally known strip joint. Even though I was the only white guy in the place—or within a ten-square mile radius—I was welcomed there. I had been there quite a bit in the past, and I was known there as being okay. It's a tough crowd though where trouble can spark at any moment. If the girls there didn't do such a good job of keeping the guys' attention, there would be trouble.

Ray and Cortez had a great time. Jason and I just kept our eyes on each other's backs to make sure there wasn't any trouble for us or the recruits. We dropped Ray off. He said he would sign a contract with us tomorrow as planned and thanked us for showing him around. My first mistake was not signing Ray right then. I learned a key lesson: You must sign the player on the spot if he is ready. Don't give him the chance to change his mind.

After dropping Ray off, we were on the way to taking Cortez home. Cortez asked me if I had signed Ray. It seemed like such a given and a formality that I said yes. I didn't think much of it until later when Jason asked me if I thought it would be a problem. I felt that as close as Ray and I were there was no way something as insignificant and harmless as that would come between us. He said he was going to sign with me the next day anyway.

Well, I was blind. I shouldn't have assumed anything or exaggerated the truth. I made a mistake and I paid for it big time. It turns out that Cortez and Ray had been talking to several agents later that evening, and Cortez told them what I had said about having signed Ray. When word got back to Ray later that night, he went nuts. He got on the plane and flew home without letting me know. I went to pick him up at his room to get him to sign the contract and he had checked out—he was gone for good.

The feeling I had when I was told he checked out was one I will never forget. I knew I had made a mistake and there was going to be hell to pay for it. I had lost my first-round pick, damn! I had made a mistake by allowing my hunger to impress another player (Cortez), to affect my chances of signing a player (Ray) I was likely to get. What I said was unnecessary. I meant no harm and I believed it would ultimately be the truth, but there are no excuses for mistakes in this business—ever.

I finally reached Ray on the telephone in North Carolina, and he told me how upset he was. He said he would never be able to trust me again. He hung the phone up on me after chewing me out. I knew he and Bobby Houston were going to the Senior Bowl, so I thought I would try again to see them after I flew to Honolulu to watch Tiger and Eric Green at the Hula Bowl.

Hawaii was no vacation. I had spent that week entertaining players and competing with the other agents who were also there for the players' time. I got no sleep and I hustled constantly. I couldn't let losing Ray affect the recruitment of the other players in Hawaii. It was tough.

After an exhausting week in Hawaii, I flew to the Senior Bowl in Mobile, Alabama to try and see Ray. I took the red eye to Mobile, believing that once Ray had seen me and acknowledged my effort of flying out there to see him, he would have a heart and give me a break. I hoped he would treat me like the friend I thought I was. When I had arrived at their hotel, I waited in the lobby for Ray and Bobby to come in. I must have waited two hours for these guys. I was exhausted physically and mentally.

Finally, they showed up and started walking through the lobby. I yelled, "Ray, Bobby—I made it out here guys." I was so excited to see them I could barely control my enthusiasm. All the other agents in the hotel were looking at me. They could see how haggard I looked. "Hey Drew," Ray quietly said as he looked away and walked right past me. Bobby Houston didn't even say hello. They just ignored me and kept walking. I didn't care about the humiliation in front of other agents who got a good laugh at my expense. I didn't care about the disrespect of being treated like some other agent.

I was devastated at having lost that first-round pick that I had so desperately wanted and worked for—all because of a split second slip of the tongue. I wanted to take it back. But I couldn't. I had been beaten. I had lost. Not to another agent, but to myself—there's a difference. It was a long plane ride home. I was sick with anxiety and agony. To come so close and let it slip away killed me. I didn't want to have the kind of year that the other agents would have. I wanted to stand out and have a great year. But it wasn't going to happen.

I could not accept being ordinary or average. I would be the best or die trying. I learned very quickly how harsh this business can be, and there is no margin for error. I vowed never to make the same mistake again. I realized that as a beginner I was going to make mistakes, but as a winner, I wouldn't make the same mistake twice.

When I got back, I didn't give up. I kept calling Ray, and I finally got him to agree to hear me out and meet with me. It was late at night and in the pouring rain, but I got in the car and drove over to see him. On the way there, I was doing sixty or so when I hit a puddle, hydroplaned and spun. My car went off the side of the road and flipped over in the mud. It was one of the scariest moments of my life. For a second, I was at the mercy of fate.

The car rolled over and was on its driver's side. I climbed out of the passenger's side and jumped off. I was a little shaken up and bruised, but I was fine. The car was off balance and shaking from the wind and rain of the thunderstorm. I was drenched with rain and mud. For the first time in my life, I had brown hair. The side of the road was tilted downward so it was easy for me and the rain to push the car back over on its wheels. A little muddy and dented, the car started right back up and I went on my way—slowly.

I pulled up to Ray's apartment in a wet, muddy, beaten-up car. I looked like John Rambo as I was covered with mud. I had hoped that Ray and Bobby would lighten up after seeing me in this condition. I had hoped they would be impressed with my perseverance and determination. I had hoped—but it was all for nothing. Their minds were set and they didn't even pay attention to what I had to say. They just let me say what I wanted and then said they had to go.

I may have been knocked down pretty good by Ray Agnew, but like Rocky Balboa, I wasn't going to go down for the count. I wanted a shot at Bobby Houston. I understood Ray's distant attitude toward me, but not Bobby's. Bobby was very unfriendly to me. After Ray left, I asked Bobby why he was acting that way. He told me point blank that he didn't like me because of my previous affiliation with Levine. He told me he was going to sign with another agent.

I countered, "Brett Perriman was one of Levine's clients. He fired Levine several months after I had quit and was no longer working for him. Brett hired me because he knew firsthand I had nothing to do with any of that stuff.

"Look Bobby, if you don't trust me, I'll put my money where my mouth is and I will trust you. I will write into the contract that you can pay me whatever you think I deserve. Think about that for a couple days and I will get back with you."

I could tell I made a dent. And I did. Bobby went on to hire another agent, but shortly after the draft, he fired him and hired me. This is a funny business. The guy I thought I was most likely to sign, Bobby Houston, became a client. As for Cortez, he told Jason and me that despite our friendship, he wanted to go with someone more experienced. Jason was pretty friendly with Cortez, and it was painful that we just weren't able to get it done.

Ray ended up being an early first-round pick to the New England Patriots, Cortez was the third pick of the draft to the Seattle Seahawks. Had I kept my mouth shut and not told Cortez that I signed Ray when I had not, then I would have gotten Ray. It is possible that I could have gotten Cortez, too. I could have had a phenomenal year.

In each case, I was close and came in second place. Not to mention that I missed out on Eric Green, who also went on to become a first-round pick. I was disappointed about Eric. He was a great kid. I made several trips to see him at

Liberty. Liberty is a very religious school. No swearing, no sex, no outrageous behavior. I obviously didn't fit in there when I visited Eric. But I behaved myself in order to have the opportunity to sign Eric. Eric told me that I was second choice, but that was no consolation.

I could have had three first-round picks and been the man. Instead, I watched the draft go two full rounds and go off the air without any of my clients being drafted. It was heartbreaking. The year before I was on the draft and was a player. This year, I was nowhere.

Second place really sucks.

Jason kept my spirits up, and when Tiger and Jimmie were eventually drafted, we were so happy and relieved that we jumped in the canal near our house and celebrated as if they were first rounders. Make no mistake, we were very happy to have excellent clients like Jimmie and Tiger, but it is in our nature to want more. Still, we were both disappointed and made a pledge that next year things would be different.

I realized that the agent game isn't the same as the game of horse shoes. Close is not good enough. There is no award for runner up. The second-place consolation prize means having to watch the one that got away make millions of dollars and have it rubbed in on NFL Sundays for years to come on national television. Then you get to see a rival agent gloat and use it against you in recruiting next year.

As I said before, in this business you either win big or lose big. And in this business, no matter how good you are, you will lose. If you are good and lucky, you will lose time and time again, year after year. If you aren't lucky, than you will never lose again—you'll be out of the business. Almost isn't good enough.

But I learned to never burn bridges because you never know when you might have a chance to represent the player again in the future. I had a feeling that these players might change their mind down the road. When you lose, you can feel sorry for yourself and eat your heart out or you can come back with a vengeance and make 'em all pay.

I chose the latter.

8

Batman and Robin

ALTHOUGH THE 1990 DRAFT WAS BRUTAL TO WATCH, I didn't have time to feel sorry for myself. I had several final exams to take. I hadn't studied or gone to class as much as I would have liked. But I pulled some all-night study sessions, and although popular opinion was that it couldn't be done, I graduated on schedule.

My family came up for the graduation. It felt good to have both sets of grandparents there. Both of my grandfathers, Irving Rosenhaus and George Jackman, had been practicing attorneys at some point in their careers and had made a major impact on me. I was the first in the family after them to graduate from law school. My parents were very proud. My younger sister Dana told me she was going to go to law school when she graduated from college. And that is exactly what she did.

My experience at Duke was over now, and Jason and I had a fourteen-hour drive home to Miami. Jason and I talked about business and strategy all night throughout the drive. We felt like Batman and Robin again, ready to take on the new challenges that would be facing us. Jason was very positive, reminding me of how far I had come and how anyone else would be coming home feeling like some kind of war hero.

I listened to him and explained how we were not like everyone else. We were not going to be satisfied with anything less than becoming the superstars we idolized as kids. When I got back to South Florida, I kissed the ground. It was great to be back on Miami Beach. I was home.

After getting a good night sleep in my old bed, I woke up reenergized. I went for a swim in the ocean, and I felt like the sea breathed a whole new life into me. I had so much energy and hunger back I couldn't contain myself. It was time to go to work. One of the things that is great about this business is that every day is a new challenge, and there is always something rewarding to shoot for. The positives were that I was out of school and had graduated. Of my players, Jimmie Jones was the third-round pick of the Dallas Cowboys. Bernard "Tiger" Clark went as high as we could have hoped; he was drafted in the third-round by the Cincinnati Bengals. Bobby Houston had already called me after being drafted in the third round by the Green Bay Packers, and he had become my client.

It was like we were kids again. Jason and I were back in our old room together at our parents' house. We worked together out of my mom's interior designer office. I was in a difficult situation as my credit line was starting to run low. I had the Florida Bar Exam to take, and of greater importance, I had three third-round contracts to negotiate. I also had to negotiate Basil Proctor's contract with the New York Jets. Proctor was a friend of mine at the University of Miami and was a seventh-round pick. I negotiated with Jet President Steve Gutman, who was the friendliest NFL executive I had dealt with. He was a very pleasant guy and he helped to educate me about the NFL.

The same can be said for Dallas Cowboy's executive Bob Ackles. He was also an excellent person. Although Gutman and Ackles were my adversaries, I also learned that they could be my friends. These guys showed me that you can often get more from friendly negotiations than from hard-line stances.

It is important to read your adversary. It was funny seeing

Bob Ackles work with Jimmy Johnson and Jerry Jones. Those two guys are aggressive and outspoken, while Bob was quiet, unassuming, and very laid back. It was a nice change of pace from the "tough-guy negotiators." Gutman was like a Jewish grandfather and tried to talk to me like I was a relative. It was a persuasive style, trying to lull me into believing that he was looking out for my best interests and telling me the truth. He tried to develop a bond with you and make you feel obligated to him. He had a unique style.

Tom Braatz, the General Manager for the Green Bay Packers, was also a nice guy, laid back, and nonconfrontational. He was straightforward, direct, and honest. It was fun negotiating with these different styles and personalities. I spent some time that summer going back to the University of Miami campus studying for the bar exam. It was nice to be back on that campus as an agent instead of as a student dreaming about becoming one. Studying for the bar was not nice. My priorities were my clients first. I was not going to allow my efforts in studying for the bar exam to be at the expense of my clients. I spent the bulk of my time working on the negotiations and put my studying aside. I had a job to do. I knew that if I didn't get the job done on behalf of my clients, my career would be finished. The bar was of secondary importance to me, but I still prepared for it.

I wanted the top general managers around the League to know who I was. I wanted the NFL brass to know and respect me. I wanted to develop a good rapport with the teams. So I flew out to each of the four teams to meet with the top executives. Most agents for a third-round pick don't fly out to the team to start negotiations. Those deals are usually done over the phone. But I wanted to build a relationship with these guys, and I wanted to do everything within my power to get the best contracts possible for my clients. I was fortunate that I was dealing with the top dogs on each team. You always want to deal with the executive who has decision-making power. This way if you influence him, you have won.

The toughest negotiations are when you have to deal with the hired gun negotiator who is trying to impress his boss.

It is his goal to look good by signing your player to the lowest deal possible. I learned right away to try and deal exclusively with the general manager, president, or owner of a club.

I wasn't thrilled about Tiger going to the Bengals because if New Orleans' Jim Finks wasn't the toughest negotiator in the NFL, then Cincinnati's General Manager Mike Brown certainly was. Like Finks, Brown was from the old school of hard-line negotiations. Bengal rookie contracts can be difficult to negotiate because Mike Brown is a tough owner.

Flying out there to meet with him face to face, I wasn't expecting us to get along because we were so different. I was wrong and very pleasantly surprised. Somehow, someway, Mike Brown and I got along great—we went to lunch together. I can't help but admit that I liked him. And I know that he liked me, because he prides himself in being honest and he would not have been phony with me. Why should he be? He is one of the most powerful guys in the NFL. He certainly doesn't need to impress me.

This guy was supposed to be someone with whom I would not see eye to eye but we did. We got the contract done very easily. It helped that through my research I found out that Mike Brown's brother and co-owner of the team, Pete Brown, had attended the University of Miami. Of course, I capitalized on this connection and frequently discussed my affiliation with UM. I was young and bright eyed. I often tried to use that to my advantage, hoping the older NFL executive would take me under his wing and be fair with me.

I learned you were always better off trying to use sugar rather than salt.

However, if the sugar didn't work, then you had to go to Plan B. Tiger signed a contract that held up well in comparison to the other deals in the round. I know I did some good work for Tiger. As for Bobby Houston, I flew out to Green Bay to meet with Tom Braatz, and we came to an agreement very quickly. He was cordial and reasonable, and we were able to get a good deal done. I thought that contract was another piece of work I could hang my hat on.

I supposed that because I had matched up against Finks

and held my own that these guys had respect for me. They were interested in meeting the kid brash enough to take an ESPN camera crew with him into Jim Finks's negotiating room. I assumed that since Finks was not able to intimidate me, other general managers wouldn't try. It didn't take long in Dallas to see if my assumption was correct. I was brought into Jerry Jones's office. I knew that he did a good part of the negotiating himself. He was on the phone closing out a multimillion-dollar oil deal when I walked in. I thought that since this guy was used to doing mega million-dollar deals, I could easily squeeze thousands of dollars out of him. I thought wrong. Jerry Jones sat me down and went to work on me. He told me Jimmie Jones was going to sign a four-year deal. He told me Jimmie wasn't going to get this deal or that deal. He fought with me over nickels and dimes. I couldn't believe it. I was impressed with how passionately he managed his team's finances. I wanted a three-year deal and he told me I wasn't going to get it. One minute the guy was likeable and the next minute he made you feel like you were the devil. This guy was good. I respected him enough not to interrupt him and waited for him to finish making his points. When he was done with me, I knew I was in for a dog fight. I reminded him about Massey's holdout and how I would do the same with Jimmie if given no other choice. We gave each other ultimatums and left it at that. I was not happy.

As I walked out, I saw the Cowboys head Coach, my "old friend" from UM, Jimmy Johnson. He was very friendly, joking, "Hey Drew, we meet again. You've come a long way since I saw you last. I thought I got away from you when I left Miami."

"Actually Coach, I've been thinking about moving out here since you've brought in all of the best players," I answered.

Jimmy seemed impressed that I had grown from some college kid he kicked off a practice field, to an up and coming agent who represented one of his top picks. It felt good to have made the jump to the NFL where he was as well, with both of us coming from UM. I had a feeling that we would be working together for years to come. I enjoyed the new-found respect that Jimmy Johnson had for me. In the past I was just a kid, now I was someone he had to deal with. I was determined to gain power, respect, and credibility in the NFL.

I knew I had a tough negotiation on my hands going up against those two. They wanted Jimmie to sign a four-year deal. They were real smart, knowing that after three years I could renegotiate a multimillion-dollar deal for Jimmie. They wanted Jimmie under contract that fourth year so they could get away with paying him a couple of hundred thousand dollars instead of a couple of million. They also knew that since Jimmie was their player that they coached in college they could persuade him to take the deal they wanted and undermine my relationship with him. And they almost did. Jimmie was real close with his former defensive line coach Butch Davis and defensive coordinator, Dave Wannestedt. After speaking a few minutes with the coaches, he hung up the phone and was ready to come in and sign the four-year deal. I had to drive over to his apartment and talk him out of it.

We needed a three-year deal and they insisted on the four-year contract. Like I did with Massey and many other agents at the time, I held Jimmie out. Only not too many agents have the guts to hold out a third-round pick, especially when they play for Jimmy Johnson and Jerry Jones. It was a concern that if I held Jimmie out, I might never sign another Hurricane player again because of the Cowboy coaches' connections to the University of Miami. These guys played hardball but I wasn't going to allow them to intimidate me. There were a lot of eyes on this negotiation.

The negotiation was further complicated by the fact that I had my bar exam to take. I couldn't take a couple of days off and put Jimmie's contract on the shelf in the middle of a holdout. I had to put the bar on the back burner. It was a tough call, but with all of the negotiations going on, taking the bar was a luxury I couldn't afford. To this day I can thank Jerry Jones's tough negotiation stance with me for my missing the bar exam.

My philosophy was to always put the needs of your client ahead of your own.

Even though I had studied for months, I had a responsibility to Jimmie and his family that I would give his contract status my undivided attention. It was a tough call. I just didn't have the time, and to this day, I still haven't had the time. So I had Jason do it instead. Jason had to take both the CPA exam and the bar exam while still working with me as an agent. He didn't get a free ride on my coattails, and that's how he wanted it. After over two weeks of holding out, we compromised. Jimmie signed for a three-year deal with a voidable option. That fourth year would void out based upon Jimmie's playing time. And if the fourth year didn't void out due to a lack of playing time, then Jimmie would get a bonus as consolation. Jerry Jones didn't budge much with the overall money so Jimmie and I didn't feel like we scored a lopsided victory. Both sides in this deal walked away having been a little beaten up. But once again, I was creative and found a way to get the deal done. The key I learned was to find solutions and have an open mind. Not many third-round picks had voidable years and very few second rounders had two-year deals. I was definitely leaving my signature on NFL negotiations.

Once the summer was over and all of my clients were signed, I wanted to get something accomplished. I had to think about doing better the next year. I needed that first-round pick. I knew Jason and I had to grow.

After the summer, Jason was back at UM for the fall semester of his senior year to get his degree in accounting. Jason never complained about it because after working with me in the agent world, school was a vacation for him. It was too early in the year to start working on next year's first-round draft pick, so I traveled to see my clients play. I wanted to put myself in a position to make something happen and something did.

With Jimmie Jones and the Dallas Cowboys coming to play

the Tampa Bay Buccaneers, I thought it would be productive for Jason and I to drive to Tampa. I was on the money more than I knew.

I got to the game before the crowd so that Jimmie could talk to me before the game started. That first view of the field is always something I enjoy as I walk into the stands. There weren't many players out there yet. I walked down to the very bottom row and waited for Jimmie to come out.

"Drew!"

I knew that voice. I turned around saw Michael Irvin running toward me.

"Where have you been, buddy, long time no see. I miss you," he said to me. I leaned over the rail and hugged him. I had forgotten how fond of him I really was. It was great to see him in person. It was like old times again.

"I see you have been doing well. It is good to know the guy I brought in to the business has become a success. By the way, how come you haven't talked to me about becoming my agent? Listen, we are about to play this game, but afterward I would like to talk to you about that."

Shocked and stunned, all I could say was, "Of course, Mike. I'll see you afterward. Have a great game."

Here I was, disappointed at working my butt off and not signing any first-round picks, and now someone ten times better just walked up and jumped into my lap. This was the most respected and admired athlete by the University of Miami college players, and he had asked to talk to me about being his agent. Michael was one of the most focused and intense athletes on game day, and he came over to me. This is the type of client you would work for years in advance, and he was recruiting me. This was the ultimate boost to my career.

I never felt so fortunate in my life. With Michael Irvin in my corner, I would be unstoppable and get that first-round pick for the next ten years. True, Michael Irvin was coming off a serious knee injury and had yet to realize his awesome potential, but I knew what every other Hurricane football fan knew, that Michael Irvin would eventually dominate the NFL.

It was a close game that went down to the wire. Sitting in seats that were the courtesy of Jimmie Jones, we sat with all the Cowboys' friends and family attending the game. The Cowboys fell behind late in the game and then Troy Aikman got the ball back. With just a few ticks left on the clock, Aikman threw a desperation pass deep toward the end zone. Michael ran down the side line, jumped up, and pulled the ball into his chest for the winning touchdown. I loved seeing Michael as the hero again for the first time since college. I loved rooting for the future superstar who had just asked me to be his agent.

Michael Irvin was back. And thanks to him so was I. After the game, he told me how much he respected my fighting toe to toe with the Cowboys for Jimmie Jones, and he wanted someone that tough to fight the Cowboys for him. In no time at all, I became Michael Irvin's agent. I felt great.

Here I was, hanging on by a thread, and now I had Michael Irvin, whom every single player at the University of Miami respected, as my client. By being able to sell myself as Michael Irvin's agent, I would surely be able to get all of the UM guys I targeted. I had it made. It was unprecedented for an agent to be my age and represent a player the caliber of Michael Irvin. I had it all.

It felt great to come back to Miami and tell everyone I was Irvin's agent. And yet, wherever I went and told people I was an agent, they only wanted to know if I represented any Dolphins. It crushed my ego to say no.

When Jason and I were kids, we used to go over to Dolphin camp at St. Thomas University, so going over there to watch the team practice seemed like the natural thing to do. As I watched the practice, it occurred to me that everything was different. I was no longer looking at players to see who was going to be a good player to help Don Shula and Dan Marino get to the Super Bowl. I was no longer a fan looking at football players. I was an agent looking at prospective clients.

But if I was going to be known and respected in my hometown, it would be because I represent Miami Dolphins. I also wanted to be able to watch the Dolphins and have the thrill of rooting for my own clients on the team. I didn't only want the money, I wanted the lifestyle. All I need are targets to shoot for, and now I had my mark. I wanted to represent Miami Dolphins. From that time to this time, I have represented approximately forty players who at one time or another were Miami Dolphins.

No other agent can come close to those numbers with any team. It all started for me with a Miami Dolphin twelfth-round pick out of Maryland named J. B. Brown. In a conversation I had with Bobby Houston about my daily scouting visit to the Dolphin training camp, Bobby mentioned to me that he went to high school with Brown, a cornerback with the Dolphins, and that Brown had fired his agent. After the next practice, I walked up to J.B. and told him that I was Bobby's agent and that Bobby sent his regards. J.B. was very warm and friendly and we hit it off pretty good. Throughout the year, I developed a good friendship with J.B.

J.B. had been paid the minimum salary that twelfth-round picks received, and he had managed to become a starter by his second year. After his contract expired, he mentioned to me that he wanted to hire a local agent. J.B. said he wanted to meet with me after he got back in Miami from driving up to Maryland. I didn't want to let Murphy's Law stand in my way so I didn't leave anything to chance. Yeah I was in good shape now, but who knows what could happen when he went home. I learned the hard way that anything you don't make sure will go right will go wrong. Therefore, I saw an opportunity and took it.

I offered to drive up there with him and he accepted. I talked and talked and talked. He tried everything to shut me up—he blasted rap music and jazz. He even faked sleeping. The only thing that was going to shut me up was his signature on a contract with me. After several hours of assault on the road, he finally said he would sign as long as I promised not to talk him to death on the flight home. The drive was seventeen hours and I proved my talent to J.B.

Being a Miami Dolphin fan who, as a kid, would cry when the Dolphins lost, signing J.B. was something special to me that was both business and personal. I know it's not professional, but I can't help but root for the Dolphins. At least now when I would cheer for the Dolphins, I would be rooting for a client as an agent, and not just as a fan. I knew that once I had my first Dolphin client, I would be unstoppable and many more would follow. It was a key breakthrough in the development of my career.

I had two main objectives for that year; I wanted a first-round pick in the 1991 NFL Draft and I wanted a Miami Dolphin client. Thanks to J. B. Brown, I had accomplished the second objective. And now it was time for me to get that first-round pick I had wanted for so long. The player I targeted was Randal "Thrill" Hill.

I had scouted Randal Hill all season long. He made a lot of big plays throughout the year and was known for having world-class speed. Mel Kiper and Joel Buchsbaum had Randal rated highly as a first or second rounder. Based on all of my information and conclusions, I thought Randal would be a first-round pick. Randal was my type of player: flashy, outgoing, and a big-play guy. He earned his nickname and was the prototype Miami Hurricane. These were the types of players I wanted to represent, local guys with strong ties to South Florida. I wanted to develop a network of local clients from the Dolphins, UM, and South Florida.

Coming from a strong family environment with Randal's father, Ransom, being a principal and his mother, Helen, being a teacher, I knew the key would be his parents. I have yet to meet more decent people than Randal's parents. I liked them from the start and we all developed a good relationship quickly and easily. I learned how important the family can be in recruiting. This is a key to recruiting, figuring out who the decision maker is. I once spent 90 percent of my time recruiting a player, and I didn't get him because his mom made the call. Sometimes it is entirely the parents' decision, or even a girlfriend or wife. You must determine who to target when recruiting. It takes insight, instincts, and charm to win a family over.

Recruiting is the toughest and ugliest part of this business.

The players use and abuse agents to get free meals, clothes, money, and anything else they can get out of them. And yet, I never had more fun recruiting than I did with Randal. We had a couple of business meetings and after that we had a lot of fun hanging out. He would come over my parents' house where I still lived, and we would play baseball in the backyard with Jason, or throw the football around, or go to the beach. We worked out together. We went to movies, played ping-pong and video games. It was neat having your top recruit also as your best friend. It was like I was a kid again.

In no time at all, Randal signed with me. Randal had a great Senior Bowl and impressed at the combine workout and the individual workouts for the teams. He was the fastest player in the draft. In fact, when I found out that Randal ran a fast time at the workouts, I couldn't contain my joy and started to scream and shout. The other agents and teams looked at me like I was crazy. But I couldn't help it. My enthusiasm was genuine. I was in love with my job.

I also went to the East-West Shrine Game to scout some players. I was staying at a nearby hotel in San Francisco, and at about eleven o'clock at night, I got a knock at my door. I heard the guy say, "Delivery," so I told him to come in.

It was no delivery boy. It was Harold "Doc" Daniels, a rival agent who had signed Eric Green out of college. This huge, six foot three, three hundred fifty pound man walked right into my room.

"I heard you were the guy who talked Eric Green into firing me. I came here to tell you one thing. If you ever come after one of my players again, it will be the last time. Make no mistake, I will not allow you to mess with any of my guys again."

This guy was big and angry. He obviously came to scare me, but I wasn't going to let him or any other agent intimidate me.

"First of all, Eric fired you and went with another agent, not me. Second of all, I said nothing behind your back about you. I don't recruit players by talking negatively about agents behind their backs. So your problem isn't with me. If one of your players comes up to me and expresses an interest in me, then I will pursue it. You do what you have to do, and I'll do what I have to do. But I will tell you this. You don't have to lose sleep at night worrying that I am calling your players and trying to steal them away from you. I am not going to come after your guys. You do your job and they won't want me to represent them. You do your job and you and I won't have to butt heads."

I earned his respect and he left my room in a friendlier state of mind. Had I showed weakness and fear, every agent in the business would have heard about it and told all the recruits and the media. As it was, every agent knew not to try to intimidate me, it wasn't going to happen. When I got back to Miami, I liked where things were headed for Randal. It was awesome walking around the All-Star Games and Combine as the agent for Randal. He was one of the top players in the draft and I felt like the man.

In particular, I saw that he impressed Don Shula and the Dolphin scouts. I knew the chances were slim that Randal would be drafted by the Dolphins because they drafted pretty late in the first round. Nevertheless, I could dream. I talked with several of the Miami Dolphin scouts and developed a good relationship with Tom Heckert, one of the team's top personnel men. He told me there was a chance it could happen. I didn't allow myself to get too excited, because I never allowed myself to lose sight of the fact that what was best for Randal was to be a high first-round pick and not necessarily a Miami Dolphin. There was justice in the world again for me as I had my client in position to be a first-round pick. And more, Jason signed his first client, Robert Bailey, who was drafted by the Los Angeles Rams in the fourth round and is still playing in the League. I was proud of Jason. He had made his move and signed a client for us as he was getting ready to graduate college. He tied my record of being the youngest agent to negotiate an NFL contract for a rookie draft pick. I felt good. "Robin" had made his mark.

And then Draft Day arrived. With the way the draft shook

out, Randal had one chance to make the first round—it was Miami. After seeing it through my eyes this time around, it is easy to understand why Jason and I went nuts on Draft Day when Don Shula called and made Randal Hill the Miami Dolphins' first-round pick. And after seeing it through my eyes again, it is easy to understand why I was so crushed and defeated when Shula traded Randal away.

I had my first-round pick and I had my Miami Dolphin. I had all that I wanted. I was going to be able to watch Randal catch touchdowns from Dan Marino for the next decade. I had that exciting lifestyle I wanted for Jason and me. And then I had it taken away from me. Along with that came the public humiliation and reproach.

If I thought the previous year was tough with Ray Agnew, Cortez Kennedy, and Eric Green, then Randal's trade took it to a whole new level. How was I ever going to be the man now? While watching the movie *Conan the Barbarian,* which involved Oliver Stone behind the scenes, I was captivated by a Friedrich Nietzsche quote he used in the film, "That which does not kill you makes you stronger." As much as I cherished the meaning, I did not necessarily agree with it. In my not so humble opinion, I think it is more accurate to say adversity makes the strong stronger and the weak weaker. I wanted to be the shark that survives the attack and comes back for revenge another day. Like a young Dick Grayson and Bruce Wayne in the Batman comics, Jason and I became men on a mission. Our mission was to sign more Miami Dolphin clients. Women, fun, drinking, friends, relaxation, peace— none of it mattered as much. I wanted blood. I could think of nothing else but avenging myself by becoming the agent that dominates this business.

Everything else to me was unproductive. I had to find something productive out of this disaster. I had to turn this nightmare into a pleasant dream. But how? What angle did I have? I took a long hard look at my negative. Several Miami Dolphin players held out that year and the fans were upset with the players for doing it, but they were upset with the team for being stingy and not paying the players. Those players included Randal Hill, J.B. Brown, and Pete Stoyanovich. Since two of those players were my clients, and I was so visible, to sports fans in South Florida, I was the bad guy.

Agent, considered a four-letter word, or referred to as the "A word," is synonymous with being a sleazeball lawyer. I became the face for this picture. I became the poster boy for greed in sports today. I wanted to be famous; I became infamous. The fans were very angry with me, and the Miami Dolphin coaches and management were upset with me as well. My contract negotiations were brutal and bloody. How could I possibly create a positive out of this negative?

That was it, that was my positive—that I had the guts to face management and fight toe to toe for my clients. I had proved that I was as tough, no tougher, than any other agent out there. Although I was disliked by everyone else, the players on the team respected me and liked me. The veterans saw that if I were to represent them, then the Dolphins would know to give me their best offers early, because I wasn't afraid to hold out to get it. They knew that after having gone to war with the toughest negotiators in the business, I would have the team's respect.

The veterans realized that with me as their agent, the teams would have no choice but to give their best efforts or face an ugly holdout. Real power is being able to use the threat of force to manipulate outcomes without having to use actual force. I now had power in the NFL. Teams knew I would hold players out and this threat forced them to do the deal to avoid the holdout. I needed to make the Dolphin players recognize this. I had found my positive and its name was power. Power was all I had in my arsenal. That and a gut filled with a hunger to get more Dolphins.

I had one Miami Dolphin client left during the 1991 season—J. B. Brown. I did a good job for J.B., getting him the two-year deal he wanted. He appreciated my hard work and the results I got, and he let everyone know it. With my one Dolphin client left, I swore I would get more Dolphin clients.

This was the most critical point of my career. My competing agents reveled in the popular opinion that I was out of the business. To everyone, I was finished. Everyone said I was through, everyone except the one guy in the media that I felt was in my corner—Jim Mandich. Jim was one of the few people I knew that I could call a friend.

Jim Mandich was color commentator on the Dolphin radio broadcasts; he also had a weekly television show on Sunday nights called *Sports Rap.*

Shortly after Randal was traded, Jim put me on his television show where I could put my spin on the trade. All of the other television personalities crucified me. Jim was fair and objective with me.

Everyone was right, I was going to take a hit for Randal's trade. The problem was, I didn't want to take any more hits, I wanted to give them. If I was going to be back, it would be because I was going to sign some veterans who were smart enough to appreciate my work ethic and desire for success. I had been able to get big-time veterans like Michael Irvin and Brett Perriman and that was invaluable in being able to sign more clients. I needed to sign Miami Dolphins to stay in this business. Once I signed a key veteran, I could go back to the rookies and get them, too. But I needed the premier veteran first. The situation was clear—I was either going to sign that top veteran or fail in this business. I was at a real crossroads, and the scarecrow who was going to point the way was Pro-Bowl defensive end Jeff Cross.

9

Swimming with the Dolphins

AFTER RANDAL HILL WAS TRADED, I WAS REDUCED TO ONE Dolphin player—J. B. Brown. But that wasn't to be the case for long. After a long, hard workday, I called J.B. on a Tuesday night in 1991, and he mentioned to me that some of the guys on the team were going to a nightclub in Fort Lauderdale. J.B. mentioned that he heard Jeff Cross fired his agent, and that Jeff was going to be there. I didn't have a rapport with Jeff, and I knew that I wasn't going to develop one by staying home and getting a good night's sleep. As tired as I was, I went out hoping to put myself in a position to make something happen.

Jason and I jumped into my sports car and hit the Fort Lauderdale strip. The club was packed, the music was loud, the lights were flashing, and the women were drunk. I spotted Jeff right away. How could I not? There was this six-foot-four, two hundred eighty–pound handsome athlete surrounded by several big-chested blondes. I could see right away that the women loved this guy.

He looked preoccupied, so I decided to wait for the right moment to introduce myself. It wasn't too hard to find a nice skirt to keep me company until I could make my move. It wasn't long before I saw Jeff go to the men's room, and I

114

followed him in there. He splashed some water on his face and I did the same. He recognized me and said very matter of factly, "Hey, Drew. How's Randal doing?"

"Judging by the way those women keep falling over you, I'd say he's not doing as well as you," I said.

Jeff laughed, "I saw the girl you're with Drew, and you're not doing too bad yourself. She's the hottest girl in here."

"She's not with me. You want to meet her?"

"Hell yeah!"

I ended up buying a couple of hundred dollars worth of liquor for his friends. It is times like these that make me reconsider my rule against drinking alcohol; but I wanted Jeff to see I was a machine that was always thinking and on the job. I was aware of the fact that drinking could be a bonding experience, but I didn't want to be his drinking buddy, I wanted to be his agent. I wanted him to know that wherever I went, whatever time it was, I was always razor sharp.

I love it when I am around other agents at parties and clubs. They are a joke. They are smoking cigarettes and getting blitzed on beer and alcohol, looking like barflies rather than sharks. While these agents are getting blitzed, blurting out their sentences, slurring their words, talking one inch from a guy's face, and spitting all over him in the process, I am quick as a whip and ready to move in for the kill. They are no match for me. They're ordinary, like every other guy. Jason and I, we never lose the discipline. We always stand out and distinguish ourselves as serious professionals, even at four in the morning in some nightclub with women and players all around us.

It was wild hanging out with Jeff and the other Dolphin players in those clubs. Everybody wanted to know who Jason and I were. Women were attracted to the big, handsome athlete and also to the sharp, smooth agent. People thought we were Secret Service or Mafia hit men. It made people very uneasy to see us so serious while they were trying to relax. And women loved trying to tear away our phones or beepers and trying to get us to relax like everyone else and have a drink. This was work but it was also fun.

Jeff invited me out again and again over the ensuing weeks, and my social life improved quite a bit as we spent some time in the clubs. I didn't talk much about his contract, but we talked Dolphin football constantly. Jeff was one of the few football players who liked to talk about football all the time as if he were a fan as well. A very articulate and well-educated guy, Jeff gave me a player's perspective on the game.

Having gotten off to a good start with Jeff, I started to feel a positive momentum swing my way. The more I went out, the more I would bump into two other Dolphin players whose contracts were going to be renegotiated in the off season—Mark Higgs and Shawn Lee. They were both looking for agents as well and J.B. had recommended me. You see, all you need is one happy client on a team and then BOOM, there is a chain reaction. Soon it would become fashionable for many of J.B.'s teammates to sign with me.

Mark Higgs, better known as "Higgy," became South Florida's favorite new athlete. The muscular but short five-foot seven-inch running back had won over the hearts of the Dolphin fans big time. Higgy had a great year, bursting onto the scene to become the Dolphins' starting running back. Shawn Lee was one of the starting interior defensive linemen for the Dolphins and was a big, mean nasty-looking guy. I wanted to regain my stature with the Dolphins in the worst way and signing these three guys would give me that and then some.

The 1991 season was awesome. Michael Irvin had a Pro-Bowl year. I negotiated a Nike deal for Michael and began negotiations on Michael's behalf with the Cowboys. No matter where I was and what I was doing, I would call Michael at midnight every single night to give him updates. Yes, midnight. I work late hours; this is a late-night business.

The Cowboys weren't offering enough money to do an extension so I recommended to Michael that he play the season out. I knew he would have a great year and would be able to command a contract worth five times the dollars they were offering. Michael knew I was right and he agreed with me. But shortly after the season ended, I started to feel a little alarmed as Michael and I didn't communicate on a regular basis. He started to become increasingly difficult to reach. It got to the point where I could never reach him on the phone. All I could do was page him and wait for his calls. I was uncomfortable about the lack of communication, but we were friends so I didn't panic.

At that point, I flew to Dallas to see him, and I could tell he was not the same. Michael and I had always been able to talk about personal things, and he would open up to me, especially when he was at the University of Miami. I could connect with him. There was always a bond that I could trust. But not this time.

I asked him over and over again if there was a problem, and he assured me everything was fine. I didn't believe him. He didn't look me in the eyes when he reassured me I was his agent. Every time I could get him on the phone I sold him over and over again as hard as I could. I knew what was at stake here and I could not afford to lose Michael.

Michael had been invited to the Pro-Bowl in Hawaii and I went there to see him. While out there, I heard from several sources in the media that Michael was interviewing with several different agents. When I confronted Michael again, he told me to relax, that he was with me and to ignore the rumors. What else could I do?

Two weeks later, it became impossible to reach him. After not talking to him for a week, I called Mark Levin in the research department at the NFL Players Association, and he told me that he just received a contract between Irvin and another agent that day. I was crushed, devastated, humiliated, beaten, disappointed, and betrayed. Michael Irvin never even called to tell me or to talk to me about it. I had heard from his friends that he cared about me and hated to do it to me but he wanted an agent who was based in Dallas. No one worked harder for Michael than I did, and no one would have seen to his success off of the field like I would have.

He did not make a wise decision. He wasn't very loyal or appreciative. I was there for Michael while he was struggling and injured, and I helped him to get back on top. But when

117

he made it as a superstar, he wanted a local agent in Dallas. This was a major blow and really made me wonder if I could trust another person in this business. If Michael Irvin, whom I had known for several years and who was responsible for getting me into this business could turn on me, then anybody could. I saw firsthand how quickly life in this business can change.

To make matters worse, it was February—the heart of recruiting season for college kids. I had told all of my recruits that they should go with me and that I was Michael Irvin's agent. Now my competitors were telling them that Michael had fired me. The Randal Hill trade didn't help to impress the rookie crop either. How was I going to sign rookies now?

I knew that if it was going to be tough with the rookies, my only chance of survival was signing Dolphin veterans such as Jeff Cross and Mark Higgs. Disgusted and angered, I became maniacal. I went out to every club and bar I could to find Dolphin guys out on the town. This became a late-night job and I was working eighteen hours a day. But the nightlife was good to me, as I was in an environment where it is easy to do business. Some people like to do business on the golf course. I prefer doing business in a South Beach nightclub.

It was hard to call my work during the night just that, but it was productive. Amidst the Michael Irvin saga, I was able to sign Jeff Cross, Mark Higgs, and Shawn Lee. I felt avenged. Jeff and Higgy were the key off-season Dolphin contract negotiations, and they had signed with me. Plus, there were more new Dolphin clients to come.

When I was robbed of having Randal as my first-round pick Dolphin, I swore I would get more Dolphins. When they traded Randal, the team thought they got rid of me. The media and the fans thought they had seen the last of me. And now, by signing Jeff and Higgy, I had made good on my oath to come back with more Dolphins. Just when they thought it was safe to go back in the water—the shark resurfaced.

My new Dolphin clients and I made a great team. As intelligent as any Duke law student I debated against, Jeff shared a lot insightful views with me on what the coaches were thinking. Information has always been the most valuable of commodities to me, especially at the end of the 1991 season when the Dolphins' front office was in a transition phase. The fans were tired of holdouts and so were the Dolphins.

Charlie Winner had been the Dolphins' negotiator for as long as I could remember. There were many acrimonious holdouts in those days, and it hurt the team from a morale standpoint and from a fan standpoint. I had my share of tough negotiations with the team, including Randal and J.B., so I was very pleased when the Dolphin ownership, headed by Tim Robbie, decided to soften its stance on player negotiations.

Eddie Jones and Bryan Wiedmeier were promoted from within the front office to handle negotiations. This was the best move Tim Robbie and his siblings ever made. Eddie Jones, now the Dolphins' President, and Bryan Wiedmeier, Vice President, did an outstanding job of getting their players signed on time and for fair contracts. To this day, the Dolphins haven't had an ugly holdout since my battles with them in 1991. I believe that my tough negotiations with the team in 1991 had such a strong impact on the front office that I was, in part, responsible for the Dolphins making organizational changes that benefited the club and the fans. I definitely had a huge impact on my childhood team. And when Wayne Huizenga became the new owner of the Dolphins, I knew his deep pockets would mean even smoother negotiations. It was Don Shula's bad luck that just as he got an owner who was willing to pay the big bucks, the NFL salary cap was put in place, limiting what the team could do financially.

Although things were going well with my negotiations with the Dolphins, I knew I faced a Herculean task to sign any rookies. My difficulty was because rookies had no experience with agents. Any agent can make a great sales pitch. And many rookies believe everything they hear. When enough agents tell a player this rumor and that rumor, they start to believe it. This is an element I don't care for in the business. I don't tell recruits rumors about other agents. I never, ever, go into a meeting with a recruit and his family and say one negative word about any other agent. I sell myself. I don't bad-mouth my competition. Most of the time the recruits respect my approach and lose respect for my competitors for having a negative attitude.

There were several players I wanted to sign from the University of Miami, but the player I wanted the most was offensive lineman Leon Searcy. I could see that Leon had the makings of an All-Pro. He was big, mean, strong, physical, and tough. He was the prototype tough guy in the trenches. I worked hard to get Leon and was very close to signing him. However, at the time his parents had someone else in mind who Leon was also high on. Once again, I was the runner-up.

Leon had a lot of respect for his parents' opinions and they made the difference. I had made a mistake here by not recognizing the importance of his parents' involvement in Leon's agent-selection process. This was one lesson learned the hard way. By this point in my career, after just a few years, I had experienced more highs and lows than most agents ever will. In the last six months, I had my top client traded away from the Dolphins, I had been fired by Michael Irvin, and I did not sign one single rookie draft pick.

Jason and I watched the 1992 NFL Draft from my apartment by ourselves, with no fanfare. We weren't proud of our accomplishments. It was a day I will never forget. Three years ago, I was all over the draft coverage with Robert Massey, being televised on ESPN. Last year, I had a first-round pick with my hometown team. This year, I was a nonfactor. I was no one. It was humiliating every time someone asked me who I had in the draft. I answered by saying that I was focusing on signing some Dolphin players. My enemies rejoiced in the fact that I didn't represent any rookie draft picks, but I knew I would be back to make them sorry the next year. I avenged myself that summer by securing excellent contracts for Cross, Higgs, and Shawn Lee. And I was able to do it without any holdouts. I learned the important lesson that experience teaches agents in this business: Get the deal done. When you know you have pushed the team as far as they will go, when you know that there is no more money on the table, then do the deal. I learned holdouts are almost never effective and are always to be averted. Holdouts are the last resort in a crisis situation. I was no longer seen by the teams as the holdout tough guy. Instead, I became known as a deal maker who wasn't scared to pull the trigger and do the deal.

By the start of training camp, the Dolphins had a new training facility at Nova Southeastern University. It was state-of-the-art, and still is. During Randal's and J.B.'s lengthy holdouts the year before, I would be in the Dolphin parking lots, waiting to talk to guys and the media. The new facility had been specifically designed to restrict access and improve security. Coach Shula disliked what he called "the negotiations in the parking lot," where I was always around talking to clients and the media.

I liked going to see the guys and waiting for them in the parking lot after practice. I liked hanging out in the parking lot to meet with the guys and being around for something positive to happen. I would often hear how this player fired his agent and was looking for a new agent. All I would have to do at the old facility at St. Thomas University was wait for them. I now had a problem. My problem was the security of the new training facility, specifically Director of Security Stuart Weinstein.

Since my days as a kid, I had seen Stu run guys out of there who were twice his size. Stu was tough. He kicked Jason and me out of there a couple times when we were kids, so you can imagine how he salivated at the idea of our trying to get into the new facility as agents. The big test of the new facility was to see if it was "Drew proof." Well, the very first day of training camp, much to my surprise, Jason and I walked right in. I saw Stu smiling and waiting for us. Apparently, the fact that we signed our Dolphin veterans on time without any holdouts or negative publicity had changed the organization's view of us. He told us that we could wait in the lobby, and he would let the guys know we were there. He was professional about it and I appreciated that.

I saw Coach Shula after practice, and he was cordial and pleased with the fact that we didn't create any holdouts. I had a newfound respect for Coach Shula at that point. Of course, I admired him as a football coach and a leader of men, but I learned something from him. I had caused him a lot of aggravation in the past and he could have held a grudge against me, but I could see that everything in the past was water under the bridge. I learned from Coach Shula that when something is done, it's done; address it, move on, and be productive.

I had turned the corner with the Dolphins; I made my move to gain power and I had done so. But if I was going to truly dominate this business, I was going to have to get dominating rookies. And the most dominating college player in the 1992 season was Florida State middle linebacker Marvin Jones.

10

When Preparation Meets Opportunity

ALTHOUGH MY HARD WORK HAD ALLOWED ME TO SCORE points as a deal maker with the Dolphins and other NFL clubs, my reputation among South Florida fans still needed improvement. Whatever Dolphin event I would attend, there would always be someone there to yell, "Drew, get the players signed and in camp on time." I was constantly heckled and harassed by the fans. On the radio, they would call in on talk shows to talk about how much they hated me. They even insulted my brother, Jason. I had really made a name for myself all right.

So I was a big shot in town with all my new Dolphin clients, but I had missed my mark. I felt an insatiable hunger to get the best damn player in college football.

But I needed some luck. I thought about a sign that Jimmy Johnson put up in the Miami Hurricane football gym for all the players to see. The sign read, "Luck Is When Preparation Meets Opportunity."

I loved that message and I needed my opportunity. It just so happened that a Florida State football player by the name of Marvin Jones grew up in a house twenty minutes away from the house where I grew up. I was from Miami Beach and he hailed from nearby Coconut Grove. Dennis Erickson, then the head coach of the Miami Hurricanes, said, "Marvin Jones is the best linebacker I have ever seen playing college football."

I watched Marvin play that 1992–93 season and he was simply awesome. He was the most dominating defensive college football player I had ever seen. He was fast, explosive, and had an incredible knack for hitting brutally hard. Marvin went on to win the Butkus Award, the Lombardi Trophy, and the College Player of the Year Award. There can be no doubt that Marvin was the most outstanding college player that year without exception.

I wanted this guy to be my client so bad I couldn't sleep. I woke up at dawn every morning trying to strategize my recruiting pitch. The facts that I had represented a local first-round pick before in Randal Hill and that Marvin played at the same high school as my client Brett Perriman was impressive.

So when I called Marvin's house, I was told that Marvin's older brother Fred Jones, a police officer, was going to be advising Marvin in the agent selection process. I remembered Fred when he played at Florida State. He was a tough, hard-nosed linebacker like Marvin, except he lacked the speed and quickness. Since I generally get along well with football players, I thought Fred's involvement would make things easier for me.

I thought wrong. Fred returned my call to tell me that he was too busy to meet with me. He said that he was going for a jog at 6:00 in the morning and would be working a twelve-hour shift. He continued to say that by the time he got home, he would be too tired to do anything but enjoy some quiet time with his wife.

"Fred, thank you for returning my call. I understand and hope to meet with you soon."

Well, Fred was more than a little surprised to see me and Jason at his front porch at 6:00 A.M. that next morning.

"I said I would see you soon."

He was not in a very good mood.

"Come on," is all he said as he started to jog.

Jason and I were in top shape from practicing karate. With Fred being such a big man, I thought Jason and I could stay up with his jogging pace. For the first mile, Jason and I kept up with Fred. After the second mile, Jason started to fall behind. After the third mile, I fell behind and Jason was so far behind us we lost track of him. Fred cruised home, took a shower, and ate breakfast. Jason eventually caught up to me as we both walked back in extreme pain.

As the pain became manageable, Jason and I realized that we were in the middle of one the toughest neighborhoods in Miami. Even early in the morning, there were prostitutes, homeless people, and drug addicts everywhere. There were people sitting out at the corner drinking and smoking like it was the nighttime. We didn't know where we were. We didn't know how to get back to Fred's house. We were exhausted, and this wasn't the type of neighborhood where taxicabs or even police cars drove through.

I said to Jason, "Fred's a police officer. He'll come back for us." I was half right. Fred's brother, Nathaniel Jr., a.k.a. Snake, pulled up in his car laughing, and drove us back. As we walked in to talk to Fred, he was leaving and said, "I'm busy again tomorrow too," and then left. Jason and I looked at each other, knowing this was not going to be easy. Despite having sore legs, Jason and I ran again that next morning with Fred and continued to do so until he finally said more than ten words to us. "I'll be fishing later today. You can talk to me then. I'll be at that second bridge we jogged past this morning. I will call you to let you know when."

Finally, we had our chance. I cleared up my afternoon schedule and waited for the call. Jason and I sat around waiting until midnight. Fred called and said to meet him at the bridge at 2:00 A.M. Sure I was tired, exhausted, and hungry. Jason had been up almost twenty-four hours and was asleep. I woke him up and dragged him with me to meet Fred. The only thing biting at that bridge was the mosquitoes. It was late; our stomachs were growling and burning with acid from not eating; we were fatigued from jogging earlier and had aches from not sleeping—and we loved it. As tired as we

125

were, as difficult as those conditions were, we took advantage of the opportunity and thrived. It was no different than from our old karate days. We learned to deal with pain and find a way to win. This is what we were. This is what we were trained to be. My dad told Young Soo Do to make his boys tough and that is what he did.

During my presentation to Fred I was on fire. I was screaming and yelling my points of argument to Fred. I was on a roll. I was unstoppable. I wanted it badly and I showed him how much heart I had. I told him my whole story and won him over. I kicked and punched the concrete walls and chopped the steel rails out of anger as I discredited all the lies that my competitors told him. At four in the morning, while our competitors were sleeping in their beds, we showed Fred Jones what the Rosenhaus boys were made of. Fred looked in my eyes and saw that I was honest, smart, loyal, and hard working. Thus, with Fred's endorsement, Marvin Jones, the best college football player in the country, became our client.

But that wasn't enough for me. I wanted more. I signed University of Miami superstar wide receiver Kevin Williams. I signed Miami Dolphin kicker Pete Stoyanovich who was one of Coach Shula's and South Florida's favorite players. Jason signed University of Miami linebacker Jessie Armstead who later became an All-Pro linebacker with the New York Giants. Jason was very clever to sign Armstead. The NFL scouts did not rate Jessie very highly because he was coming off of major reconstructive knee surgery from his sophomore year. But Jason remembered the talent that Jessie had before injuring the knee and saw that he still had great speed. Jason believed in Jessie and saw a young man with a lot of heart and determination, not to mention something that NFL teams are starting to place more and more value on today which is character. Today, Jessie has emerged as one of our highest paid clients, earning over $3 million in the last year. He is the type of client that is loyal and appreciates our hard work. It's clients like Jessie that keep me in this business.

My first task in representing Marvin was to help him get

ready for the draft. Marvin had a chance to be the first pick of the draft, but for that to happen he would have to work out for all the NFL teams before the draft in March. Marvin decided that he was going to train in Miami, because there were too many distractions at Florida State University for him to concentrate. I trained with Marvin and Fred six days a week. Just keeping up with those guys I got in the best shape of my life. I thought I was ready to work out for the teams. Now that Marvin was getting in shape, I had to set up his workout. Since Marvin didn't work out at the Combine, I had to make my own Combine.

The first thing I had to find was a field to do drills on. So I went to a local high school stadium with a nice fast track for Marvin to run his forty-yard dash. I paid a few hundred bucks and had the field beautifully cut and manicured, and I had the track prepared and cleared it with the local municipality, the city of North Miami. I was going all out on this workout. I had a ton of media covering the workout. I had a whole weight set brought in for Marvin to do his bench press repetitions. I also borrowed a vertical leap scale from the Miami Dolphins. Throw in a few cones, stop watches, and measuring tapes. Presto, an instant Combine.

I also paid the video guys from the Miami Dolphins to tape Marvin's workout, professionally, just like they would at the combine, so they went all the way up in the stands and had two cameras. I would then make copies of the tape and send it to all the teams. I also put up a tent for all the scouts to stay under while Marvin was warming up, so they would be out of the sun. I catered it with food and drinks. His workout became famous. It was a one of a kind. The scouts still talk about it. It was a first-class operation. People still recalled this workout in 1993. For example, Sam Wyche mentioned it during the NBC-TV broadcast of the Dolphins versus the Jets. Marvin made a big play and Wyche, formerly coach of the Tampa Bay Buccaneers, said that the thing that stood out most about Marvin was going to the workout that I set up for him. Wyche said he would never forget how fancy that workout was.

Not only was the setup great, but so was Marvin's performance. He excelled. The scouts were very impressed. Now it was time for the draft.

The 1993 NFL Draft was a huge breakthrough for me. Marvin Jones was the first defensive player drafted, and he went to the New York Jets with the fourth overall pick. Kevin Williams was Jimmy Johnson's first choice for the Cowboys. But as usual with my career, there was some suspense along the way. Marvin was projected to be the third pick by the Jets. While we were in New York for the Draft, the local Jet fans were very fired up about selecting Marvin. However, Drew Bledsoe, Rick Mirer, and Garrison Hearst were moving up the charts. Therefore, with our hearts pounding and the ESPN cameras focused right on us, the Jets traded from the third pick to the fourth. The Jet fans were chanting from the Draft Ball-Room for the team to take Marvin. And after fifteen minutes of painful waiting, the Jets made Marvin the fourth pick. I was elated, but this time I kept my composure on the national TV cameras. It was great to be the "King of New York."

While I was with Marvin in New York, Jason was in Dallas with Kevin. The Dallas Cowboys sent a representative to be with Jason and Kevin during the Draft to make sure Jimmy Johnson and Jerry Jones could reach Kevin by phone. Well, as the Cowboys first pick came, so did the call. Jason answered the phone, and talked to Jerry Jones on the other line. Jerry said, "Son, we are prepared to make Kevin a Dallas Cowboy and pay him a lot of money. If you are willing to take a four-year deal similar to what last year's player got, I will make Kevin a Dallas Cowboy."

Jason called me and got me on the phone with Jerry Jones. I told Jerry we needed a fair increase over last year's pick, but if we got that, we should be able to do the deal. Jason went over to the Dallas Cowboys' facility with Kevin to do a press conference. Jimmy had just won his first Super Bowl with Jerry. The Dallas Dynasty had begun. Everyone thought Jimmy and Jerry would become an unstoppable team. Everyone should have watched that press conference, and they would have gotten a glimpse of what was to come. Jerry and Jimmy were sitting together on an elevated table on top of a stage. When Jerry introduced Kevin as their top draft choice, Jerry moved his chair back a little. Well, he slid the chair back a little too far as it went off the edge. The chair slid backward and Jerry Jones started falling on his back in the chair. Jerry tried grabbing the table but to no avail. He was on his back reaching for someone or something to pull him back up. Jimmy, seated right next to him, just looked over and started laughing. The Cowboys' public relations director raced over to Jimmy and, along with several other Cowboy employees, tried to pull Jerry up.

Jason called me and told me what happened. He and I knew that it was just a matter of time before that situation imploded. Nevertheless, Jerry Jones eventually gave us the deal we needed. Kevin Williams was the first player ever to sign a contract during the new rookie cap era. Jerry, Jimmy, Kevin, and I had made history. I had the guts to pull the trigger on the deal while everyone else waited to see what the other guy was going to do. I like setting trends, not following them.

For all the flack that Jerry Jones takes, the Dallas Cowboy fans are very fortunate to have him as their team owner. No owner wants to win more than Jerry Jones, and he does whatever it takes to make his team the best.

As for Marvin, I negotiated with the Jets' Steve Gutman on a five-year contract worth close to $7 million. If Gutman acted like he was trying to be my friend during Bobby Houston's negotiation, he was like immediate family during Marvin's negotiations. Our talks were very amusing. He liked to be very personal and friendly. When all was said and done, Marvin got a massive $3.25 million signing bonus and a voidable fifth year. It was a good deal for both sides.

Marvin's contract was very creative. It was one of the first contracts to employ a voidable year concept. A voidable year is one that allows a player to dissolve his contract and become a free agent. Marvin's negotiations were tricky because he was picked after Drew Bledsoe, Rick Mirer, and Garrison

Hearst—two quarterbacks and a running back. These were the highest paid positions in the NFL. As a middle linebacker, Marvin's position was one of the lowest. My solution was to compromise and go with the voidable years. The NFL League Office thought Marvin's contract circumvented the salary cap, and they examined it. After almost rejecting it, the contract was finally accepted and Marvin's deal became official.

I had gotten Marvin's and Kevin's deals done and it felt great. I came back from oblivion to have a great year, and my competition was left with nothing to do but watch me. From there my career took off. I left my competition in the dust as I shot off like a rocket. I was on a roll.

Miami Dolphin wide receivers Mark Duper and Mark Clayton were my childhood heroes. The "Marks Brothers" were as prolific a wide receiver tandem as any in the history of NFL. They were a big part of Dan Marino's record-breaking Hall of Fame career and should both be considered for the Hall of Fame themselves. I can still see Duper and Clayton catching Dan Marino's game-winning touchdown passes, as Jason and I cried tears of joy and screamed and yelled in what had to be our greatest moments as Dolphin fans.

Being the Dolphin fanatics that Jason and I were, it was special for personal reasons to sign both Clayton and Duper. When I became their agent it felt great, but also bittersweet: sweet because they were my childhood Dolphin heroes; bitter because Don Shula did not want either of them back. I signed Clayton to the Green Bay Packers and Duper with the Cincinnati Bengals where Dave Shula was the head coach. Although their time of glory had come and gone, it was great to be held in high regard by them. It was the ultimate compliment that such experienced veterans wanted me to be their agent in the twilight of their career.

I was now known as the agent to the Miami Dolphins. Everybody now knew me as the man who represented the top Miami Hurricane football players and top South Florida players like Marvin Jones. I had the notoriety and lifestyle I wanted. I was hanging out with Pete Stoyanovich at different restaurants and nightclubs. A handsome and well-known guy, Pete had the air of a movie star about him. He had a great presence and women swooned over him whenever we went out. I spent a lot of time with Pete who always appreciated the efforts and work I did for him.

One time in particular, I went with Pete to a charity Miami Dolphin softball game. At the game, wide receiver Tony Martin came up to me and asked me to be his agent. At the time, Tony was a practice squad player, but I could see he had a lot of potential and could develop into a good player so I took him on as a client. After the season, the Dolphins' top free agent was safety Louis Oliver. If he was the top Dolphin free agent, then it was only fitting that he sign with me, and that is just what he did. The Dolphin players kept on coming as I simply dominated my competitors with the Dolphins and Hurricanes. My momentum kept picking up.

The top University of Miami Hurricane prospect in the 1994 NFL Draft was fullback Donnell Bennett. When I first signed Donnell, he was projected to go in the third or fourth round. I worked hard to get him drafted as high as possible. The NFL scouts told me that he needed to lose weight and improve his forty-yard dash time and his agility drills. I worked day and night with Donnell, encouraging him to train for the workouts. He worked with the University of Miami track coach, he ate properly, exercised, and did all of the right things. In one month's time, he lost ten pounds and improved his forty-yard dash time significantly. He worked hard and listened to me and his father, Donnell Bennett Sr., and it paid off. The Kansas City Chiefs made Donnell their second-round pick, and we were extremely pleased.

Donnell went as high as we could have hoped for. As we waited for the call, Donnell was driving in a car behind me and we were heading back to my office. When I got the call from the Chiefs that they were selecting Donnell as their second-round pick, I was so happy I pulled to the side of the road, ran over to Donnell's car in traffic, and hugged him as I delivered the good news.

As elated as I was at having the Hurricanes' premier player in the draft, I still wanted that first-round pick. To me the mark of a top agent is having that first-round pick year in and year out. I didn't get that first-round pick that year, and even though I signed the top Dolphin free agents in Pete Stoyanovich and Louis Oliver and the top Hurricane draft pick, I still wanted more.

Well, the team that took away my first-round pick (Randal Hill) brought me a new one, and his name was Tim Bowens. I first met Tim at the annual Dolphins Banquet in June 1994. Tim came from a small town in Mississippi called Okolona. Coming from Ole Miss University, Tim was not at all comfortable in the bright lights and big city of Miami. He didn't know anyone on the team and was very uneasy being around so many strangers at the banquet who were trying to talk to him and be friendly. Seeing that he was having a miserable time, Jason and I asked a couple of his teammates to pull Tim away from the crowd that was mobbing him. Our client Jeff Cross took Tim under his wing and showed him around. Tim was very bright and articulate, but because he kept to himself you would think he was very quiet. After seeing how Jason and I handled so many different affairs for our clients, Tim decided he wanted to have agents who would personally take care of business for him. Naturally, he wanted to go with us. Who else was there? We represented so many of his teammates, why not him, too?

I had my second Dolphin first-round pick and was determined to make sure that the negotiations went smoothly this time. Things went so smoothly that Tim was one of the earliest first-rounders to sign. Instead of holding draft picks out like I had done in the past, I was now getting them signed at a record pace. In fact, since Marvin's contract in 1993, I have not had a rookie miss a single day of training camp.

The Dolphins seemed pleased that I was Tim's agent because they knew we both wanted Tim to become a great player. Tim has tremendous size, speed, and quickness. They could see he would become one of the best defensive tackles in the game and had the potential for greatness if he worked hard. They knew I would stay on Tim to help him with whatever he needed so that he could concentrate on working out properly. Jason must have hung out with Tim every single day for the entire summer while he showed him his way around Miami and Fort Lauderdale.

We work with our clients to help them reach their potential. Teams know we will work with our clients to ensure that they work hard and take care of their business off the field. Tim picked things up fast and learned all he needed to know after the first week. Tim didn't like to be around many people, he liked to do his own thing; but Jason was the one guy who didn't get on his nerves. As for me, he told me straight out I talked too much for him.

I remember one time Jason and I drove Tim to the airport, and Jason had accidentally cut off this black Mustang. Four so-called tough guys jumped out of their car with bats and tire irons; they wanted to fight as soon as Jason and I got out of the car. Jason and I were just smiling. We were smiling because right after those guys gave us the finger and started calling us every bad word in Spanish, Tim stepped out of the car.

He raised his arms and yelled, "What!" I guess when they saw the six foot five, all muscle, three hundred twenty pound giant, they decided maybe it was their fault they got cut off after all. Sometimes it's good to be the agent.

By the start of the 1994 season, I had made Rosenhaus Sports into an empire. Although still in law school, Jason had taken and passed the Certified Public Accounting Exam in the state of Florida. And my father Robert, who is now a Vice President at Capital Bank in South Florida, was working with some of our clients as an investment advisor. I had a well-oiled machine running on all cylinders. Representing more Miami Hurricanes in the NFL than any other agent, and representing more players on the Miami Dolphins than any other agent ever had on any team before, I was making my move to the top.

11

Expanding Empire

BY 1994, THINGS WERE GOING WELL FOR MY COMPANY, ROSEN-haus Sports Representation, Inc. To be at the top, however, I had to sign more Pro-Bowl players. While meeting with the Pittsburgh Steelers on a contract extension for my client D. J. Johnson, I was watching such a player on the practice field, and his name was Eric Green, the huge All-Pro tight end.

I hadn't seen Eric since the Doc Daniels's days, and he was real friendly as he walked over toward me after practice. Eric was the man in Pittsburgh, and, of course, since I was the man among agents, he became my client in no time at all. It was very rewarding to finally sign Eric after I had come so close to representing him while he was in college. This is why you never burn bridges. When Eric decided four years ago not to sign with me, I was a gentleman and wished him well. I was patient and waited for another opportunity in the future.

My time had come. Eric was entering the final year of his contract, and unless the Steelers gave him an extension, he would play his contract out and become an unrestricted free agent at the end of the season. I dealt with Dan Ferens of the Steelers, who was a very talented negotiator.

Outside the negotiating room, he was cordial and hard not

to like. Inside the negotiating room, he was very tough with little flexibility. He knew that Dan Rooney, the owner of the Steelers, did not like to overpay players, and Ferens was looking to keep things that way. I have to take my hat off to the Steeler organization. Every year they lose top players to free agency, and every year they bring in new players and stay competitive. They have drafted as well as anyone over the years and keep producing big-time players who fit their scheme. Their head coach Bill Cowher is one of the best coaches in the business.

His guys go to war for him. He is a leader by example, and his players respect him for it and want to win for him, every single one of them. It is that mutual respect and desire to win that makes the Steelers a special organization. Eric liked playing for the Steelers and Cowher, but he did not want to be underpaid.

The Steelers named Eric as their "Franchise Player," which limited us from negotiating with other teams. On a long-term contract, the Steelers weren't offering what we needed in the form of a signing bonus or early year salaries. The bulk of the money was put in the base salaries toward the end of the five-year contract. The problem with contracts where the big money is paid out in the third or fourth year is that the team can cut the player after his second year, and the player will get nothing. Even worse, he will have been underpaid the first two years. With Eric having some injury concerns, we wanted him to get the big money in his first and second year, so if he was released, he would have already made his fortune.

As hard as I worked, we weren't able to get the Steelers high enough on a long-term offer, so we accepted their offer on a one-year deal. I was in a tough spot as one of the few agents in NFL history who had to deal with the dreaded "Franchise" label on Eric. We wanted Eric to become a free agent.

So we decided he should play out the 1994 season and hit the open market. If Eric would go on to have a great year, we would win; if Eric had a poor year, we would lose. He was willing to gamble and I was behind him all the way. It was frustrating dealing with the Franchise Tag because the Steelers had his exclusive rights. An unrestricted free agent can go to the highest bidder, and it is completely at the player's discretion for which team he wants to play. But with the Steelers making Eric their franchise player, they had his exclusive rights, and we were not able to deal with other teams. But we were patient, and as you will soon find out, that patience paid off. Having signed one Pro-Bowl veteran client in Eric Green, I went out to New York to add another. I had two New York Jet linebackers who were my clients already: Marvin Jones and Bobby Houston. Marvin and Bobby told me that Pro-Bowl linebacker Mo Lewis had fired his agent and was looking for a new agent.

I liked Mo the moment I met him. A black belt in several different forms of the martial arts, Mo was my kind of guy. Mo was as funny and witty a guy as you'll find. I could see he was not only a tremendous football player, but he was also a man of character which was the combination I look for in a client. Needless to say, I had to make him a Rosenhaus Sports client.

I represented all three Jet starting linebackers. In time I singed their back up, Glenn Cadrez. It was cool representing the entire Jet linebacking corps. They called themselves the "Drew Crew." And it wasn't long until my Jet clients hooked me up with the team's starting running back, Adrian Murrell. A classy guy, I was thrilled to have Adrian as my client, especially since he was making his move to become one of the best running backs in the NFL.

Continuing with the All-Pro players, I signed Brian and Bennie Blades. Since I knew these two from my days at the University of Miami and from working with Levine, it was very gratifying to represent the Blades Brothers. Both of them were excellent players whom I got along with really well. My local competitors went after those two hard, but since I represented the top players from South Florida, I was the man to beat and I kept my title. The Rosenhaus Empire was expanding rapidly. by 1995, I negotiated over $100 million in player contracts. I was ranked by several publications as one of the top four agents in the business, based on my clients and negotiated contracts.

Because I was signing so many new clients, I stepped on a lot of toes. All these great veteran clients I picked up had previous agents. These agents got fired and watched me walk away in the limelight with their clients. It was bad enough that I had stolen the show by getting all the hype, now they were watching me on TV with their ex-clients, too. My competition hated my guts. They hated me either because they had lost a client to me or they were afraid they would be next. Because of me and my work ethic, agents could no longer be complacent. When other players saw how I was with my clients, I made their agents look lazy and uncaring. The other agents could no longer get fat off of the blood, sweat, and tears of their clients. Now they had to go out and work hard, too.

With all the venom my competition was spewing at me, I received a massive dose of publicity. My competitors said my ethics were the lowest and that I was a scumbag. There were numerous investigative articles and exposés on me. Reporters took negative quotes from my competitors, but they could not find one player in the NFL, my client or not, who could say that I wronged him in any way. That's right, my competitors said that I was the unethical bad guy. And yet it's these guys who screw their clients over by negotiating short-sided deals, putting their clients into bad investments or failing businesses, mishandling their taxes and overcharging them. It's also these guys who don't protect the players and fail to help the players budget their money for the long term, and it's these guys who abandon their clients when their football careers are over.

These guys are the so-called good guys in the old-boy network, and because I squash them like bugs, I am the bad guy. And I have always been squashing them, from day one. My competitors can only explain my success by claiming that I cheated. I ask you, how do you cheat in signing smart, experienced veterans like Mo Lewis and Pete Stoyanovich? I ask you, why is it a twenty-two-year-old Duke law student gets more hype in his first year by bringing ESPN into his home on Draft Day than they did in their entire careers? I ask you, why is it this same rookie was the first and only agent ever to bring in an ESPN camera crew to film an actual NFL contract negotiation? I ask you, why was I able to gain so many clients, in such a tough business, in such a short period of time?

Why? Because I outsmarted and outworked my competition—it's that simple. And if outworking my competition and going that extra mile to do right by my clients creates more enemies among my competitors, then so be it. I am not going to stop. In fact, I am just getting started. I have Jason working with me full time as my partner now that he is an attorney and a certified public accountant. With Jason watching my back, no one is going to stop me. This is my home and I'm kicking everyone else out the door.

My competitors were on the outside looking in. They were anonymous, they were in hiding, they were lurking in the shadows while I was in the bright lights. I was appearing on television every Sunday as an NFL insider on Jim Mandich's local television show and the CBS affiliate WFOR with Jim Berry.

Jason and I were in the limelight for all to see on networks such as ESPN and CNN, having fun hanging out with Tim Bowens, Marvin Jones, Eric Green, and Brian Blades. I became the prototype and the image that people envisioned when they pictured an agent. When my competition would introduce themselves as an agent, they would hear, "Oh, like Drew Rosenhaus," and I loved it. I was everywhere and they could not escape me. By singing all these veterans, I was crushing my enemies, seeing them driven before me, and I heard their lamentations as I put them out of business. Yes!

So, remember, when you hear complaints about my ethics and morals, you aren't hearing what the players say, you are hearing my competitors' whining. And unfortunately for me, some writers in the media who don't know me are often too lazy and unprofessional to talk to me to hear my side. Some members of the media only hear the wimpy crying from other agents, and like their readers, they believe what they read. So I am often criticized unfairly without the writer even knowing the facts. But, hey, those guys don't want to let the facts get in the way of a good story. And controversial agents are stories that sell. You'll notice that the media in South Florida is much more fair toward me because they report and write the facts as they are. They are journalists, not sensationalists like too many high-profile reporters are. But this all comes with the territory.

You are going to take a lot of heat when you dominate the veteran market like I did. Now it was time to dominate with the rookies. And the most dominating player in college football was University of Miami defensive tackle Warren Sapp. Sapp was the biggest legend on the UM campus since Michael Irvin.

He was the fiercest of all competitors, quicker than the offensive guards in front of him, meaner and nastier than anyone on the team. This kid was unstoppable. He single-handedly won football games for his head coach Dennis Erickson. Playing on national television, Sapp became a household name and one of the most popular players in college football. Sapp was rewarded for his outstanding play with the Lombardi Trophy and the College Defensive Player of the Year Award. As I watched him play his junior season, I was in awe of his talent. It didn't take an NFL scout to realize that this was the best player in college football. As the Orange Bowl game approached, the Hurricanes were to play the Nebraska Cornhuskers for the National Championship. I couldn't wait. And I wasn't the only one.

Toward the end of the 1994–95 season, Jason and I went to a Dolphin game at Joe Robbie Stadium the Sunday before the Orange Bowl game. We were sitting in a sky box when we noticed the entire Nebraska football team seated just below us. At half time, the announcer informed the Dolphin fans of their presence in anticipation of the game.

At first, the Miami fans started booing. Then, louder and louder, I heard the crowd chant, "War-ren Sapp! War-ren Sapp! War-ren Sapp!" over and over again. Sapp wasn't there, but the crowd was letting the Nebraska team know they were in for a brawl. I had never seen a crowd chant a college player's name like that in any NFL game, and I probably never will. Jason and I knew we had to get this guy. Sapp was the man in this town, and so would be his agent.

My title was on the line. I obviously wanted to represent Sapp not only because I knew he would be a great player but also because of the prestige of representing such a local hero. I had worked so hard to be the man in my hometown, there would be a new "sheriff" in town if someone else got Sapp.

Shortly after the Dolphin game, Jason and I went with Pete Stoyanovich to Sylvester Stallone's Christmas party at his luxurious estate in Vizcaya. Gloria Estefan and her husband were there, as was Daisy Fuentes, who was very obviously hot for Stallone. Being the huge Rocky fan that I was, it was very gratifying to be in Sylvester Stallone's home on Christmas Eve. I had met Sly several times before through a mutal friend named Jason Binn.

Binn was one of the owners of *Ocean Drive Magazine* which was the hot magazine in South Beach. I had hung out with Binn a lot with Pete at different clubs in South Beach, and he would often be accompanied by Stallone.

Jason and I noticed a lot of Rocky memorabilia and artwork in Sly's house. His house was very impressive not just for the overwhelming size of the estate, but for the interior design and artwork as well. When Stallone came over to greet us, I was anxious to congratulate him on his art collection, but I didn't get the chance.

"Drew, are you going to sign Warren Sapp as your client or what?" Stallone was a real gentleman and a pleasure to converse with, but the second he ended the conversation, I wanted to get out of there. I wanted to go find Warren Sapp.

Finally, the Orange Bowl game came and went, and Sapp played one of the best games I had ever seen a defensive lineman play. Soon after the game, Sapp announced he was entering the NFL Draft to come out early as a junior. I got up the next morning and waited by the phone until I thought it was late enough in the morning for him to be awake. At high noon, I made the call.

"What!" I heard a grumpy voice say.

"Warren, congratulations. You had a tremendous year," I said.

"Who the hell is this!" he demanded.

"Drew Rosenhaus."

"I'm not talking to agents right now, bye," he snapped.

"Hang on Sapp. I'm the man, I represent all your buddies."

Sapp responded, "I'm the man and I don't care who you represent!" And then I heard the dial tone. I couldn't believe it, the most popular University of Miami player in years and the guy hung up on me. I was in serious pain. The thought of a rival agent getting Sapp made me sick to my stomach. I could not let that happen. In the worst mood ever, I was determined to get another shot at Sapp. I didn't know how or when, but I knew it had to be soon because it wouldn't be long before he would hire an agent. All I could do was go out to the clubs the players went to, put myself in a position for something to happen, and hope to get lucky.

After being awake over twenty-one hours, Jason and I got lucky. At 1:00 A.M., Sapp walked through the doors of Club Amnesia at South Beach. Sapp had a reputation for being hard on people he didn't know. My client, Jessie Armstead, and a couple of others who were there, told me that Sapp had a real mean streak in him. They warned me he would be tough if I were to approach him in a bad mood. Considering the fact that I had already pissed him off, that was not good. But you know how we were trained by Young Soo Do to feel about adversity: it is an opportunity to be seized for great victory. Not knowing what this tough-looking two hundred eighty–pounder was going to do, Jason and I walked up to him. It was obvious he didn't want to talk to me, and I knew it was possible he could be angry with me for bothering him. But I wasn't concerned about anything but winning him over, so I came at him. He looked at me like I must have been crazy for going within ten feet of him.

This was good. I wanted him to see I could not be intimidated, even by him. I wanted him to see how much I wanted and deserved to be his agent.

"Sapp, I apologize for the other morning. I didn't mean to upset you. I called to ask you for the chance to meet with you and your family about becoming your agent."

"Not interested. Bye," he said as he waved me off and started walking away.

Jason stepped in front of him, "Sapp, ask your teammates about us. Ask Jessie if we did right by him. He's standing right here."

I stepped in, "Sapp, you've got us all wrong. We're not the bad guys everybody tells you we are. We are the hardest workers in the business and we'll fight and kill for our clients. Just ten minutes of your time is all I'm asking for. After that, it's on you."

"Damn, Jessie, how do you deal with these guys?" Sapp joked.

"The Rosenhaus boys are good guys. You'll love 'em," Armstead said.

"I doubt that, but you'll get your ten minutes. Call me tomorrow."

"Thanks Sapp. You won't regret it," I said.

"Can I go now?" he asked.

Jason and I laughed as he walked past us. We had our shot, thanks to a client who went in the eighth round and at that time hadn't made any real money. Even though Jessie wasn't a star yet, we always went all out for him. We knew some day he would become a great player for the Giants, but at the time he was climbing the ladder from the bottom up, and we were there every step of the way to help him. Not only did Jessie become one of our top clients, but because we were with him when everyone else forgot about him, he was more than happy to do right by us with Sapp. That was a perfect example of how working hard for every single one of your clients ultimately pays off.

The next day, Jason and I went over to Sapp's apartment but never got the chance to talk business. Instead, we played NHL '94 on the Sega computer system. Jason and I had previously played the game to the point where we were experts. Our clients always wanted to battle, so we were already darn good at the game. I said, "Sapp, I am going to show you what domination means. I am going to kick your ass. And when I am done, Jason's going to mop up whatever's left of you."

No one spoke to Sapp like that. Especially not the offensive linemen he beat up on every day. I saw the steam in his eyes. I saw the fury. I knew he was outraged and wanted to put my head through the wall. But I also did my homework and knew that above all else, this kid was a competitor. I had challenged him, and no matter how much I pissed him off, I knew he couldn't resist.

"Come on," was all he said to me.

I never wanted to win a video game so much in my life. This was a game that was hundreds of thousands, if not millions, of dollars to me. I had to beat him because I knew he wouldn't let me leave his apartment until he got his revenge. And yes, I took him out. He was so upset, I thought he was going to tie the TV cord around my neck and throw us out the window. Instead, my gamble paid off. We played again and again. We played for hours. Jason just watched us. It was a marathon battle. Eventually we both adapted to each other's styles and started to stalemate. Jason finally got in there and let Sapp beat him in overtime. Jason was no dummy either. He wanted to put Sapp in a good mood. Sapp had his suspicions, but he wanted that win. Sapp had tested us, and not just over video game skills.

After he had left the club the previous night, he had called ten of his former teammates who were our clients. Our clients really went to bat for us. Whenever our clients thank us, we always remind them to save it for our recruits when they call. Well, they remembered and Sapp was impressed.

And then he impressed me. He pulled out the statistics of what the NFL salaries were and went over each and every contract I negotiated in the last five years. He grilled me and was very tough. He had heard all the criticisms about me and asked me about them one by one. I loved it. He gave me every opportunity to show him what I had, and I could see that by the end of the night I had won him over. Now we had to impress his mom.

Sapp gave us his permission to drive to Plymouth, Florida, to meet with his mom, Annie Roberts. The minute I met Annie, I could see where Sapp got his strong presence. Annie was the nicest, most pleasant person I could ever ask to speak with, and yet I could see that she was an extremely strong-willed person. This was a woman who was going to do whatever she set her mind to. Sapp had much to be grateful for. Shortly after meeting with Annie, I signed the immortal Warren Sapp. My competitors tried to recruit Sapp by offering limousines and fancy dinners; I did it with a video game challenge. Of course, it wouldn't have gotten me very far if I didn't have what it took to represent the best player in the country, but it gave me the shot at the title which was all I needed.

Sapp turned out to be one of the most loyal, trusting, and generous clients I've had. It's very simple: Until he knows you, Sapp is extremely skeptical and challenging toward you. But once you're in, you're in all the way for life.

I knew this because at the NFL Combine in Indianapolis in February 1995, Sapp was barraged by agents. My competitors came after Sapp and told him anything and everything they could to try to alienate Sapp toward us. Sapp didn't even bother with them. They couldn't make a dent in Sapp's loyalty to me. He was there to take care of business at the Combine.

Every college player that the teams have a strong interest in is invited to work out for what they call the NFL Combine. The players are placed under a microscope by all the NFL teams at this big workout in the RCA Dome. All the scouts, coaches, and general managers in the NFL are there to meet with and observe the players' talents on and off the field. The players are given a thorough medical and physical examination; they run drills, lift weights, take IQ tests, and drug tests as well. Since every big time player is crammed into this one small area, every agent and wanna-be agent are there as well. As you could imagine, I was not going to win any popularity contests there. The long and not so distinguished list of agents who have been fired by clients I now represent are all there, so I found myself walking right in to the lion's den. Except that in this den, I'm the predator.

Waiting for Sapp to come out of a meeting, I was in a hotel lobby in Indianapolis at the Combine. The lobby was filled with agents and a couple of scouts were there, too. Everywhere around me, I saw agents looking at me and talking about me with pure hatred. If there was a rope around somewhere, these guys would have tried to hang me. I wasn't concerned because I knew they didn't have the guts to take me on. There had to be twenty agents there, all in unison, talking about me and continually looking over toward me.

One agent in particular was upset that one of his clients was threatening to fire him. Since the player had ties to Florida, of course the agent blamed me.

As I was talking with Jason and an NFL scout, the agent shouted some insult toward me, claiming I was calling one of his clients. This was too good to be true. Finally, one of these weasels had the temerity to say something to my face, even if it was from ten feet away as he was surrounded by a bunch of his coconspirators.

I was FURIOUS and shot back, "You punk! I have kicked your ass every single time we matched up. All you do is go around my back like a wimp and tell lies about me." I yelled at him, as we were face to face.

Although Jason is my younger brother who I look out for and protect, he always tells me that most of the time he feels like he's my bodyguard. He had been waiting to get a piece of a competitor, too, and couldn't help himself. He jumped between us, and pushed the agent out of my face.

Jason knew better. I told him never to get into a confrontation with these losers. I had instructed Jason many times before to always pull me out of a situation like that before making a scene. Now Jason had made it physical. Now I was even madder. This guy was threatening Jason, telling him to never touch him again. Jason had put his hands on him, but the other agent did nothing. Jason had regained his composure and just smiled at the guy right in his face, daring the agent to take it to the next level. When he saw the other agent was scared, Jason turned his back to him, grabbed me, and walked me out of there.

After Jason got me out of the room, the agent started yelling again.

I went back in there and reminded myself that I was acting unprofessionally because there were NFL scouts around. I was embarrassing myself monkeying around with this schmuck. Dick Haley, the general manager of the New York Jets, and his assistant Pat Kirwan were waiting for me next door at the bar. But like a caged Shark that hadn't eaten for far too long, I smelled blood and wanted that kill.

In front of the entire room, I challenged him man to man, "Let's settle this outside! Come on! I'll kick your ass!" I drooled at the thought of being able to pummel his face into the frozen dirt. I wanted red snow. Jason wanted this so bad, he did not follow, making sure the agent would not have an excuse to back out by saying it was two against one. Jason knew I wouldn't need any help.

I started to walk outside, opened the door, and yelled, "Let's go!"

Staying where he was, the agent answered, "I'm not going out there. It's too cold."

The agent was overdressed in a big overcoat and I was in a black jacket and T-shirt.

I looked in his eyes and saw a coward. He saw that I knew it. If it's true that a hero dies but once, and a coward dies many times, I killed him that day. End of story.

Drew with karate instructor *(From the author's collection)*

Little Drew in his pee wee league football uniform *(From the author's collection)*

Young Drew, sister Dana, and Jason (front row, from left) at their house in Miami Beach with Dolphins Duriel Harris (back row, second from left), Joe Rose (back row, second from right), Fulton Walker (back row, first from right), and family friends *(From the author's collection)*

Drew with his father, Robert, at Duke Law School graduation *(From the author's collection)*

Drew Rosenhaus and Robert Massey ponder Massey's fate in upcoming NFL Draft

Drew and client Robert Massey appearing in the April 19, 1989, edition of *The Durham Sun (Courtesy of* The Durham Sun/*Jim Sparks)*

Photo by Steve Wilson

"When you're faced with a no-win situation, it's my opinion that your best approach is to change the rules of the game," says Drew Rosenhaus, a third-year law student at Duke and NFL agent. "And I did that."

Drew while at Duke Law, appearing in the September 25, 1989, edition of *The Triangle Business Journal,* taken at Duke football stadium *(Courtesy of* The Triangle Business Journal/*Steve Wilson)*

Front-page photograph of Drew (front right), Jason (back left), and client Randal Hill (seated on left) in the April 22, 1991, edition of *The Miami Herald.* Taken at Joe Robbie Stadium after Randal was drafted by the Dolphins *(Reprinted with permission of* The Miami Herald.)

Drew speaking to his beloved south Florida media *(From the author's collection)*

Partying at Miami night club in 1994 with clients. From left: Randal Hill (Dolphins), Jeff Cross (Dolphins), Jason, Pete Stoyanovich (Dolphins), J.B. Brown (Dolphins), Drew, Marvin Jones (Jets), and Mark Higgs (Dolphins) *(From the author's collection)*

A gathering at Sylvester Stallone's house in Miami Beach. From left: an unidentified friend, Jason, Stallone, Pete Stoyanovich, and Drew *(From the author's collection)*

Drew and Tom Cruise in Los Angeles during filming of *Jerry Maguire*. The autograph reads: "Stop—I said stop trying to look like me. Seriously, thank you for participating in *Jerry Maguire*. Tom Cruise." *(From the author's collection/Photo by Andrew Cooper)*

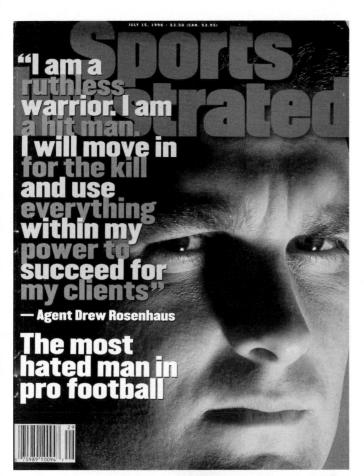

JULY 15, 1996 • $3.50 (CAN. $3.95)

"I am a ruthless warrior. I am a hit man. I will move in for the kill and use everything within my power to succeed for my clients"
— Agent Drew Rosenhaus

The most hated man in pro football

Sports Illustrated cover featuring Drew *(Courtesy of* Sports Illustrated/*Brian Smith)*

Drew and actor Jay Mohr, who played Bob Sugar in *Jerry Maguire;* taken at premiere in New York City *(From the author's collection)*

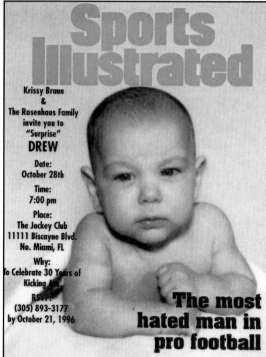

Sports Illustrated

Krissy Braun
&
The Rosenhaus Family
invite you to
"Surprise"
DREW

Date:
October 28th

Time:
7:00 pm

Place:
The Jockey Club
11111 Biscayne Blvd.
No. Miami, FL

Why:
To Celebrate 30 Years of
Kicking A___

RSVP:
(305) 893-3177
by October 21, 1996

**The most
hated man in
pro football**

Invitation to Drew's thirtieth birthday party in Miami *(From the author's collection)*

Drew with client Stanley Pritchett of the Dolphins at Drew's thirtieth birthday party in Miami *(From the author's collection)*

Modeling card of Drew's girlfriend, swimsuit model Krissy Braun *(Courtesy of Koren)*

Photograph of Yatil Green (seated on left), Drew (middle), and Robert (right) in the April 20, 1997, edition of the Fort Lauderdale *Sun-Sentinel*. Taken in Lake City after Yatil was drafted by the Dolphins *(Courtesy of* Sun-Sentinel/*Dede Smith)*

Yatil Green and Drew at Miami Dolphins press conference after the draft, featured in the April 20, 1997, edition of *The Miami Herald (Courtesy of* Miami Herald/*David Bergman)*

Drew and his family in
1996. From left: Robert,
Jill, Drew, Dana, and
Jason *(From the author's
collection)*

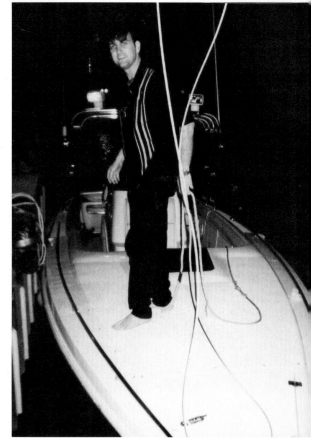

Drew, dripping wet after
jumping into the water
with his clothes on to
rescue his clients from a
drifting boat during the
1997 Super Bowl *(From the
author's collection)*

12

Seeing Green

THE SPRING OF 1995 BROUGHT A NEW SEASON OF POWER FOR agents, with free agency coming on strong in only its second year under the new collective bargaining agreement. I was a force to be reckoned with. Not only did I have the best rookie in the upcoming draft, Warren Sapp, I also had one of the top veteran free agents in tight end Eric Green. As I said earlier, at the start of season, Eric and I received a five-year offer from the Pittsburgh Steelers for $10 million with a $1.6 million signing bonus. The average was what we wanted, but the problem was the amount of money Eric would have received in the first two years. After talking it over with Eric, we decided to turn the offer down and play out the year for the $1.4 million franchise offer.

"Green Gambles on Future," read the headlines all over the country. We were gambling on Eric having a strong year, so that we could play the free agent market. It took a lot of guts but we rolled the dice. Eric came through like a champ. He had a great year, went to the Pro Bowl, and was a hot commodity on the free agent market. I knew that once free agency began in mid-February, my phone would be ringing off the hook with NFL teams calling for him.

The team that was calling the most was the Miami Dolphins. Don Shula wanted Eric Green. The thought of a two hundred eighty–pound tight end catching passes from Dan Marino was extremely tantalizing. I thought Eric would become a Hall of Famer playing in that offense with Marino. With Eric, Miami looked like a Super Bowl Contender. I also knew that playing on natural grass would be good for Eric's knee. In addition, Eric lived in Orlando, so playing in Miami would be ideal geographically.

The teams playing in this game were the Steelers, Cleveland Browns, Oakland Raiders, Washington Redskins, Green Bay Packers, and the Dolphins. Eric originally wanted to stay with the Steelers, but the Steelers weren't very competitive with their offers to him. Eric visited the Raiders, Redskins, Packers, and Dolphins. The pressure was on. Eric and I had passed on a $1.6 million signing bonus from the Steelers, and I needed to make something happen. It was up to me to get them to open their wallets.

This is what an agent gets paid for. It was my job to create a bidding war and sign with the highest bidder. I had four teams make competing offers for Eric and went back and forth with them trying to drive the offers as high as I could. It was fun dealing with Al Davis, owner of the Raiders; he was my boyhood idol. Davis was counting on the Raider mystique to get Eric to sign. Eric was impressed with the Raider tradition and attitude, but Davis's offer was minuscule compared with the Skins, Packers, and Fins.

The Redskins' effort was led by GM Charlie Casserly and Coach Norv Turner. They are both great guys who look out for their players. They flew down to Miami to give their sales pitches to me in person. It was also a pleasure dealing with Ron Wolf, the great GM of the Packers. He is widely regarded as one of the most astute executives in the NFL.

My most interesting negotiations were with the Dolphins and Coach Don Shula. When Eric visited the Dolphins, I sat in on a meeting with Shula, Marino, and Eric. I took the initiative and really sold Shula and Marino on signing Eric. I persuaded them that Eric would be a huge addition to the team due to his receiving skills, run blocking prowess, and pass protection. Eric was unique. Nobody else in the NFL could do the things he could do at his size. I also promised Shula and Marino that Eric would work hard on his weight and conditioning. Even though I knew the Dolphins wanted Eric, it was still my job to sell them on giving him a monster contract offer. This was awesome. I was working with a tremendous talent in his prime and with four great organizations. Eric would have been happy playing for any of the four.

It is not very often for an agent to have all of the leverage in this system, so when you have it, you have to take advantage of it. The agent is often at the team's mercy and has to take what he can get. In this case, I was running the show. And I ran it well. Eric told me my job was to bring him to Miami.

I negotiated day and night with all three teams—the Skins, Packers, and Fins. I was able to solicit very similar offers from all three clubs. Eric and I set our goal on a $3.5 million signing bonus, and I had to get one of the teams to bite. The negotiations were nerve-racking. I had great offers on the table that I didn't want to lose; however, I wanted to make sure I got every penny there was to get. After long, intense negotiations over a period of three weeks, we got what we set our sights on and agreed to a deal with the Dolphins.

The $3.5 million signing bonus was a record for a Dolphin free agent, and the total of $12 million over six years was the highest contract ever for a tight end in the history of the NFL. This was one of the highlights of my career. I was the man who brokered one of the finest contracts in the NFL, and I did it with my hometown team.

The second I got off of the phone with the Dolphins, I flashed back to being a kid. In those days, I would read the sports page and dream of being able to make the big deal with the Dolphins. And now I had done just that.

Eric's signing was being hailed as the move the Dolphins needed to get to the Super Bowl. I came through for Eric big time. Our gamble paid off to the tune of over $2 million. Instead of getting $1.6 million up front, he would be getting

$3.5 million dollars. This way, if Eric were to get injured after his first year, he would be protected.

I was a hero. I helped my client and may have brought a championship to my hometown team. I was on cloud nine. One of my top clients would be right there in Miami with me for six years, and I would be able to turn him into a marketing giant. I owned Miami.

Dolphin fans weren't the only ones watching the Eric Green saga. An old friend of mine was watching, too. Leon Searcy, who had just fired the agent that he selected out of college, was one of Eric's former teammates with the Steelers. Leon was impressed. Although I didn't keep in touch with Leon, whenever I would bump into him with Eric, I was always friendly. Even though Leon made a business decision to hire someone else, I still liked the guy. It was hard not to like Leon. And I also didn't want to burn any bridges. After seeing how I fought toe to toe with the Steelers, and how Eric came out on top with the Dolphins, Leon knew I was the agent for him.

It didn't take long for Leon to sign with me, making the Eric Green contract even a bigger deal for me personally. As if it wasn't enough that free agency allowed me to negotiate the highest contract ever for a tight end, it also yielded the best right tackle in football to me.

Ironically, Leon was in the same position Eric was in one year earlier. Leon wanted me to get him that multimillion-dollar deal like I did with Eric. I knew Leon had a chance to become my highest paid client, and I went to work to make it happen.

Leon had one more year on his contract with the Pittsburgh Steelers, and their best offer at the start of the season was about $2.2 million a year with $1.8 million to sign. It was a take it or leave it situation. The $1.8 million up front was a lot of money to turn down, but we wanted more. After talking it over with Leon, we agreed that if he were to have a great year and stay healthy, we would make much more. I knew Leon was the best right tackle in football, and he was going to prove it. Again, I rolled the dice with my client and played for high stakes.

Leon came through in a big way. The Steelers won the AFC Championship and Leon had a phenomenal year and a great Super Bowl. Leon mauled people. He was as physical and tough as any offensive lineman in the NFL. And the Jacksonville Jaguars, with a great young left-handed quarterback, noticed. I knew Jacksonville needed a right tackle to protect Mark Brunell's blind side, and I knew that as an expansion team they had more money to spend than anyone.

At midnight, the first minute that the Jacksonville Jaguars were permitted to talk to me about Leon, I got a call from their Vice President of Operations Michael Huyghue. I was expecting that call and Michael knew I would be waiting. I told him about the offer we had turned down, why and what we had gone through. And then I told him what we wanted. He knew signing Leon would take the Jaguars to the next level. I knew he would find a way to make Leon a Jacksonville Jaguar. We left things that night with a mutual understanding that we would talk first thing in the morning and try to get the deal done.

Everything about that organization was extremely impressive. Coach Tom Coughlin was a straightforward, likable guy who was determined to win. Between Huyghue and Coughlin, I was very comfortable sending Leon over there under their leadership. Leon wanted to play for a winning team and Jacksonville was only entering their second year, so Leon had some concerns. But after talking with Coughlin and Huyghue, Leon was sold. We both foresaw Jacksonville winning right away, not down the road. Leon was ready if we could get the dollars we wanted. The other competing teams were, of course, the Steelers, the Philadelphia Eagles, the Jets, Indianapolis Colts, and Houston Oilers. The Eagles were aggressive, but the Jaguars were not going to be beaten out. Huyghue and I talked late at night and then all day long. After going back and forth, over and over again, with the different teams, I knew Leon and I had a chance to get an unprecedented contract. Doing what was necessary to close the deal, Huyghue made his best offer. To steal a line from one of my favorite movies, *The Godfather,* it was "an offer we couldn't refuse." The Jags wanted Leon so badly that the deal was done the very first day of free agency.

The offer was a $17 million deal with a $5 million signing bonus. Yes, $5 million to sign. That contract was record breaking, making Leon the highest-paid offensive lineman in the history of the NFL. Great agents get great contracts, and that was what I did. One of the best people in the NFL, Leon was now the highest-paid offensive lineman in the NFL.

The only thing that Leon wasn't happy about was having to leave Coach Bill Cowher in Pittsburgh. I called Coach Cowher to give him the news and explained to him how much Leon wanted to stay and play for him, but the money was millions of dollars higher than what the Steelers had offered, leaving Leon with no choice. Cowher knew he was losing a great player and was disappointed. He tried to change my mind to the very end. He said that winning and playing for a great organization was more important. I respected his point, but I knew Leon was going to a great organization in Jacksonville and that they would win as well. If the Steelers' offer would have been even close to the Jags, then Leon would have stayed in Pittsburgh. But we weren't talking about a hundred or even hundreds of thousands of dollars, we were talking about several million dollars. Careers can end on one play and Leon had to do what was best for his family's future. I knew Leon made the right move, especially when he got that $5 million check, and we never looked back.

Free agency was the best thing that could have happened to me and my clients. It gave the agent and player the power to control their destiny. Randal Hill had wanted control of his destiny for years. I was unhappy with the way things worked for Randal Hill since his trade from the Dolphins. Yes, I had survived the trade and still became one of the most successful agents in the business, but I couldn't help but wonder what Randal might have become if he had stayed with the Dolphins.

Redemption at last. In one of the feel-good moments of my career, I brought Randal home. The Dolphins and I agreed to a one-year deal bringing Randal back to Miami. Randal was going to have his chance to show what he could do. He and his family were very happy and so was I. I felt like I had righted my wrong. In a similar move, I re-signed Louis Oliver that year with the Dolphins as well.

I was feeling on top of the world. I had approximately eighteen Miami Dolphins on the roster, including stars like Tim Bowens, Eric Green, Pete Stoyanovich, Jeff Cross, J. B. Brown, Randal Hill. This was my team, as I represented one out of every four players. I had a very productive working relationship with Don Shula and did multimillion-dollar long-term deals for Jeff, Pete, J.B., and Chuck Klingbeil.

There I was, sitting in Coach Don Shula's new office. As a kid, I would have given anything to do a deal with the legend who had been with the Dolphins through four decades. He was the winningest coach in the history of the NFL. He had done what no other head coach had ever done before by staying on top for so long. And most importantly, he did things the right way—his way—with class and integrity.

I was thrilled to look to my right and see my client Eric Green sitting there next to me, receiving the highest signing bonus the Miami Dolphins had ever paid to any free agent player. I knew at that moment that I had made it to the top.

Coach Shula said to me, "Drew, I am glad we were able to get this done."

Just over a year later, I found myself sitting in that very same office, although it wasn't Don Shula I was sitting across from, it was his replacement, Jimmy Johnson. And that seat to my right—empty.

"Drew, we're not going to win on this one, but there will be others," Coach Johnson said to me as if to console me. After Don Shula's Miami Dolphins paid Eric Green about $4 million in the 1995 season, Jimmy Johnson had decided to let my client go. Eric had the misfortune of injuring his knee toward the end of the season and then again in the off season. Coach Johnson felt that the risks outweighed the rewards. He didn't want to honor Eric's remaining years on the contract due to Eric's injury.

There had been a changing of the guard. The extremely well-organized, immaculate office, with the pictures and memorabilia of the 1972 Perfect Season when the Dolphins went undefeated to become the Super Bowl Champions, no longer belonged to Don Shula. Gone was the Head Coach of the Dolphins who had been with that team for over twenty-five years. Gone was the legend who did everything he said or accomplished in his entire career, with pride and dignity. Gone was the man with whom I had developed a productive working relationship. Gone was my domination of a team where I previously represented one out of four players. Gone were many of my clients.

When Jimmy Johnson took over, I knew things were going to change. Under Coach Shula, players who just signed new contracts knew that they could not get cut because of salary cap ramifications. They also knew Coach Shula wanted to win now and wasn't going to go with youth and start from scratch. Certain players lost the fear of Shula's wrath because they knew he would not cut them. Well, all bets were off now with Jimmy Johnson as the new sheriff in town.

Jimmy Johnson sent Shula's favorite players such as Bryan Cox, Troy Vincent, Marco Coleman, and Irving Fryar packing to other teams. Right away every player got the message that no one was safe.

Shortly after Johnson made his moves, I saw a report by John Clayton on ESPN. He said "Johnson's toughest task in taking over the Dolphins would be dealing with Drew Rosenhaus." Clayton said Johnson would have his work cut out for him because I had a stranglehold on the team. I could see that a lot of prominent members of the media were pitting me against Jimmy Johnson for some type of battle.

What was forgotten was that Johnson and I had already battled before. I held Jimmie Jones out of camp several years earlier when Johnson was coach of the Cowboys. Three years later, I had Johnson's top Dallas rookie draft pick in 1993, Kevin Williams. Kevin was the first draft pick to sign under the new rookie cap system, and it was a deal that was one of the better deals in the round. I showed Johnson that I had the guts to be the first agent to do a deal and that I wanted Kevin to get off to a good start.

Since then, I have had what I consider to be an excellent working relationship with Coach Johnson. But that relationship was put to the test that first year he was in Miami. After releasing Eric Green, he released Chuck Klingbeil, J. B. Brown, Pete Stoyanovich, and ultimately Jeff Cross.

Johnson released eight of my clients that season and reduced my Dolphin client count to ten. He said that I was personally responsible for screwing up the Dolphins salary cap by getting the previous regime to overpay my veteran clients. Johnson decided to go with a younger, less expensive team.

I had definitely taken a big hit in this changing of the guard. If Coach Shula had remained, J.B., Pete, Eric, Jeff, and Chuck would still have been on that team. I had just negotiated long-term contracts for all of them, and now they were no longer Miami Dolphins. In the NFL, the only guarantee is change, where the players will come and go. That is why it is so important for the agent to get the client as much money as possible as quickly as possible. Eric Green had only been with the Dolphins for one year, but I protected him for life by getting $4 million that first year.

Even though all my guys that Jimmy let go had just received big signing bonus money, they were disappointed because they had grown so accustomed to living and working in South Florida year round. I, too, was disappointed. I had worked extremely hard to sign those Dolphin players, and now they were gone. I got very close to those guys and seeing them leave Miami was like saying good-bye to a family member. Once again, I had what I wanted taken away from me. Once again I vowed to get back what belonged to me.

To take a quote from Dan Le Batard, a columnist with the

Miami Herald, "Only a few things would survive a nuclear holocaust. Astro-turf, cockroaches, twinkies and Drew Rosenhaus." The writer was correct, I was a survivor and would adapt to the changes brought on by Jimmy.

I actually enjoy dealing with Jimmy. He is a very positive and upbeat person. He is willing to listen and give you the opportunity to state your point. He is very friendly and open-minded once he respects you. I believe I earned Jimmy's respect because he knows that I am fair and want to see my clients succeed. He also knows firsthand that I am a hard worker, and I have come a long way since my UM days. In fact, Jimmy was quoted as saying "I like Drew, he is a character."

I am fortunate to work in a market that has coaches and executives like Jimmy Johnson and Pat Riley of the Miami Heat. I recently was at a charity function and Riley said that he was a big fan of my TV work—though he was glad I didn't represent NBA players. Riley was about the smoothest guy I had ever met. He is a man of distinction, and I have ultimate respect for him.

Before I could take on any new Dolphin clients, I had to take care of business. And the core of my business is signing the top University of Miami players year after year. The top University of Miami player gearing up for the 1996 NFL Draft was Ray Lewis. Ray had come out early as a junior and had switched agents twice already before I stepped into the picture. In what was a no-brainer for him, he hired Jason and me, and he went from a projected second rounder to being the first-round pick of the Baltimore Ravens.

We got Ray a great contract. Ray was one of the few players in the draft to get the final year of his contract voided out by play time. Ray's contract was originally for five years, but by midseason, Ray's fifth year voided out and his contract became a four-year deal. When the contract expires, Ray will become an unrestricted free agent and will be in a position to become one of the highest-paid linebackers in the NFL.

Having signed the top Hurricane rookie for the third straight year and having done Leon's blockbuster deal, I was ready to claim what belonged to me. Coach Johnson's first draft as the Miami Dolphins' head coach was outstanding. Of the rookies he drafted, seven ended up starting. These rookies didn't necessarily start because of a lack of depth, but because they were very good players.

When Tim Bowens came to town as a rookie first-round pick, he saw how hard I worked for his teammates and wanted me to do the same for him. The following year, in Shula's last year, I signed Norman Hand, another Dolphin rookie draft pick for the same reasons. I had hoped that the new crop of rookies would see what Norman and Tim saw and do what Norman and Tim did. Well, I worked hard for my clients and put myself in a position for something good to happen. When it did, I was prepared and made the most out of it.

Four rookies—fullback Stanley Pritchett, running back Jerris McPhail, defensive lineman Shane Burton, and safety Shawn Wooden all switched that year to a local agent. Guess who?

After being knocked down to ten Dolphin clients, by the end of the season I was back up to fifteen. I expect to take more hits next year because Johnson is building with youth, but in time, I will eclipse my mark of eighteen that I had with Shula. The Shark will continue to swim with the Dolphins.

13

Feeding Frenzy

THE LIFEBLOOD OF THIS BUSINESS IS SIGNING TALENTED ROOKIES
each year, and even though I had signed some outstanding
young Dolphin players, I needed to go to work and sign the
best 1997 rookies. The first thing an agent does as he gears
up for recruiting is to determine which players to go after.
You want to recruit players who will do well in the draft
and will succeed in the NFL. And of those players, you have
to recruit those you can get. You can recruit the ten best
players in the world, but if none of them sign with you, you
have lost an entire year where you passed up other good
players.

I targeted two players in particular. The first was Hurricane
wide receiver Yatil Green. Of the players coming out of the
University of Miami, I knew he would be the first player
drafted because he had superstar potential written all over
him. The second player I targeted was Troy Davis. Troy
played at Iowa State University but had played high school
football in Miami. Troy Davis ran for over two thousand
yards in back to back seasons. He did things that Hall of
Fame running backs such as Barry Sanders and Emmitt
Smith did not do in college. He was the Heisman Trophy
runner-up by a narrow margin.

I still can't believe a running back can carry the ball almost four hundred times and run for 2,185 yards against teams like Nebraska and Colorado, break NCAA rushing records, and still not win the Heisman Trophy. I knew that because Troy was five feet seven inches tall he would not go as high in the Draft as he would deserve. But this kid was the toughest football player I had ever seen. I also knew that he had incredible quickness, strength, balance, vision, and instincts. The guy is a real warrior who just wants to play football. He got hit over four hundred times last season, and got up faster than the defender each and every time. Whether he would be a first-round pick or not, I wanted Troy because I knew over the course of his career, he would become one of the best running backs in the NFL.

Troy's season ended early in December and he declared for the draft. Jason and I met with Troy and his father William Webster who figures very prominently in South Florida's high school football circles. They weren't interested in limousine rides, free dinners, and all that other jazz my competitors like to use. They were interested in talking football and having an agent in their backyard. I obviously was their man. After signing Troy as a new client, my mission was clear—sign Yatil Green. I felt Yatil had solidified himself as a first-round pick after he made a spectacular touchdown catch in the Blockbuster Bowl. Several days after the game, Yatil declared he was coming out early as a junior to enter the 1997 NFL Draft. The chase was on.

Jason and I met with Yatil. I hit him with everything I had: "We represent the top UM player every year. We represent more Hurricanes by far than any other agent in the business. We represent more Dolphins than any other agent. We are the hardest workers in the business. We negotiated the top free agent contract last year for Leon Searcy. We represent Hurricane wide receivers Brett Perriman, Brian Blades, Randal Hill, Kevin Williams, and A. C. Tellison. We represent your friend Warren Sapp. We have negotiated more contracts for more money than any of my direct competitors. We will be in Miami and work with you every day to help you train for your workouts. We will be with you in Miami every step of the way to market you for the NFL teams as you work out and meet with them. Those scouts don't know what they are talking about when they tell you that you will be a second-round pick. They don't know you are going to run a 4.3 forty-yard dash at the Indianapolis Combine. If you work with me and take my professional advice, I know you will be a first-round pick. Look at Sapp's contract. Look at Leon's contract. We would make a great team with Jason and me working every single day to help you focus on doing all of the right things. We are the top agents in the state of Florida."

By the end of the night, Yatil said we were his guys. I had the contract in my pocket, but he said he wanted to go home to Lake City, Florida, to think things through. I knew I had won him over that night, but as I knew all too well, anything could happen tomorrow—and it did.

Over the next couple of days, the other agents worked Yatil over good. They told him to sign with anyone but the Rosenhaus brothers. They told him we negotiate bad contracts. They told him we have too many clients to do a good job for him. They told him we were bad guys.

They said anything they could as many times as they could. They knew I was the guy to knock off the top of the hill. Yatil started to buy into the big lie and no longer took my calls. Every time I called he was either out of town, in the shower, out for the night, or on the other line. He was avoiding my calls.

At six foot two, over two hundred pounds, faster and able to jump higher than any other top receiver in the draft, I knew Yatil had greatness. The NFL scouts compared him with Michael Irvin except Yatil was faster and could leap higher. Michael may have gotten away from me, but I wasn't about to let Yatil do the same.

After not speaking to him for a couple of days, I knew things were going down hill. But I wasn't about to call it quits just because Yatil made up his mind to go with someone else. I wasn't going to let my competitors get the best of me.

I called Yatil again, and he said he would call me right back. After an hour went by and the phone didn't ring, Jason said, "Drew, we're in trouble here. We gotta go there immediately before it's too late." I looked at my office wall where I have newspaper pages hung up with pictures of me and my client on Draft Day. I saw me with Randal, me with Marvin, me with Sapp, and stared at the empty space I was saving for Yatil. I wanted to put the picture up of us celebrating on Draft Day. I looked at Jason, and said, "Grab the keys and let's go."

Jason and I jumped into the car and drove six hours straight into Lake City, to find Yatil. I called his mom, Sonya Butts, to ask if I could meet with her, and she said to come over her house. Jason and I were already in the neighborhood when we made the call. Surprised that I was there so quickly, Sonya and Yatil's sisters welcomed us into their home and made us feel very comfortable. Sonya had spoken with several other agents, and she talked to me about some of the concerns she had.

She said she wanted to meet the "infamous Rosenhaus Boys" about whom all the other agents had so many bad things to say. She even showed me this videotape that another agent made about me. She showed me clippings of newspaper articles from twenty different cities that other agents gave her about me. She wanted to know why all the other agents hated me so much.

I responded by showing her the *Sports Illustrated* issue with me on the cover, titled, "The Most Hated Man in Pro Football." At that moment, Yatil walked in the door. He was surprised to see me, and when Sonya asked him to come over and sit down and talk, he said he would like to but he had some friends in the car waiting on him and that he would be back later. He turned around and started to leave.

Jason and I drove six hours to get there. We talked with his mom and sisters for two hours until he showed up. I wasn't about to let him walk out the door. Jason and I asked Sonya if she would excuse us as we followed him out the door.

"Yatil! Jason and I drove all this way to see you."

"I'll be back in five minutes, wait inside with my family."

"Yatil, you have been ducking my calls and avoiding me. You haven't returned any of my pages or called me back. Other agents are going around telling people that they are going to sign you. I came here to talk to you face to face, man to man, to find out what's going on. I came here because I know something's not right. What's up?"

"Okay Drew!" and then he started laughing. "I can't believe you came up here just like that."

Then he got professional, "The deal is I am going to sign with another agent. I like you and your brother, but I heard all these bad things about you from the other agents." He went on to say some ridiculous lies that my competitors made up.

Jason interrupted him, "Yatil, all that is completely untrue. Whoever told you that looked you right in the eyes and lied to you. What's more, they think they can trick you into signing with them by lying to you. That is the type of people you have been talking to."

I jumped in, "Yatil, everything we have said to you is true. I have not lied to you nor will I ever. You can always count on me to tell it to you straight."

Yatil said, "Well, a lot of people are bad-mouthing you."

"Yeah, well, a lot of people are saying you aren't going to be a first-round pick. Do you believe that as well?"

"No way. Those guys are full of it."

"That's right, and that's what those other agents are. They don't come to you like men, like we do and sell themselves. They come toward you like cowards and say anything they can to bad-mouth me behind my back. I don't respect that and I don't respect them. That's why when they see me coming they cross the street to the other side and look away. They don't want to be your agent like I do and they aren't willing to pay the price. But the hell with them. The minute Jason and I saw that we were in trouble with you, we didn't mess around. We got in the car right away and drove straight here to find you. That's how much you mean to us."

Yatil responded, "That means a lot to me. It does. That's not an easy drive and I don't know how you found the place."

I could see Yatil was starting to be the Yatil that I knew. He was being himself again. I could see I was wearing down his resistance toward me. I saw I was breaking through. Here was my chance. I had to turn it up. Right in the middle of the street, I started screaming and yelling, fighting and kicking, doing anything and everything I could to let him see how much heart I had inside and how much I wanted to represent him. I looked him in the eyes when we were speaking and made sure we never lost I contact. Anybody who looks me in the eyes will become a believer in me.

"It wasn't easy getting here. I wasn't sure that I would be able to catch up with you. But I always find a way to get the job done. I always do. And if you give me the chance, I'll bust my ass every single day working hard for you. I won't stop until you go in the first round. I won't stop until you get one of the best contracts in the round. I won't stop until you become a superstar and get the best endorsements. I won't stop until you retire and you and your family are financially set for life. I won't stop period. I can't be stopped. You are on your way to the top and I am going to help you get there. Why? Because like you, I am the best at what I do. I will outwork and outsmart any competitor I go up against."

I was on a roll: "I beat those guys every year to represent the best players out of UM and I am going to do so again with you. My competitors hate me because I kick their ass over and over again. All they can do is whine and tell lies. Be smarter than that. See through that. Go with your gut and do what you think is right. Look at me, I am screaming out in the middle of the street, fighting to represent you. Fighting to save you from making a big mistake. Fighting to help you become a first-round pick. Fighting to help you become the best receiver in the NFL. I am fighting to show you what I have in my heart. Fighting to show you how much you mean to me. Fighting to show you that I am the best agent for you. Can't you see how much you mean to me? Can't you see the fire in my eyes? Can't you see how I will annihilate anyone that gets in our way? Can't you see that as a team we can't be beat? See it! I'm not leaving this street until you see it—until you look me in the eyes and say that I am your agent."

Moved, Yatil starts laughing, "You really are Jerry Maguire, aren't you?"

Jason and I stayed over and spent the next day with Yatil. He told us he was driving upstate and would call us when he got back to Miami. Jason and I didn't want to leave Lake City until Yatil would give us his word, but he told us what he wanted us to do, and we respected it.

We were up tight for the next couple of days while we waited for Yatil to get back. In Lake City, Yatil had said he would be driving home and would get in around midnight. Having heard nothing from him, Jason and I decided to drive to his apartment and wait for him to come home.

I know it seems desperate to wait by his apartment, but you never know if it can make the difference. At about three in the morning, Jason spotted Yatil's car driving past us. We waited for him to get inside and then called him.

"Yatil, Jason and I have been waiting around for you all night, we're right across the street. Can we come over?"

"You can come over, but I have some bad news for you."

"We'll be right there."

Damn! It looked bad for us. It looked like we were done.

"Look, Drew, I know Yatil pretty well. Keep your poise in there because there is a chance he may be testing us," Jason said to me. I looked at him like he was dreaming. I tried to keep my chin up but I felt like I just got punched in the gut. "Jay, I'll give it all I have. Maybe we can still change his mind." I knocked on Yatil's door and he told us to come in, it was open.

He was sitting down on his couch watching television and said point blank, "I thought it would be best to tell you guys in person. I like you guys a lot, but I am going to sign with another agent. Thanks for recruiting me. I wish you good luck."

"So you've made up your mind?"

"I have and I thought you would respect that if I told you face to face."

"Yatil you're making a big mistake." I went on and on for another forty minutes, giving it everything I had. And when I was exhausted and shot, Jason took over and did the same. In the middle of Jason's attempt, the phone rang. Yatil answered it, told us it was his agent, and to hold on a second.

"Yeah, the Rosenhaus Boys are here and I'm telling them that I am going with you. Yeah, they are pretty upset and trying to talk me out of it. No I won't let them. I said I was going with you and that's that. I am not going to go back on my word."

I looked at Jason and saw that he finally gave up on his idea that Yatil was just trying us. It was over. When he got off the phone, he said he was tired from the drive and was going to sleep. He walked us to the door. As sick as I was, as crushed as I was, I said to him one last time, "Yatil I respect you and like you, but you are making a mistake."

Jason said to him, "Yatil, I'm disappointed. I thought all along that we were your guys. You're making a mistake and I wish I could change your mind, but I can't. You know we've tried."

As angry and upset as I was, I handled the defeat with composure. It is always my motto not to burn any bridges. Jason and I started walking to the car. As Yatil turned back toward the door, I looked at him one last time, and I said in excruciating pain, "Yatil, you are a good person. I wish you nothing but the best."

"Thanks, buddy, and good luck to you too," he said as he walked toward the door.

Jason and I were beaten. I said to him, knowing how much pain he was in, "Don't worry. We'll be back stronger than ever. We'll beat them all next year and make them pay."

"I know . . ." Jason said, keeping his head up, although he looked as low as I've ever seen him. "We always come back."

Then out of the blue I hear Yatil say, "Hey Drew! Jason! Come on back. I was only kidding."

Afraid it was some cruel hoax, Jason and I looked at him,

and saw him screaming, yelling, and punching. "What! You know you're my boys. I had to test you guys. And you passed! Where's that contract at!"

"Yes!" Jason and I were almost crying out of joy.

"Yes!" we screamed again in the middle of the night as we ran over toward Yatil. We woke up the whole apartment complex and didn't care. We all hugged each other. I was the happiest man alive. And then I was the hungriest man alive. I was so thankful to him that I wanted to go right out then and there to tell all those general managers, coaches, and scouts that Yatil is the best receiver in the draft, and they better get ready to open their wallets. We were going to make an unstoppable team. Yes! Yes! Yes! We won!

14

A Roller Coaster Ride

So THERE I WAS. DRAFT DAY, APRIL 20, 1997. I FOUND MY-self sitting in a tent at Winfield Park in Lake City, Florida. Ready for battle I tested my phone lines at the tent. I made sure my laptop computer with fax modem was on line and hooked up to the Internet. I made sure my two cellular phones and nationwide pager were ready for action. I checked in with the teams to make sure they had the correct numbers to find me and Yatil. I looked back at the phone, stared at it, and remembered how it was with Randal.

On this all important day with Yatil, I was determined for us to win. Yatil had seen several draft reports that projected him to be perhaps the seventh pick of the draft to the New York Giants. If he didn't go eight to Tampa Bay, the experts said he would go ten to New Orleans. Other draft projections had him going twelve to Seattle. Seeing that he could go as high as seven—that was what everyone was pulling for.

I had spoken to draft experts Joel Buchsbaum and Mel Kiper the night before. Kiper was somewhat optimistic that Tampa Bay would take Yatil in the top ten, but he did not have a strong conviction. Buchsbaum told me he did not think the Giants or the Bucs would draft Yatil and cautioned me to be prepared for the fact that Yatil could wind up at twenty.

Concerned, I called Rich McKay, the general manager of the Bucs, and he said Yatil had a shot to be their eighth pick, but I could hear it in his voice that the shot wasn't as strong as I would like it to be.

I rationalized that if the Giants and Bucs passed on Yatil, New Orleans would probably take Yatil at ten. A couple of days earlier, Yatil and I had gone to New Orleans to meet with Coach Mike Ditka. Coach Ditka told me that he would draft Yatil if he was there and joked he would kick my ass if I held him out.

I asked Iron Mike, "Coach, do you really think you could take me?"

He laughed.

I knew that if all else failed, Yatil's old college coach Dennis Erickson would be our insurance policy with the Seattle Seahawks at number twelve.

Everybody was expecting the best possible scenario to happen as if it was a given. Pick number seven was where all the people were rooting for Yatil to go. They had forgotten that when I first stepped into the picture, Yatil was hoping to be a late first-round pick. They had forgotten how most of the experts like Buchsbaum had Yatil rated in the middle of the first round. Instead, everyone at the park set their sights at seven because that was the highest prediction they had seen. There is nothing wrong with hoping for the best, but in doing so, you should always be prepared for the worst.

I was prepared. I did my homework and was ready. All my information in the last few days told me Yatil could slip all the way to twenty.

It would be disastrous if Yatil were to go as late as twenty. But I didn't think that could happen. Especially with the Dolphins at number fifteen. Jimmy Johnson had publicly made some negative comments about Yatil, so many people thought that Jimmy wasn't interested. I knew better. I knew Yatil would be a perfect fit in Miami's offense. I knew that because when Jimmy Johnson made some negative remarks, there was the chance that Jimmy was playing a little poker, hoping teams would not think Jimmy wanted him.

Why would Jimmy do that? Because if the team at number twenty wants Yatil, but they think Jimmy is going to take Yatil at number fifteen, then the team at twenty would trade up to fourteen and snatch Yatil away from Jimmy. Like I said, I thought Jimmy was playing a little poker.

As if there wasn't enough pressure on me already, the situation in that Lake City celebration brought a little extra strain to the day. With Yatil's high school teammate, Florida State defensive end Reinard Wilson, and his family, under a tent just a few yards away, there was an unsaid tension/competition to see who would get drafted first. Both Yatil and Reinard are friends who want to see the other do well, but on this day they were competitors.

There was competition between us agents as well. Reinard was represented by another South Florida–based agent, competitors of ours who recruited Yatil. But I wasn't concerned with Reinard and his agent, I was concerned about my client.

It was some scene at that park. There had to be a thousand people there, and under each tent there had to be at least a hundred family members watching. The tents had to be separated by only about twenty-five yards or less. It got hectic.

I could see that Yatil was not likely to go as high as his family was hoping. I could see that I had a difficult day in front of me. I could see that this day was going to work out either really great or really bad. It was going to be one or the other, and I was ready.

With NFL Commissioner Paul Tagliabue taking the podium at the NFL Draft Headquarters in New York at noon, the draft was on. "Here we go, Yatil," I said to my client.

It was on and I was ready. I looked at my phone and told it to get ready too.

As Draft Day unfolded, everything was going well for us through the first five picks. All the can't-miss prospects were taken, and we were in a position for Yatil to be next. But then with pick number six all hell broke lose. The Jets traded pick number six to the Bucs and then the Bucs traded the pick to Seattle. Seattle now had the sixth pick, the Jets were at eight, and the Bucs would be at twelve. So with pick number six, the Seahawks went for what they needed most and drafted Offensive Lineman Walter Jones.

They needed an offensive lineman much more than they needed a receiver, but I knew Coach Erickson liked Yatil a lot and I'm sure it was a close call for them. Although we weren't all that confident that they were going to take Yatil at six, it still wasn't fun for us to watch Dennis Erickson pass on Yatil.

Well, we just got set back for several reasons. We were hoping Tampa Bay would draft Yatil at number eight, but they traded down and switched spots to number twelve. So now we would have to wait until twelve for Yatil to be taken by Tampa. Seattle, who would have drafted Yatil at twelve, moved to take another player. With that, we lost our insurance policy protecting Yatil from slipping past twelve. Our blanket protection of Dennis Erickson at twelve was gone. And as far as the Jets go, who have the number eight pick now instead of the Bucs, they did not need a wide receiver. So now it's starting to look like Joel Buchsbaum's prophecy of Yatil going at twenty could happen.

Our hope was now that the Giants were going to take Yatil at number seven. I knew they needed a receiver but I was not feeling good about our chances because they were not high on Yatil. Instead, they surprised the world and took another wide receiver, a Florida player, Ike Hilliard, who no one had projected to go any higher than the twenty-fifth pick. All of Yatil's family started to carry on and get riled up. There were dozens of reporters and media people around with TV cameras, as well as photographers, all looking for a reaction. It seemed like hundreds of family members were all staring at me, wanting to know what was going to happen to Yatil now.

I was sitting there right next to Yatil, glued to the TV, when Paul Tagliabue made the announcement, "Ike Hilliard, wide receiver." We were angry because just about every other team I spoke to had Yatil more highly rated, but it only takes one team to get drafted. The reporters were stunned. No expert had predicted Ike Hilliard would go so high. The reporters on ESPN said, "Wow, what a shock."

The reporters started to say that the Giants shied away from Yatil because he had some nagging injuries during the course of the year, and they wanted someone more durable and steady. The Giants wanted to play it safe and be happy with that. They said Yatil had the great potential to be a star and be a much better player than Hilliard, but Hilliard was a safer bet.

The pressure was starting to kick in. To make matters worse, right before my eyes, I got hit again. The Jets at number eight took a linebacker, James Farrior, and on ESPN the broadcasters said that the Jets were trying to trade Marvin Jones—one of my other clients. On national television, the reporters came out and said that Marvin Jones was being shopped right now on national television. So, not only do I get nailed by Yatil not being picked at number eight where we were hoping he would be picked by the Tampa Bay Buccaneers; but I have to sit and listen about my player, Marvin Jones, becoming the subject of trade talks. I also have two other linebackers on the Jets, Mo Lewis and Bobby Houston, so the Jets drafting another linebacker with their first pick did not bode well for me.

Inside, I was churning. But on the outside, I tried to keep my cool, keep my composure. I worked to comfort Yatil and his family because I felt we were looking good for number ten with the Saints. "Ditka told us he was going to make you a Saint at number ten. So get ready," I said.

We waited fifteen minutes for the Saints to be up at number ten. The broadcasters were again showing highlights of Yatil, saying this is exactly what the Saints need. They pointed out that Yatil visited the Saints and that Mike Ditka is going to get the big play maker for the NFL's most anemic offense. The Saints had just made a trade for a new quarterback, Heath Shuler, and this would be the perfect complement.

We knew that when Yatil visited the Saints, the coaching staff told us that they were going to take Yatil if he was there at ten, so everyone's expecting the name Yatil Green to appear on the screen. The Saints get on the clock and just as Paul Tagliabue is about to announce their pick, I jump up on a table, and say simultaneous with Tagliabue, "The Saints pick . . ."

As I said, "Yatil Green," Tagliabue says, "Chris Naeole." I felt and looked like an idiot as I was standing on the table speechless. The draft experts on ESPN were in shock—not because the Saints passed on Yatil, but because the Saints took an offensive lineman with the tenth pick that no one predicted would go that high. All the experts were saying Naeole was a questionable pick. This pick came out of nowhere. No one saw this coming.

Yatil and his family once again were getting antsy. Now after seeing the Giants bypass Yatil for another receiver at seven, witnessing the trade at eight with Tampa moving down and Seattle moving up, and seeing our hopes of being taken in the top ten dashed as New Orleans picked someone else, we were getting edgy.

I looked at Yatil and I started to see pain set in. Despite my last minute cautioning, Yatil wanted and expected to go in the top ten. He was devastated. He couldn't sit still anymore and started to walk around. My father Robert was with me and I told him that we were in big trouble. I called Jason who was with our client Troy Davis in Miami Beach and said the same thing.

Trying to keep Yatil's spirits up, I said, "Don't fear. Tampa Bay at number twelve is going to select you. We're going to make it happen."

Atlanta was at eleven. We didn't expect Atlanta to select Yatil, but we were confident that with Tampa at number twelve we'd be in business.

It was just the week before when Tampa's general manager, Rich McKay, and Director of Personnel Jerry Angelo, hung out with me, Jason, and Yatil. We had invited them to spend the day with us getting to know Yatil.

We took the boat out for a ride in the ocean. While we were coming back from the ocean, the engines shut off because seaweed got caught in them. Not wanting to waste a day being stranded in the ocean, Jason stripped down and jumped into the water, pulling the seaweed out of the propellers. In a few minutes we were up and running and on our way. We ate lunch at a place on the waterfront. Eating the best food and smoking the finest cigars, we had a great day. When we got back to the house, I played ping-pong with Rich and let him win to make sure he was happy. It was a real sight to see one of the NFL's toughest general managers put on a pair of shorts and a T-shirt to ride our Yamaha wet bike. I could tell Rich wasn't scared to do something a little adventurous. He and Yatil got along very well. And yet, on the ride back to the airport, when Yatil told Jerry how much he wanted to be a Buccaneer, they cautioned him not to be hurt if it didn't happen. I could see Jerry liked Yatil and wanted to prepare Yatil for what could be a real heartbreak. As much as we enjoyed ourselves, after hearing that, I knew it wasn't a slam dunk that the Bucs were going to go with Yatil as their top pick.

On the surface, with the GM coming to visit with Yatil right before the draft, it looked like a given that Yatil was going to be a Buc; but that little voice in my head told me it wasn't going to happen.

Ignoring that little voice, we waited another half hour for Tampa to be on the clock and were anxious. All the broadcasters were saying again, "Yatil Green's going to go to Tampa."

Finally, Tampa gets on the clock. The strain was immense, the cameras were focused on us waiting for Yatil to get that phone call. I'm staring at the phone. Just as had happened six years earlier, a friend calls. I picked up the phone and hung it up immediately. We were trying to keep the line clear for the team. I start looking at my cell phone, trying to will it to ring, begging Tampa to call us. My mind keeps flashing back to Randal on Draft Day. I had the same feelings all over again. Once again I was working the phones at a feverish pace. I called Tampa, Miami, every team I could think of, promoting Yatil.

Then we watched on ESPN and they're inside the Tampa war room, and we see that they're on the phone with a player and we know it's not us. The family was all tense. Everyone was asking, "Drew, are they going to pick him?"

All the experts, as well as Yatil's family, were convinced that the Bucs were going to take Yatil—it would be a popular pick. The announcement comes, Commissioner Paul Tagliabue says, "Tampa Bay selects Warrick Dunn, running back, Florida State University."

Yatil's family is crushed. At that point Yatil got up, angry, and went out to sit in his truck to calm down and get some space. Our camp was totally silent. Everybody's optimism was gone. Tampa also had the sixteenth pick in the draft. The fact that they didn't take Yatil led me to believe that Tampa projected Yatil to slip down to sixteen where they could take him with their second first-round pick.

Talk about taking a beating. As bad as I was feeling for Yatil, I was feeling worse for another reason. The selection of Warrick Dunn would not help my cause in representing Buccaneer running back Errict Rhett.

Within an hour, my star rookie was passed over several times and two of my veterans appeared vulnerable. Although I was dying a slow death, I was in front of the national media, so I had to look like I was feeling no pain. Yatil and his family were looking to me for support and were counting on me to be positive. I couldn't look scared. I had to carry the flag and wave the troops onward.

But that wasn't so easy. Remember, this whole town was caught up in Yatil being drafted and our celebration was quickly turning sour. There was a live band playing; they were barbecuing food; it was festive. Not anymore. Now, all of a sudden this happy occasion has turned into a nightmare where people were getting paranoid, frantic, and nervous.

They were all looking at me and saying, "What are you going to do?"

My father was sitting there sick and suffering. There was nothing he could do but watch as I had all that pressure heaped upon me, feeling this whole community's weight on my shoulders.

At this point, Yatil came back over and sat down next to me. He was leaning against me for support and positive reassurances. We were helping each other fight our way through this.

I took charge and stood up on the table and told everybody to relax, to take a walk around. I told them there was no doubt that with the next pick at number thirteen, the Houston Oilers would take Yatil. I started wondering if I should stop saying that, but that was the way I felt and I was looking to breathe some life into the despondent crowd.

Besides, the Oilers said that they would draft Yatil if he was there. But in my mind, I was already envisioning the worst case scenario: Yatil dropping all the way to the Kansas City Chiefs at eighteen. The Chiefs spent a lot of time with Yatil, and they needed a wide receiver.

Then like a bolt of lightning another blockbuster trade went down as Houston swapped picks with Kansas City. Kansas City, who was my guarantee that Yatil wouldn't get past number eighteen, had now traded up. They were a lock to take Yatil at eighteen because the guy they wanted most, Tony Gonzalez, surely would not be available. But he was available now, everyone knew they were going to take him. The Chiefs sent their pick to the podium, "Tony Gonzalez, tight end, University of California."

So in one fell swoop, two of the teams I was banking on to take Yatil were now out of it. Houston passed on Yatil and Kansas City took a tight end.

I felt like I was thrown into a bottomless pit. I was going down hard with no hope in sight. And then I remembered the last time I felt like this was six years ago, and I started to think—Miami.

Oh my God! We needed the Dolphins to come through. That was the only way this scenario could work out for the best. All Yatil's mom wanted was for her son to be a Dolphin and Yatil wanted it, too. That was our only hope. Miami was at fifteen. That would be better than going top ten.

I said to myself, "Just two picks away. Please come through for me. Just like with Randal, Miami can turn this nightmare into a happy ending."

Wanting to take control of the situation, I placed a call to the Dolphins. I couldn't get through, they were on the phone.

The Cincinnati Bengals were now on the clock with the fourteenth pick. I'm hoping Miami's trying to trade up and get Yatil with the fourteenth pick. Everybody's whispering and saying forget about Yatil going to the Dolphins because Miami wanted Reinard. Miami indicated to Reinard Wilson that they would take him.

Inside, I couldn't imagine a more painful prospect for Yatil. If Miami passed on Yatil to take Reinard, Yatil would be in agony. Yatil's family was nerve-racked. I hoped that fate would not be that cruel to me and my client.

In that fifteen-minute span, I felt like my career, my reputation, and my client's future were all on the line. The pressure seemed immense, and it's not like I was sitting in my room alone.

I've got all the media looking at me, talking to me. Just when I think it can't get worse, I hear a roar from the next tent. The Cincinnati Bengals just picked Reinard Wilson. They were cheering and celebrating and singing like there's no tomorrow. And we were over in our tent saying, "I wish we could be celebrating like them."

Although Yatil was genuinely happy for Reinard, he couldn't help but be crushed as he watched Reinard's family partying and celebrating.

Everyone's cries and pleas blacked out as I focused on what had happened. From the depths of despair, I felt an overwhelming rush of adrenaline. My eyes opened wide as I realized that I might have just gotten the break we needed. With Reinard going to Cincinnati, the path had been cleared for the Dolphins to take Yatil.

I was filled with too much adrenaline to sit still. I felt uncontrollable energy and a strong desire to force the Dolphins to take him. Yet it was their call. I had done all I could to market Yatil to the Dolphins and I knew I did my best.

Just a few weeks earlier, I persuaded the Dolphins to bring Yatil in for a private workout and interview. The meeting went very well, lasting for several hours. I knew we did our part, now it was up to Jimmy Johnson.

Yatil needed this. I needed this—bad. The Dolphins were my one chance to get out of this nightmare. Even though Yatil slipped a couple of picks, if Miami were to take him, all would be well. No, all would be unreal. All would be phenomenal. All would be magnificent.

This would be a hometown team picking a University of Miami star. It would be a dream come true. Ever since Randal, I wanted the Dolphins to call on Draft Day to have a Dolphin first-round pick. I wanted to have a superstar like Yatil in Miami.

It would be perfect. Almost too good to be true. He'd be the man in Miami and I'd be the man if they picked him. This was the same situation with Randal, except instead of wanting to hear Shula's voice, I was hoping to hear from Jimmy Johnson.

I silently vowed that if Miami drafted Yatil, the negotiations would go smoothly and there would be no holdout.

I walked around with my cellular phones, waiting for the right one to ring. I called my brother on the phone and said, "Jay we've got to get this. Miami's got to pick him."

Jason was screaming and yelling, "Come on Miami! Take him! Do it!" at the television set. He knew what was at stake and wanted it with everything he had.

Remember, no one projected that the Dolphins were going to take Yatil. In fact, Yatil wasn't even mentioned among the top fifteen most likely candidates to be drafted by the Dolphins. Jimmy Johnson had even said at a press conference the previous week that he was not likely to draft Yatil even if he were available. Jimmy said he had questions about Yatil's health and his desire.

The draft experts and media bought it. I knew Jimmy well enough to know he wouldn't say that unless he wanted Yatil. I knew there was a real chance.

I hung up the phone and saw the clock was ticking. I knew

that if I didn't get that call from the Dolphins right then and there, it wasn't going to happen.

I looked at the phone and prayed, "Ring phone. Ring."

In deep concentration, I almost walked right into a tree. Realizing that at this point, with so much time having gone by, the Dolphins were not likely to make the call, I felt like I had been punched in the stomach. This was my life—my career—and whether I was going to be a winner this year or not was going to happen right now.

Feeling beaten, I kicked at the tree and for some strange reason, I stared at the grass. Screaming out at me was a four-leaf clover pushing aside the tall blades of grass.

"I remember you . . ."

Only this time I wasn't going to lower my head and go home without fighting back. Like I did when I was twelve years old, I yanked at that four-leaf clover.

"Bring me luck!" I screamed to myself.

Ring. Ring.

My head jumped up. My eyes opened wide with anticipation.

Praying to hear Jimmy Johnson's voice on the line, I answered my cellular phone immediately. It was Jeff Smith. In the back of my mind I knew Jeff Smith was from the Dolphins. Still, I asked Jeff what team he was with. He said the Dolphins. In a state of shock, I calmly said, "Jeff, how can I help you?"

He said, "Drew, I need to speak to Yatil."

"Jeff, tell me you're going to pick Yatil. Please tell me you're going to pick him."

"Drew, we're thinking about it but I've got to talk to Yatil."

At this time Yatil was over in the tent getting ready to congratulate Reinard. Yatil was talking to Reinard's agent asking him if there was any explanation for what's going on here.

I ran over to the other tent screaming at the top of my lungs for Yatil. I had to yell as loud as I could because Reinard's people were partying.

I looked at Yatil and our eyes met. He could see the look

in my eyes and he knew right away there was a chance for something good. I said, "Yatil I've got the Dolphins on the phone."

He got on the phone. We must have looked like one of those two-headed monsters, with both of our ears plastered to the tiny receiver. We were hugging each other as we listened closely, and we were praying hard. Yatil gave the Dolphins our number at the tent and walked calmly over to the phone. I was trying to keep it together.

My whole body was tingling in anticipation. I wanted it so bad I could taste it!

Then, just as we were talking with the Dolphins, we looked at the ESPN broadcast and they were showing Jimmy Johnson in the war room with Jeff Smith on the phone with us. As we were talking with Jeff, I saw Johnson motioning for the telephone, and when he gets to the phone I scream. I yelled at the top of my lungs because I knew in my heart that Jimmy Johnson was going to take Yatil.

The whole tent erupted. I waved for them to be quiet because nothing was finalized yet. I called Jason to give him the update and we were both praying. I held the phone down to my side and could still hear Jason screaming at Johnson to take him.

Everybody in our tent was going insane. Johnson gets on the phone with Yatil and says "Yatil, I'm thinking about trading this pick."

For a moment my stomach sank, and then I knew Jimmy was just negotiating with us. Yatil could barely hear Jimmy because everyone was screaming. Yatil screamed for everyone to be quiet, "He hasn't taken me yet and he says he's thinking about trading the pick."

The whole place fell silent. Then Jimmy said to Yatil, "I've got to know that you're not going to have an injury problem. I've got to know that you're going to work hard for me. I need this commitment from you."

Yatil said, "You've got it coach, whatever it takes."

Then Jimmy said to Yatil, "I want to talk to Drew."

I took the phone from Yatil and said, "Coach, we've got to

get this deal done. We've done a lot of business before. You've got to come through for me. You can't let this kid down. We've got to get this guy on the team. I'll make sure he's a great player for you."

He said, "Drew, I need to know that there isn't going to be a holdout. I need to know we can reach an agreement on this. I need to know that we're not going to have a problem. I need to know that you're going to give me your word that Yatil will be reasonable in the negotiations."

Obviously, Randal's situation was flashing through more than just my mind. I said, "Coach you have my word. Make the pick, we'll get it done. You have my word that this will go smoothly. You have my word that Yatil will not hold out, just be reasonable and fair with us."

"Drew, if that's the case then you have a deal."

At that point I scream, "Yatil's a Dolphin!" and the whole tent erupted in total ecstasy. My dad and I went ballistic. Jason was going nuts in Miami Beach. Dressed in his best suit and shoes, he ran out the back door screaming and dove headfirst off of the dock and into the bay.

My dad was hugging me. It was one of the happiest moments of sheer joy in my life. Not only has my client been drafted by my hometown team, but by my favorite team; not only do I know that he's going to get a $6 million plus contract with about $3 million up front; not only do I know that he's going to be the talk of the town, but it gives me great exposure with other Dolphin players, and great exposure with future clients from the University of Miami and other local guys. It was the best thing that could happen to me and Yatil.

I weathered the storm. And the cameras caught the whole episode. That was the ultimate victory. I looked back to the night two months earlier when I went to Lake City, the very same place, and was screaming and yelling at Yatil to give us a shot at representing him. His neighbors all thought I had lost my mind. But I wasn't going to lose Yatil. I pleaded with him and sold him with my best pitch, spoke from the heart, looked him right in the eyes, and exerted all my energy.

As I watched him hug his family, I thought of the same guy who said he was going with other agents just to test us to see how we would respond. I thought of all Jason and I had gone through and how it had worked out better than I could have hoped.

Caught in a trap, the Shark found a way to break free. Once again I was victorious and celebrating on Draft Day. Stronger than ever, these jaws wanted something to bite. That next challenge would be Yatil's negotiations.

Now that Yatil's dream had come true, it was my job to make it reality. I had been in this situation before with the Dolphins and Randal Hill. This time I wanted to make sure the negotiations went smoothly. I wanted Yatil signed early so that he could start working out under the supervision of the Dolphins' strength coaches and be in top condition to make his move for the starting job. I wanted Yatil to get off to a good start. So I went to work.

The Dolphins also wanted to get Yatil signed early. Jimmy Johnson hates rookie holdouts. Since we were both sincere about getting a deal done, the outcome looked bright. After about one month of marathon negotiations, we struck a deal in June.

Yatil would receive $3 million up front and a total of $6,250,000 over five years. The Dolphins needed some salary cap room and restructured Dan Marino's contract to come up with the money to pay Yatil. With that one contract, Yatil would have enough money to make him financially secure for the rest of his life.

This time in Coach Johnson's office, he wasn't trying to brace me for the news that he was letting my star client go. This time that seat next to me wasn't empty. This time Yatil was there and he picked up a $3 million paycheck. This time it was all smiles. Jimmy Johnson was right a year ago when he said there would be other deals I would win on, and this was one of them.

We were all happy and upbeat. Jimmy and I talked about

fishing and scuba diving. Jason talked with him about the saltwater reef tank that Jimmy had in his office. Then we talked football. All the Dolphins would soon be running the forty-yard dash to see who was the fastest guy on the team. Coach Johnson mentioned running back Jerris McPhail and wide receiver Kirby Dar Dar as two guys who could run a 4.2 forty-yard dash time.

The local media had been hyping up the day of the race so there was a lot of excitement about it.

I told Coach Johnson, "I keep getting calls from guys off the street asking me to get them in that race, saying they can run a 4.3."

"Please . . ." Coach Johnson says rhetorically, "when I was coaching at Oklahoma State, some big, fat guy came up to me at a restaurant and asked me for a tryout, saying he could run a 4.4. I laughed and said he couldn't even beat me in a race. He challenged me and I said, if you can beat me, I'll give you a shot with the team. Well we raced the next day and as I pulled ahead of the guy, he faked a hamstring injury. He didn't get his shot."

I said to Jimmy, "Hey, Coach, Yatil will take that bet."

He laughed as we headed into the press conference room to announce Yatil's signing. As I stood there watching Yatil and Jimmy standing together, Jason said to me, "This is the perfect ending to the roller coaster ride we've been on."

I said to him, "No Jay, this is just the beginning. We're just getting started."

15

Booby Traps

Y OU'RE A ROOKIE PLAYING FOR THE DALLAS COWBOYS. YOU COME from a small school and small town where the girls you grew up around were small-time. You're new in Dallas and find yourself in a nightclub hanging out with some of your team-mates who know the place. Your girlfriend back home, who you have dated since high school, is short, a little over-weight, and not particularly good-looking.

All of a sudden, your teammates summon this incredibly beautiful girl with a body like you've never seen. As they introduce you to her, you can't help but notice that her breasts are barely concealed by her top. Her lips tempt you as she smiles and asks you to buy her a drink.

You think you are dreaming. You think you are in the movies. You look at her legs and are in heaven. She belongs in one of your wildest fantasies—and then she brings her friends over who look even better than her. Yes!

As she gets a little drunk and comes on to you, you reject her, telling her about your girlfriend back home. Yeah right! You take her home and have the best night of your life.

Welcome to the NFL, where the women are everywhere. And they are some of the hottest, sexiest, most desirable women you will ever see. With the faces of models, and the bodies of aerobics instructors, the women that surround NFL players are unbelievable.

And that's just when you are a no-name rookie. Just wait until you are the hometown hero. Just wait until all these women find out you are making millions of dollars. Just wait until everyone watches you on TV making great plays. Just wait until you go to one of those team parties where there are nothing but cheerleaders, models, actresses, TV broadcasters, female fitness instructors, and one or two strippers.

Let me tell you what happens. They come to you. They try to seduce you. Some of the women there are thrilled just to have sex with a famous athlete. Some of the women there want to make you theirs by being the best sexual experience you ever had. They want to dominate you sexually and have you wrapped around their finger. They want to blow your mind and make you feel like you've never felt before. They'll let you do things you've never done before and then they'll do them to you.

And then you go out the next night, and start all over again with someone even better looking. It's that easy. It's that good. These NFL guys walk into a nightclub, and if they have any game whatsoever, they can have just about any girl they want. It's great to be an NFL player.

And just as good to be an agent—if you're like Jerry Maguire. In the movie, you saw all of the hot women he dated on the video at his bachelor party. And you also saw his sexy fiancée Avery—Kelly Preston. Agents have a tremendous opportunity for women because they are around the players at all the right places. Agents are known for having money and being big shots. Women love agents—at least the smooth-looking ones.

It is awesome being an agent right now. Whenever Jason and I go out with the guys, the women say, "Oh, you're like Jerry Maguire. I loved that movie. Is that how it really is?" You throw in a line or two about doing some cameos with Tom Cruise or working behind the scenes of the movie as a consultant and it's all over. You're in. It's so easy, so good, and so tempting that it can dominate your life if you let it.

Me, I didn't become the only agent ever to be on the cover of *Sports Illustrated* by spending all my time getting women. I'm a ruthless warrior who takes care of business first, and then I'll let women take care of me.

I was trained for this, but a lot of players aren't that disciplined. A lot of players come from high schools and colleges that don't have many beautiful women. A lot of players haven't had much success with women prior to entering the NFL. Some players may be great athletes, but they may be overweight or not very handsome. Not every NFL player is particularly handsome or has had a lot of success with women. Some of the guys are big and brutish and haven't had a lot of women before, so when a real pro throws it at him, he's done. He's in love or addicted to the sex and she has him. It's real tough for a guy who has never been able to get a decent-looking girl to all of a sudden have a seductive sex machine all over him.

Say you are one of these players that has had to settle for the not-so-attractive women that you were lucky to get. Now, imagine you're in the NFL and you are dating the girl of your dreams who is giving you the best sex you have ever had by far. Life's great.

Naturally you fall in love, not with the girl, but with sex. It's so great, you can't get enough. Before you know it, you'll be thinking about having sex with her all of the time. You start wanting to get out of practice early, and instead of knowing your play book, you're playing around with her. You'll spend all your time and money trying to keep her happy so she'll keep your Johnson happy.

Next thing you know, you're not playing as well as you were. You are tired all of the time. You are not as motivated. You lose your starting job. You start getting into arguments with your girlfriend and you are distracted and frustrated. Then you get cut by the team. Then your girlfriend leaves you because you are broke and no longer on the team and she starts dating your former teammate. Life sucks.

This is the story of the biggest career-ending injury in the NFL—women, the female booby trap. Fall into the wrong one and you're finished. I've seen more careers ruined by guys chasing women than you would believe.

I love women as much as the next guy, but more players have lost their careers as a result of picking the wrong women than from torn knee ligaments or anything else. This really happens. This is the trap players fall into.

I know for a fact that in the NFL the right woman can make you and the wrong woman can break you. The movie *Jerry Maguire* was on the money with its description of Rod Tidwell's marriage. You saw how much support, confidence, happiness, and hunger Rod gained from his relationship with his wife, Marcy. For her, he wanted to have a great year so he could support his family by getting a multimillion-dollar contract. From her, he found the confidence to be the best. From her, he mustered the courage to risk being injured and play out his current contract, so that at the end of the season he could get the big signing bonus. She helped make Rod Tidwell the success that he was. She deserves almost as much credit as he does.

Unfortunately for the players, not every woman out there is a Marcy Tidwell. There are some real predators out there that eat these NFL studs for breakfast. These women use sex to manipulate the players and have them at their beck and call. They get the players to buy them clothes, jewelry, cars, and even condos. And when the bank account balance starts to disappear, they are out the door.

Now, I'm not telling you these players are all innocent victims. There are players who are out there having sex with three different women a day several days a week. I don't know how they do it, but they do. They'll sleep with dozens—if not hundreds—of hot women in the course of their career. But sooner or later, it will catch up with them.

The night life is something else for a player in the NFL. It's everything that it's cut out to be. I can go out any night of the week with my clients in South Beach or any NFL city, and there is no shortage of women. The women flock to them like you would not believe. Sometimes we have to brush them off us like gnats. They're attracted to their fame, fortune, magnetism, and size. It's unbelievable. People ask me all the time if it is like the movie *North Dallas Forty* with all the crazy parties filled with groupies and hundreds of women. YES IT IS. It can be wild.

I'll never forget these two blonde girls in particular who kept hanging around at Dolphin parties. They were financial planners and were trying to seduce a lot of the players. Their game was to persuade the players to let them handle their investments in return for letting the players handle them. The players went along with it and had their way with them over and over again, giving them the old "check is in the mail" line. The two women didn't get a dime. The funny thing was they were banging the guys who were broke. What a joke.

There are agents who use women to get players as clients. Prostitutes, escorts, strippers, and so on. There are also female agents who go under the covers to get clients. They probably won't succeed because they degrade themselves by trying to have sex with a player to obtain his business. But crazy things do happen in the NFL.

You can't take anything lightly in the NFL. A career in football is short-lived. There is a very small window of opportunity to make a very large amount of money. And as an NFL player, you're considered a very good catch. Women love these guys, I see it. A football player has a chance to land a real beauty who is a great catch in her own right. If the player is smart, he'll marry the right one who will take him to the top. If he's not smart, he'll wind up with nothing.

Remember what Al Pacino said playing Tony Montana in *Scarface,* "First you get the money, then you get the power, THEN you get the women." By taking care of business on the field, the money will come and so will the women. It's simple. The more fame and money you have, the more women you'll have. That's part of the reward of being in the NFL. The problem is, the more women you have, the less money you'll have. It's a fine line that too many players cross over.

I always ask my clients, "What's the most expensive piece of real estate in the world?" They'll say some building in Manhattan, Japan, or house in Beverly Hills, etc. And they are wrong. The most expensive piece of real estate in the world is that four-inch patch of real estate between a woman's legs. I want my single clients to see that and appreciate where their hard-earned dollars are going. It's true, guys spend more money on that, whether to lease it or own it, than anything else. That's not a wise investment.

Make your investment in business. Put your money away. Spend your time playing ball and being successful, then you can snap your fingers and get all the women you want. The truth of the matter is, whether you are a kicker or a punter or a superstar quarterback, hot women across the world will bend over backward for a football player. Guys are never the same on or off the field once they meet the wrong woman. For this reason, I encourage my players to get married. I encourage them to settle down and have a family. I practice what I preach, for the most part.

I admit when I was in college and law school I was a playboy. But once I became an agent I settled down. I'm thirty and still a bachelor, but I'm not out there dating a hundred different women. I've had two main girlfriends over the last few years.

Although I'm not ready to get married or settle down with a family because I'm dedicated to my work, I set an example for these guys because I don't spend my time chasing women. I tell them, "I work for you. How would you feel if, when I should be working on your contract, I'm out there chasing women all the time!"

For example what if a clients asks:

"Drew, how's my contract negotiation going?"

"Oh, I'm out on the boat right now with Bridgette."

"Drew, how's my investment coming along?"

"Aah, I'm getting some right now. Let me call you back."

"Drew, how's the deal coming along?"

"Oh, man, I'm hittin' it right now. I'll have to call you later."

Please, as Jimmy Johnson says sarcastically, if I said that to a client I'd be fired before I could hang up the phone. I flip the coin, and say, "How's your team going to feel when you should be studying your play book or focusing on your meeting or saving your strength for your game and you're exhausting yourself and expending your time and energy on women?"

And the NFL teams know about it. They know when a guy is throwing his career away over women. They know when a guy is out all night, hanging out in the clubs, drinking and looking for women. The NFL teams do their homework and shy away from womanizers in the draft and in free agency. They're looking for family men or one-woman men. They do not want guys who are running and chasing women all the time. These guys may have lost their focus and discipline. They know these guys may be mentally weak, and a weak mind is a weak body. They know these guys might fall apart and won't last. It will cost a player money in the draft and in free agency.

I tell my clients to be smart and to marry a good person who will be a supportive wife and a loving mother. The most important move a player can make isn't on the field. It's off the field, in choosing the right woman.

16

It's Not Just a Job

I WORK HARDER THAN ANYONE ELSE IN THIS BUSINESS NOT JUST BE-
cause this is my job, but because this is my life. My clients
put their futures and the futures of their families in my
hands. This is a tremendous responsibility that must be met
head on. What am I prepared to do? Everything within my
power to succeed for my clients. There is nothing I won't
do—even risk my life.

For instance, this past year, on the night of the Super Bowl,
I had about twenty clients come over to my house in Miami
Beach. At half time, everybody wanted to go out on the boat
for a quick ride. Jason and I figured we were going to take a
quick spin because we certainly did not want to miss the second half of the Super Bowl. That's the last game we would
want to miss. We grabbed a portable TV and brought it with us.

So I loaded twenty guys on my thirty-foot Scarab sports
boat. It was crowded but we went for it. Jason drove while
I made sure everybody was enjoying the night ride. Well,
what was supposed to be a quick ride in the middle of the
night turned into something much more.

As Jason gunned the boat through the intracoastal waters,
the guys wanted to jump some waves in the ocean. The guys
were yelling, "More, more, more."

Although it was a rough, chilly night, I didn't want to let the guys down, so we went for it. It was a full moon so at least we had good visibility. We proceeded to take the boat into the ocean. We go into what's called the Haulover cut, which is a channel inlet with rocks and jetties.

Leaving the bay, we went underneath the bridge, drove through the channel of large rocks, and braved the Atlantic Ocean. As we got through the rocks, the waves picked up, and the boat was jumping so high the back engines were continually bursting out of the water. It was wild. Jason and I were loving it, but we could see that the guys had enough fun for the evening so Jason slowed the boat down.

Well, we were having so much fun, that Jason didn't realize the gas gauge had malfunctioned, and we were completely out of gas. What looked like a full tank was actually empty. Just as Jason turned the boat around to steer us through the two rows of jagged rocks, the engine cut off.

Jason knew right away that we were in trouble. I didn't know what was going on until Jason calmly asked me to check something out.

Jason quietly said to me, "We've got a problem. We're out of gas . . . no reserve, nothing."

I tried to restart the engines but they wouldn't turn over. I looked at the current and it was bringing us back toward shore. That was good. I looked at the rough waves and saw that they were driving the boat right toward the rocks. That was not good.

Jason said, "Drew, we have to go in or we're going to hit the rocks. And if we hit the rocks . . ."

I looked at those rocks and then at the dark, white-cap water. I flashed back to a couple of nights before, when I had been fishing in these waters with a couple of young players— Daryl Porter, Derrick Harris, and Marcus Wimberly. We were going for bonita. We kept getting a hit—then all of a sudden, nothing. When we reeled up the lines, we were surprised to reel in only the heads of big bonita whose bodies had been bitten off. So I hooked the bait differently and this time reeled up the fish as fast as I could.

191

As I started to see the bonita being pulled up under my bright spotlight, I thought I had beaten whatever was down there to the punch. I leaned over, grabbed the line, and had my gaff in place to pull up the fish. All of a sudden, right before me, a huge tiger shark, ten feet in length, pounces on the poor fish, clutches it in its razor sharp jaws, pulls it down, shakes it, gnaws on it, and tears the body away from the head. Blood was splashing everywhere. I was drenched in it. That tiger shark was the meanest, ugliest, scariest looking creature I had ever seen.

That was just a couple of nights ago and not far from where we are now. And Jason tells me he wants to jump in. I see him pulling his boots off and shirt off.

"No way! You're not going in. No way! Stay on the boat!" I ordered.

As always, Jason listens. And then I listened to what he said two seconds ago—that we were going to hit the rocks.

If we hit those rocks, our seventy-thousand-dollar boat would be destroyed, but who cares! We have twenty of our clients on this boat. The rocks are slippery except for where they have razor sharp barnacles on them. Our clients would not be able to climb onto the rocks. They would be smashed and sliced against those rocks. What's more, when a boat sinks, it sucks down the water with it. And not just the water, but all the people on the boat with it. Not to mention that most of the guys were inexperienced swimmers. This was disastrous. This was a nightmare. This was for real. This was life and death.

After seeing me yell at Jason to stay out of the water, the players could tell something was up. We were drifting hard and fast as the waves were driving us toward the rocks. Whether they could swim or not, sharks or not, they knew those rocks would hurt them just real bad, if they were lucky.

"Our options?" Jason asks me cool as ice as this gets ugly.

"We can't let these guys get hurt. They could get seriously injured and drown!" I said to Jason. I could never live with myself if any of my clients got hurt. I had to protect them. Jason and I would have made it as we are excellent swimmers, but our clients wouldn't have. We couldn't leave them stranded.

This was a bad time not to have an anchor on the boat. Using my cellular phone to call for help would be pointless—the boat would be smashed to pieces long before they could arrive. I saw another boat nearby. I saw the spotlight on and the balloon attached to the baitfish—they were shark fishing. They were too far away to hear us with the waves pounding all around us. I looked at the balloon and saw it go underwater. This was bad. And at the pace the waves were smacking the boat toward the giant rocks, we were only thirty feet away and closing in fast. We'd hit in about ten seconds.

Pumped with adrenaline, I turn to Jason and say, "This is it boy. We're going in. Stay with me."

Dressed in jeans and boots, I jump in. I position myself between the rocks and the back of the boat to try and change the direction where we were headed. There was a strong current from the bay that was pulling the boat toward the bridge. I knew I had to push the boat toward the center where it would catch that current and pull us between the channel of rocks.

My heart was racing, my legs were kicking, and my arms were pushing. I kept thinking that I was seeing sharks coming up toward me with their mouths opening but I pressed on. I was fighting hard and changing the direction of the boat, but now the front was heading in toward the rocks.

Confused, scared, and concerned, the players didn't know what I was doing. They were calling for me to get back in the boat.

Ready, Jason takes off his shirt and boots. He says, "Watch my back guys," wraps a rope around his shoulder and waist, screams all types of profanities, and dives in head first off the front of the boat.

A former high school lifeguard like me, Jason was swimming strong. I heard him yelling and screaming as he was taking on the waters. The Rosenhaus boys were doing it. We were fighting for our lives and our clients' lives with everything we had. Jason was pulling the front toward the center, and I was pushing the heavy back of the boat out away from the rocks.

Hollering for their lives and scared to death, the players cheered us on. Getting the boat in the center of the channel now, it looked like we were in the clear. The current from the bay caught us and was bringing us toward the bridge. Now we had a whole new problem. Exhausted, Jason was now being pulled by the rope from behind the boat, and we were headed for the concrete side of the bridge, which is not the passage for boats.

The guys threw me a rope and tied it to the front of the boat. Tired as all hell, I swam past the boat, got out in front of it, and yanked on the rope just enough to guide it in between the bridge opening.

Seeing Jason and I were in shark-infested waters, the fisherman raced over toward us and pulled me out of the water. The players pulled Jason in and picked him up out of the water. He looked blue but was still yelling about our heroism.

The fisherman gave us a tow. I couldn't help but notice the two large sharks in the back of their boat. I jumped back on our boat and stood tall.

"You see how much you guys mean to me? You see what I've got in my heart? Jason and I risked our lives for you guys. More importantly, we risked ours and saved yours. At the moment of truth, when it came down to life and death, we were men! We showed no fear! Those sharks were scared of US! We were heroes! This is what you guys have as your agent! This is why you believe in us! This is why we're the best agents in the business!"

The guys loved it, and what's more, it looked like we would get back in time to catch the second half of the Super Bowl. We had turned a negative into a positive.

What started out as a night that could have ruined us became the night our clients will never forget us risking our lives to save theirs. The legend continues.

Randal Hill wasn't there that night, but he can tell you

about another time where doing my job meant risking my life. He was there—sort of. He was talking on the phone with me as it went down.

It was about three years ago, and I was talking on my car phone with Randal. I was going over Randal's contract negotiations with him when the phone started to break up. He was on his cellular phone, too, and his battery was just about to die. He was trying to catch a flight so he wouldn't have time to call me from a pay phone when he got to the airport.

Although I was in a dangerous area, this was important so I pulled over and parked in a lot. I figured I could park there, sit in my car, and work on the contract with him. I was more concerned about taking care of business than I was for my own safety. I wasn't scared—or very smart. Immersed in my work, I was caught off guard as glass from my driver's side window shattered all over me.

My window had been smashed open by a thrown spark plug. The next thing I knew I was looking at the barrel of a nine millimeter pistol six inches in front of my face. I looked at the guy holding it to my head, and he looked cracked out. He looked crazy and careless enough to pull the trigger.

There were two guys screaming at me. Another guy was standing at the front of my car with a shotgun pointed at me.

I was wearing a gold Rolex watch at the time, and they yelled at me to give it to them.

With Randal listening on the phone and freaking out, I calmly handed my watch over to the guy and said, "Here's the watch. It's a Rolex. Take it. It's yours."

I didn't panic. I kept my composure but what scared me was that I could see they were scared. Scared men are capable of anything, especially when their faculties are deranged from being high on crack cocaine. I knew that they would either shoot me right then and there or take off.

I stared at the guy and he stared back. There was nothing I could do. I was at his mercy. Thinking it over, he said, "Gimme the keys."

They wanted the keys so I couldn't chase after them in my car once they ran off. They took the keys and ran as fast as they could. Before I could get out of the car, I heard Randal yelling for me to pick up the phone.

I told Randal I was all right and instinctively jumped right back into the conversation about his contract.

"Drew, what's wrong with you. You almost got shot. And you're talking to me about my contract? What are you nuts? Stop playing Super Agent!"

I was shaken up. I got jacked. But I'm an agent. That's what I do. And that's where my thinking was. I was trained to block out fear and be able to focus on the task at hand. With Randal, I was temporarily in disarray, but I recovered and went right back to work. Randal was impressed and the word got out that nothing slows me down. Not even three gunmen on crack.

I didn't let it phase me. Later that evening, I went out with my clients as if nothing happened. However, one thing did change. I now wear a silver Rolex watch instead of gold. I may be brave, but I'm not stupid.

But sometimes tragedy does strike, and as an agent, you need to focus on aiding your client despite everything that's going on around you. I'll never forget the phone call I got in the middle of the night on the Fourth of July. It was from Rosa Blades, Brian Blades's mother. She was crying hysterically and was beside herself in anguish. She told me Charles Blades, Brian's cousin, had a horrible accident. She said he was dead.

At the time it was late at night and I was in the middle of—celebrating, with my girlfriend Krissy. Not knowing what was going on, I drove over there to see if I could be of help to Brian and his family.

I was not prepared for what I saw. How could I be? People were crying and yelling and screaming. Brian was in such uncontrollable pain that it was hard to look at him. Brian's mother had passed out. It was a frightening experience. I tried to console Brian, but he was in shock and could not be reached with words.

I was no longer just being a contract advisor or athlete agent or athlete representative or attorney or whatever other names there are for agents. I wasn't negotiating a contract here, I was doing much more. *Brian's career and life was at stake here* from being involved in this tragic accident. I had to take control. I was there for a reason—to do what he would want me to do—help him and his family.

I stayed there all night, calming everyone down and helping them go home. I talked with the police for hours. I tried to talk with Brian all night, but I could only pity him. He was in agonizing grief.

And then the media came after him. The public was tired of athletes getting into trouble and the media wanted to sell their story. He was part of a tragic accident but people were accusing him of something more than that. He had been charged by the state for accidentally shooting his cousin.

I took him to Bruce Zimet and Fred Haddad, the best criminal defense attorneys around. This was the best way I could help him. Brian was competently advised by his attorneys not to talk to the police unless he was legally required to do so. He was also advised not to talk to the media. Well, Brian did what any smart client would do: he kept quiet and did as his attorneys advised him. Then, the media crucified him for not speaking.

They said he had something to hide and painted him in the same picture with every other athlete who had gotten in trouble.

So I spoke out for Brian and took the heat. I stood up for my client in his time of need and took a beating from the media and public for it. I was there for Brian.

I'll tell you who else was there for Brian—his coaches. That's right, in a league where coaches send players in to get beaten up, used up, and then replace them with someone younger and cheaper, Seattle Seahawks head coach Dennis Erickson and offensive coordinator Bob Bratkowski stand alone. These guys care.

Erickson called Brian and spoke with Brian heart to heart. I don't know what Coach Erickson said to Brian, but I know it was genuine and I know it made Brian feel better. I knew Coach Erickson from his college days at Miami, and I can tell you he looks out for his players. He wants to see them succeed not just in the NFL, but in life. He has a huge heart and that's why his players love him.

As for Coach Bratkowski, he actually flew to Miami from Seattle to be with Brian at Charles's funeral. That's class.

The jury for Brian's trial delivered a verdict of guilty for manslaughter, and Brian and his family were crushed. At that point, Brian had all but adopted Charles's son and the two embraced in tears. Brian's mother and father were devastated. I turned to Bruce Zimet, and he reminded me that the judge was going to make a ruling after the weekend, on Monday, on a motion he made to dismiss the case.

I told Brian to hang in there over the weekend and pray for good news on Monday. I promised him that we had a good chance on Monday and encouraged him be strong. I had been with Brian and his family every step of the way from the night of the fatal tragedy, so of course, I was there with him Monday.

When the jury found Brian guilty of manslaughter, his future looked bleak. With a heavy heart, Brian was still too sad to realize how bad a position he was in. So we walked back into the courtroom on Monday and the first thing the judge did was rule on the motion. Speaking in legalese, Judge Lebow ruled in Brian's favor and dismissed the case.

We jumped up and hugged his family. The room erupted with emotion. Everyone was hugging everyone and had tears in their eyes. Brian's mother and father must have hugged Jason and I ten times. I looked at Charles's son, and he hugged Brian and would not let go.

It was one of the most emotional moments of my life. Despite the darkest of days, we had prevailed. Although the case would still be pending on appeal, Brian would be allowed to go play football that season for the Seahawks. And wouldn't you know it, Brian would go on to catch the winning touchdown pass late in the fourth quarter to beat the Dolphins in Miami. I was the only Dolphin fan cheering him on.

I thought about all that Brian had endured to be there. I

thought about the pain he had suffered over the year. I thought about the times Brian called me to talk and tell me how much he missed his best friend. I remembered how distraught he was sitting with Charles's son and family at the funeral. And now I was watching him run free into the end zone on the best play of his entire career. "Yes!" I cheered.

When I think of what I went through with Brian and his family, I feel humbled and reminded that I'm not immortal. It's too bad I wasn't reminded two years earlier when I was in the wrong place at the wrong time.

Jason and I were in the projects of Liberty City in downtown Miami on a warm night in January. We had a meeting with a recruit, and so, of course we were dressed professionally. We were dressed in thousand dollar suits, wearing Brioni ties, black boots, and carrying leather briefcases. The apartment we were going to was in the middle of a walkway in a big complex. We couldn't drive up to it, so we had to walk about a hundred yards to get there.

As we parked our black Lexus SC 400 coupe, I told Jason, "Anything could happen here. Keep your eyes open."

"We've been in tough neighborhoods like this before," Jason said as he cracked his knuckles.

I thought about the time we were jogging with Fred Jones and left behind in that neighborhood. This was ten times worse. We were going to have to walk down a dark alley where anyone could see us coming. This was the perfect place for an ambush and we were walking around with big targets on our chest.

There were people strung out on dope. There were prostitutes. There was garbage all over the place. It broke my heart to see a cute little kid walking around barefoot, with no shirt on, playing in the pile of debris. "What chance of making it does that kid have?" I said to Jason.

"Poor little guy," Jason answered.

And then, all of a sudden, six teenage gangsters with guns, baseball bats, and knives emerged from the shadows in front of us. We stopped walking. They started to form a circle around us. They didn't say anything, so I didn't know if they wanted our money or our lives. Jason and I stood back to back.

"I take it you're not with the welcoming committee?" I asked, trying to be friendly.

The kid in front of me, who looked like the leader of the gang, flipped open his switchblade and said, "Your brief-cases, hand 'em over."

I threw him both cases. They were locked. "What's in 'em?" he said.

"Paperwork. I'm sports agent Drew Rosenhaus, this is my brother Jason. Those are my notes, stats and presentation materials."

"Presentation . . . Here's our presentation," the kid said.

Just then they were starting to move in on us. I didn't think they were going to shoot us because they were in a circle and if they missed, one of their own would buy it. So they were going to come at us the old-fashioned way—with knives and baseball bats. It was still six versus two. I wished Young Soo Do was with us. But since he wasn't, I figured I had better use my head to get out of this one. I tried to remember which clients of mine are from this area. One guy jumped to mind.

"Guys, hold on!" I said, "We're with Brett Perriman. We're Brett's agents."

Brett was from around this way and is respected by every-one in the neighborhood—especially in the poor neighbor-hoods where he does a lot of charity and business work. When Brett was young and in school, he was crazier and tougher than any other kid in the neighborhood.

"Wo, you're Brett's agent. Wait that's you? Oh man, I know who you are. Shit. Why didn't you say that from the start?"

As he handed us back our briefcases, I said, "You didn't ask."

Shaking my hand, he and his partners in crime apologized and went on to escort me to the apartment where I was headed. They also told me not to worry about my car. When I was finished with the meeting, they walked me back to my car and couldn't have been more friendly.

We risked our lives that night. Ironically, we didn't sign that player, but we didn't risk our lives for him. We risked our lives because this is our life, this is what we do. We go into these neighborhoods with the idea that we are going to help some of these young guys like Brett get out of there. It is worth the risk. We will be back again.

One guy who emerged from the mean streets of Miami is Marvin Jones. Just a boy when his mother passed away, Marvin went on to have a brilliant college career at Florida State University. A very high first-round pick, Marvin was a sure-fire superstar with the New York Jets. And then on one play against the Indianapolis Colts, Marvin blew out his hip.

It was the same injury that forced Bo Jackson out of the NFL. As soon as I saw it, I jumped on the first plane to New York and went to see Marvin. When I got to the hospital, the doctors told me this could be a career-ending injury for him. Just twenty-one years old, heralded out of college as the best linebacker to come out in a long time, and there he was faced with the possibility of his career being over in his rookie year.

When I walked into Marvin's hospital room, I couldn't believe what I saw. Marvin's hip was in a body sling and he was in severe pain. Marvin is as tough as they come, but this pain was different. He had his whole career in front of him, the makings of a brilliant career, and now it was hanging in the balance.

To see this superstar athlete, this future dynamo, so helpless was a horrible feeling I will never forget. I spent the night in that room. I slept in the chair next to him. Marvin and I had been through a lot together over the last couple of months, all of it great. And now he was in traction, wondering if he would ever play again.

That's the reality of the NFL. One minute you are invincible, on top of the world, and the next minute you are praying it's not all over. It helped that I had just negotiated a contract yielding him a signing bonus in the amount of $3,250,000, but there was a lot more at stake here. There could be millions of dollars more to make. There could be the lifestyle of playing in the NFL. The fun of playing in the NFL. And there was the possibility that Marvin would have terrible arthritis in that hip and need hip replacement surgery down the road. It was a tough night.

Over the ensuing months, Marvin worked very hard with the doctors at the hospital. Not knowing whether Marvin would make it back or not made those months brutal. We talked everyday and he stayed positive. With tremendous perseverance and character, Marvin made a full recovery. This was made possible in no small part by the New York Jet doctors. The way they treated Marvin those first few days were vital to Marvin's recovery.

When I think back to that night in the hospital, I realize that I am not just an agent. I wasn't just doing my job when I slept in that uncomfortable hospital chair. I was a friend, helping another friend make it through tough times.

The NFL career is short, fast paced, and high staked. One mistake or injury can ruin a player, and often does. The odds are against these guys making it in life after their football career is over. To beat these odds, you can't do it alone. That's where I come in! I am ready to fight, risk my life, work day and night, and go to war for every single one of my clients. We are a team. I ask for their loyalty and faith, and I give them everything I have in return. It's us versus the world. We're a team. That's what I love about being an agent and that's why what I do is more than just a job.

17

Under Fire

THE NFL COMBINE ALWAYS BRINGS A SMILE TO MY FACE. NOT because I get to leave my house on the beach to stay in an Indianapolis hotel room. Not because I'm stuck in a hotel room with my brother for a week instead of my swimsuit model girlfriend. Not because I get to leave sunny South Beach for the freezing cold of Indianapolis. But because it's time for battle, and I'm ready!

I'm ready to sell my rookie clients to the NFL coaches, scouts, and general managers heading into the draft. I'm ready to match up against the NFL executives on behalf of my clients who are prepared to test the free agent market. I'm ready to hype my rookie clients to the media. I'm ready to set up marketing and endorsement deals with companies looking for fresh faces and new talent. And I'm ready for the enemy—my competitor agents.

Players, coaches, scouts, general managers, and the media aren't the only ones that go to the Combine, another group outnumbers them all—the agents. There are two main reasons why several hundred agents go out to the Indianapolis Combine. First and foremost is because the players are there. The agents are there to sign more rookies, service the rookies they already have, and protect their clients from other agents looking to steal them away. The other reason is because there is an annual NFLPA agent meeting held there that agents are required to attend. So all of the agents gather around from all over the country and get crammed into this one hotel room. And it ain't pretty.

Imagine five hundred agents all having to sit next to each other for about six hours. These are guys who compete head to head for their livelihoods. In this business, you can work for a client for several years, make a lot of money for him, and do a great job for him. And then because another agent comes into the picture with lies and scams, you've just lost your client.

Imagine the hatred that exists between these rivals. Imagine every year they compete head to head with one another. Remember, there is no second place in this business. Like I said, you either win big or lose big—there are no consolation prizes. Either you sign a client who will pay you hundreds of thousands of dollars over the next couple of years or you get nothing. What's more, you get to watch your most hated competitor make all that money and rub it in your face every time you match up again in the future. It becomes more than business, it gets personal.

And you never know which agent is acting like your friend and all the while is scheming to steal your top client away and put you out of business. This is why I make no friends among the agent community.

And at the Combine meeting, as much as they dislike each other, the other agents act like friends because they don't have the guts to be an enemy openly. And then I show up. I'm the guy that was on the cover of *Sports Illustrated*. I'm the guy who consulted and appeared in *Jerry Maguire*. I'm the guy who was in *GQ* with Tom Cruise. I'm the guy who at twenty-two was on the ESPN Draft. I'm the guy who was also on ESPN during the draft with Marvin Jones and then again with Warren Sapp. I'm the guy that works day and night making them look fat and lazy. I'm the young guy that the players love to hang out with. I am the guy who lives on

Miami Beach. I'm the guy who has celebrity girlfriends. I'm the guy who represents their former clients.

And most of all, I'm the guy who refuses to be like them. I act with self-respect. What you see is what you get. Because I am not in their fraternity, because I am not one of them, because I succeed where they fail, because I make them look bad, because I am where they want to be, they hate me. This is why they make negative remarks toward me. This is why *Sports Illustrated* was so fascinated with my character that they put my face on their cover. And for that, I thank all my competitors.

So when Jason and I walk into the Hyatt Hotel meeting room at nine in the morning, it's just the two of us versus them all. As I look at them, they turn away until I get past them. Then when they think they are in the clear, they all collaborate and unite in their hatred toward me. They all stare and say things behind my back. The phony friendliness that had filled the room now subsides and is pushed out by the tension that is so hot that the other agents need to go get a drink. If you think I sound paranoid, just wait.

Although intense and focused on the matter at hand, I'm at ease. I don't sweat them. I'm as comfortable in the lion's den as I am anywhere else. Jason, on the other hand, was a different story. He looks like he did when he and I used to fight in karate tournaments—salty.

The night before, Jason and I watched the movie *Taxi Driver* with Robert DeNiro. We got a kick out of this Vietnam Veteran taxi driver who, when surrounded by pimps, pushers, prostitutes, and perverts, went over the edge and shot some of the bad guys.

I tell him, "Don't waste your time and energy on our competitors. Let them worry about us. Spend your time paying attention to and learning from the key NFLPA executives who are here like Mark Levin, Tom DePaso, and Trace Armstrong. That's what you're here for. I don't want you freaking out and turning into that taxi driver."

And then the NFLPA Agent Seminar begins. The seminar is very informative as it discusses the latest developments regarding the collective bargaining agreement and other League issues. They also provide you with the latest NFL statistics and other valuable documentation. But hey, business never rests. I've got players to sign. So just about every ten minutes, I had to get up and walk out to answer my phone or return a page. It's a busy time of year.

At some time around noon, I'm outside the room on the phone, when a couple of NFLPA people call me in because a new person is going to speak. As I sit down next to Jason, I notice another agent, Tim Irwin, walking over toward us and about to address the room.

Jason says to me, "This is going to be about us."

Now Tim Irwin is about six foot eight inches tall and well over three hundred pounds. He used to play for the offensive line for the Dolphins, so I was familiar with him. Dressed in a suit, he had recently retired and become an agent.

A giant of a man with a loud, booming, authoritarian voice, he needed no microphone. Having walked all the way over toward us, he began by saying that there is "a cancer" growing in this business. With his voice carrying across the room, Irwin said that the cancer was coming from South Florida. And then he pointed his finger toward us for everyone to see and said, "The problem is right here . . . Drew and Jason Rosenhaus."

The fact of the matter is he was upset because rookie Miami Dolphin defensive lineman Shane Burton fired him and ultimately hired us. He went on to accuse us of taking Shane away from him. He said we lure guys away by taking them out to nightclubs and impressing them with women. Pointing his finger toward us, he warned all of the other agents to beware of the Rosenhaus Brothers. He ranted and raved, making negative remarks about us in front of this large group of agents and important NFLPA executives. It was embarrassing. I thought about jumping up and getting into a shouting match with him to shut him up, but that wouldn't be professional. I let him say what he had to say.

He went on to ask every other agent to stand up against us and join him. He demanded that the NFLPA do something about it. In response, the whole room stood up, turned toward us, and start clapping, giving Irwin some kind of standing ovation.

I turn to Jason, and say in a Scottish accent, "It was a fine speech."

Having noticed that I imitated a character from the movie *Braveheart,* Jason burst out laughing. Here Jason and I were, the whole room standing against us, calling for our heads, and we were joking around. We were laughing and clapping with the other agents. We were all smiles.

That—right then and there, is what separates us from everyone else. Any other agent would have ran out in tears or been pissing in his pants; we handled it like men. We didn't run or hide, we faced our competitors. We showed them all that they are nothing to us. We showed them all we took their best shot, and it bounced right off us.

As for Tim Irwin, what he said was wrong. I did not steal Shane Burton away from him, Shane came to me after he terminated his relationship with Irwin. I did not sign Shane until long after he fired Irwin. He's upset because he lost a good client and I can understand that, but he tried to hurt us.

I responded by walking up to the podium with Jason, grabbing the microphone, and saying, "Tim, if you weren't six foot eight and over three hundred pounds, I'd ask you to step outside . . ." I wanted everyone to see that I wasn't shaken up and that I had stood my ground. Now it was my turn to respond. I continued, "Tim, it's unfortunate you feel that way, but what you said was not true. And as for the rest of you agents who clapped, I look forward to continuing to compete against you guys in the future." Yeah, to all you agents out there, we'll see who gets the last laugh.

As Jason and I walked away from the front of the room, I could see it in their faces that I hit a nerve. They knew that they were going to have to compete against me. They knew better than to incite the Shark.

As I we walked out of the room at the end of the seminar, I was surrounded by the media. They were anxious to get my reaction. It was the big scoop of the Combine. This event was unprecedented. Never before had an agent been singled out in a seminar and teamed up on by all the other agents there. The episode was written about in *USA Today,* in all the national wire services, most of the big city newspapers, and all over the Internet. For the most part, the NFL coaches and general managers loved how I handled it with humor. They kidded me about it for weeks. I was supposed to get riled and upset by a whole room full of agents yelling at me, instead, I handled it with composure and poise.

That night my attorney, Glenn Waldman, who is based in Fort Lauderdale, called me as soon as he heard about it, wanting blood and a little green. He implored me to go after Irwin. Hey, if the guy is my attorney, you know he's a Shark's shark.

Every year I've had an agent confrontation at the NFL Combine. People ask, "Drew, why do you even bother to show up at the Combine? So many of the agents dislike you and have it in for you."

Why? Because I'm not scared, that's why. I could be like some of these other big-time agents and go to boutique seminars where there are fifty or so guys, and it's a casual environment. The NFLPA offers several different seminars a year, and I could go to any one of them. But I don't get intimidated by anyone. I have no fear.

I don't let my competitors dictate my actions. I don't care how many other agents are there at Indianapolis. I don't care what they have planned for me, and I don't care who is waiting—bring it on! I am going to that NFLPA agent meeting, and no one and nothing is going to stop me. In February 1998, everyone will watch Jason and I walk into that room, stick our chests out, and once again take on all comers.

But hey, that environment is nothing compared with some of the situations I have had to go through during my career. You want to know what being on the spot is? Try being on ESPN live during the 1995 Draft as Tampa Bay was on the clock about to make their selection with the twelfth pick. My client Warren Sapp and I were on live TV at the Draft Headquarters in New York and were hoping the Buccaneers would take him with their pick. There were false news reports released the night before that Sapp had failed drug tests, so the media was all over us. Since Sapp and I were seated, it was easy for ESPN reporter Craig James to walk right up to us live with the camera in our faces. Despite being under a lot of pressure, I didn't back away. I took Craig on. In fact, earlier in the day ESPN had actually started their draft coverage with Craig interviewing us.

Once again Craig didn't waste any time and went to the heart of the matter, asking, "Drew, what's going on? Who are you hearing from? Who are you talking to?"

I'm about ready to answer all of his questions, when suddenly my phone rings. Hoping it's the Buccaneers, I say to the live ESPN camera, "Excuse me for a second."

Buc executive Jerry Angelo is on the phone and says, "Drew, you've got to stop the interview. We need to talk to you. Get that camera out of there."

I said to Craig, "I'm sorry, I've got to take this call."

At the same time, ESPN has got a camera in the Tampa "war room," the draft room of the Buccaneers' facility. So our conversation was being filmed on both ends. Right there on national TV I am persuading the Bucs to draft Sapp and I start negotiating his contract with them. Whew! Talk about pressure. A few minutes later, Angelo tells me that the Buccaneers are going to take Warren, and then it was officially announced.

We were ecstatic. It was a huge relief for him to stay in Florida and get drafted by a team that he wanted to play for. We knew that it would be a great system for him, and he'd have tremendous success. Once again, I was on the hot seat as I was being interviewed live on ESPN under tough circumstances in front of the whole world on Draft Day. Just about every college and pro player watched me deal with the media and the Bucs in a very difficult situation as I pulled the trigger to get Sapp drafted.

Sometimes what looks like an easy situation to handle is actually real tough. Case in point, my client Pete Stoyanovich, kicker for the Dolphins. It's midnight, February 1994, on the eve of a new dawn in the NFL. The NFLPA won free agency, and finally the players would be free to offer their services on the open market. This would be the first year of free agency under the new collective bargaining agreement. On this night in February, a historic night, Pete Stoyanovich would become a free agent. I was eager to step forward into history.

At a few minutes before midnight, I sit at my desk and prepare for the call. Pete is a hometown hero, who has won several games in the final minute for the Miami Dolphins. He is one of Don Shula's favorite players and he loves South Florida. Being from Michigan and having gone to college at Indiana, Pete appreciates the South Florida lifestyle. It's a Thursday night, so Pete is out on the town in South Beach. To make sure I can reach him and talk business, I sent Jason out with him with a cellular phone and pager. We are ready.

The phone rings at midnight on the dot. Guess who it is? Bill Parcells—the new Head Coach for the New England Patriots. And guess what he wants to do? Make Pete the highest paid kicker in the history of the NFL. What could be better than that?

The Dolphins tried to sign Pete before he became a free agent, but they never made a top-quality offer. Free agency wasn't the only new comer in the deal, so was the salary cap. As popular as Pete was in the community, as much as Shula loved Pete, as many games as Pete won, they could not make us the offer Pete needed to be set for life.

I thought Pete would get that contract on the free market. I wanted to test the waters. I was right, someone was biting, and it was the Big Tuna—Bill Parcells. My grandfather Irv, who lived for many years in New Jersey, loved Parcells for what he accomplished as a New York Giant. I admired Parcells and liked him, but hey—this was business.

Parcells told me that he wanted Pete to win a Super Bowl for them and that Pete was his number one free agent. He told me to be ready to deal the next day. I was pumped and could smell money. I called Jason on his cellular phone at a nightclub on South Beach to get Pete on the line. Pete told me to go for it and get all I could.

The next day I also got a call from Robert Kraft—the new owner of the Patriots. He was ready to pay out the big bucks and we were ready to start earning dividends. He joked that if Pete signed with the team he would throw a parade for him. They really wanted him bad. By Friday afternoon, I was able to get the Patriots to offer Pete a record-breaking $5 million contract.

I couldn't have been happier. This was a dream contract and I came through for Pete. We gambled and had what we wanted right in front of us for the taking. Nothing could be better, right? Wrong.

Pete is one of the guys who can honestly say that money doesn't mean everything. He can honestly say it because he has proved it. Pete wanted to stay in South Florida. He had a beautiful house, a great lifestyle, a great head coach, a great social life, lots of friends, and he was a local hero. He just didn't want to leave all of that behind, no matter what the price.

Now I had a problem. The Dolphins offer was significantly less, and although they wanted Pete, they weren't prepared to pay that type of money to a kicker. They admitted that they could not match the Patriots' offer.

Pete was over my condo that Friday and things looked bleak. I called the Dolphins and insisted that we meet all day Saturday to try and work out a deal. After high-charged, emotional negotiations, I was finally able to get the Dolphins' offer up to a high enough number. Pete actually decided to take less money to stay with the Dolphins. We got the Dolphins to make a deal that was for less money, but it was still a megamillion-dollar deal and the signing bonus was for well over a million dollars. It was a record-breaking contract that made Pete the highest-paid kicker in the history of the NFL.

I was happy to make my client happy. Pete was hailed as a hero; this was a big victory for us. But it was tough for me to make that call to Parcells and Kraft to say that despite

doing everything they should have and could have to persuade Pete, he was going to stay in Miami. They were disappointed but handled it with class.

This was a happy ending for Pete. Another situation that
had a happy ending was with my client Kirby Dar Dar. Kirby
Dar Dar is a wide receiver for the Miami Dolphins. He's a
guy that was primarily a special team player, and the Dolphins, after the third preseason game of the 1996 season,
decided to cut him. The next preseason game was at Tampa
Bay and I was there. I was standing on the sideline watching
the game and saw a kick returner run right by me to take a
punt into the end zone. Kirby was not on the team and as a
result the special teams suffered.

After the game, I was out by the team bus talking with
some of my clients. Jimmy knew I was Kirby's agent because
we had met when he let Kirby go the week before. Well,
Jimmy sent Dolphin security director Stu Weinstein to track
me down and send word that he wanted to see me. I was
shuttled into the Dolphin locker room and met with the
coach while he was getting dressed. They rushed me in with
so much urgency that you'd think I was getting ready to per-
form some type of lifesaving medical procedure. In reality,
Jimmy wanted to know if I had already signed Kirby with
another team.

It was then that I learned that Jimmy Johnson was so competitive that moments after winning this preseason game,
while he was half-naked and changing, I was in there talking
to him about a special teams player. He had a towel wrapped
around his waist, and I was ushered into the locker room
with players left and right around me. Of course, most agents
don't go into a locker room right after a game, but Jimmy felt
this was important. He said to me, "Drew, we want Kirby
Dar Dar back."

I told him Kirby was still available, and he said, "Bring
Kirby in with you tomorrow morning. We want to re-sign
him."

I was amazed with the urgency and importance Jimmy had
for a role player, a guy who had just been cut. Jimmy Johnson

was acting as if it was life and death, and to him it was. You would have thought he and I were about to do a deal for Dan Marino. But, you know what, it was a real smart move that Jimmy Johnson made, because Kirby came back to make some big-time special teams plays and was a big reason why the Dolphins had a great year on special teams. There's a reason Jimmy is who he is.

This was a happy ending. At first the guy is crushed after being waived, and then he goes on to become one of the best special teams players in the League. But you don't always have happy endings.

Sometimes you can work as hard as humanly possible and do everything you can to win with your client and you just don't make it. Your client doesn't get the big contract and you get fired. Take my former client Errict Rhett for instance. It didn't work out for Errict like we wanted it to. He gave me an opportunity and he didn't sign a new contract. So now someone else has the chance. Errict will be a great player. I love him, he knows it, and that's what matters to me. I wish him the best.

Getting fired is absolutely the worst part of this business. And you will get fired. It happens to every top agent. You learn from it, take your medicine, and move on. You can't be like Jerry Maguire. When he got fired by his top client, quarterback Frank Cushman, Jerry Maguire got drunk and felt sorry for himself. He even asked Rod Tidwell why Rod would want to stay with him. Rod stood by Maguire, but in the real NFL world, most players today would have canned him on the spot.

Not everyone is a Rod Tidwell—or Warren Sapp, who, when seeing that I was disappointed about the situation with Errict, said to me, "Hey, I'm sorry things didn't work out with Errict, but don't worry, you're still my boy and you'll get the Bucs with my next contract." What a class act.

But that's not the point. Never feel sorry for yourself. Never give up. Never quit. Never stop trying. I don't care what the circumstances are. I don't care how bad it is. Every day counts. Every challenge counts—big and small. You can't even get sick—whether you are or not.

A couple of years ago, I was recruiting an offensive lineman at the Blue-Gray All-Star Game during the holiday season. I came down with food poisoning and was vomiting every few hours. Before I started puking my guts out, I set up a time to meet with him for that night. This was my only chance to meet with him, and just because I was spitting up blood, I wasn't going to wimp out.

The player's name was Derrick Graham, and he is currently playing with the Seahawks. That night in December, he came over to my hotel room and we had a memorable meeting, to say the least. Every ten minutes or so in the meeting, I had to get up and go to the bathroom to vomit. It was obvious that I was very sick. What probably gave it away was when I was in midsentence and was about to puke. Being the gentleman that I am, I at least covered my mouth with my hand, excused myself, and finished the job in the john. At that point, Derrick said he had enough and couldn't bear to see me torture myself anymore.

Greener than a goblin, I said, "Derrick, you have to sign with me. Look how bad I want to represent you. I am battling this pain. Look how tough and determined I am. Don't you want a monster like me working for you?"

I didn't sign Derrick, but to this day he hasn't forgotten our meeting and still teases me about it. Even though I had this food poisoning, I insisted on meeting with Derrick. He had another agent in mind but at least I earned his respect, and he passed the word on as to how tough and disciplined I was. It didn't matter that I didn't sign Derrick. What mattered is that any other agent would have been home in bed, but not me. I was fighting the fight and passing the test. Remember, effort is measured by pain, not success.

And you will not win them all. You will lose. But with great effort, you will be back to compete and you will eventually get that win. I know, my clients have proven it to me.

I don't mind taking the heat for my clients. When the Dolphins released Eric Green, I was upset because I knew he was still injured. When I aided Eric in filing an NFLPA injury grievance against the Dolphins, the media asked Jimmy Johnson to comment. Johnson said "Whatever Drew says. Evidently, Drew is the gospel . . . I didn't know Drew took up medical practice in the last month or two." I found Jimmy's comments funny. I had to protect my client's best interests no matter how much criticism I would receive.

Another coach who made some entertaining comments about me in the media was Sam Wyche. While I was negotiating Bernard Clark's rookie contract with the Bengals, I did an interview for the *Cincinnati Inquirer,* and I was quoted as saying that I thought Clark would start and that he was going to be a leader and impact player. Sounds innocent enough right? Wrong. Coach Wyche went ballistic over these comments. He countered back with comments in the paper blasting me, saying that I should tone down my comments about Clark. Wyche, who is now a member of the media as the NBC Studio Host (it's ironic, considering how sensitive he was then), called me up and said he didn't like the fact that I said Bernard Clark was going to start. He thought it was an insult to the starters, to the veteran players on the team. Wyche was LIVID. He didn't like the fact that I spoke to the media. I told him I didn't mean any offense by it and actually developed a pretty good relationship with him.

Speaking of Eric Green, after being released by Miami, I got him a contract with the Baltimore Ravens. Art Modell is the owner of the team. About the time that *Sports Illustrated* came out with an article that called me the most hated man in the NFL, Art came up to me and introduced himself as the "second most-hated man in the NFL" because of the move from Cleveland to Baltimore. But he's a heartwarming guy to be around, an old-school owner who really cares about the players. He went to bat for Eric Green and was very generous. It was a deal that, quite frankly, may have saved Eric's career.

Here's a story about two careers that beat the odds. Jimmie Jones and Ray Seals. Jimmie came from a small high school in Okeechobee, Florida, where he barely played organized football. He was a long shot to get a college scholarship, but University of Miami coaches Butch Davis and Jimmy Johnson gave him a chance. During his senior year in college, he played in a rotation where Cortez Kennedy and Russell Maryland started. Cortez was the third pick in the draft, and Russell was the first overall pick in the draft the following year. When Jimmie played the Cowboys, he had Russell Maryland, Tony Casillas, and Leon Lett all in the defensive tackle rotation with him. And yet, in the biggest game of the year, it was Jimmie who scored a touchdown in the Super Bowl. And it was Jimmie, who in the 1994 first year of free agency, finally hit the jackpot.

At first, there was a modest amount of interest in Jimmie when he visited teams like the Chicago Bears, the New England Patriots, and Detroit Lions. And then I got a call from the Los Angeles Rams who inquired about the interest in Jimmie. I may have exaggerated a little when I said ten teams were battling over Jimmie. And I may have exaggerated when I reiterated that information to *USA Today,* but hey, I knew the Rams really wanted Jimmie and I wanted their best offer while the iron was hot.

My strategy worked, and the Rams gave Jimmie an offer of $7.5 million that was significantly higher than any other competing team. We took it right away, and it turned out to be a great deal for the Rams and Jimmie, as he played several good seasons for them. Despite having great competition for the starting job in college, Jimmie never quit. In the end, Jimmie had a great career in the NFL and was rewarded for his perseverance. Jimmie isn't my only client with limited high school football experience. In fact, my client Ray Seals of the Carolina Panthers didn't even play college ball. He is only one of two active players in the NFL who never played football in college. Ray was unable to go to college, so he played minor league football. Ray starred at this level and caught the attention of the Tampa Bay Bucs.

The Bucs signed Ray and he nearly made the team. He was then picked up by the Detroit Lions. Ray played briefly with the Lions but then was released. Ray then got another chance with the Bucs. Remember Ray was at the age when most guys were still in college. Ray developed into one of the best defensive lineman in the NFL. He signed a million dollar contract as a free agent with the Pittsburgh Steelers. But the adversity didn't stop there.

While in Pittsburgh, Ray lived with his cousin and best friend, Johnny Gammage. Ray loved Johnny like a brother. In a shocking and controversial incident, Johnny was beaten to death by some local police officers after a routine traffic stop. Johnny was a little guy who didn't have any weapons and was inexplicably beaten to death by several policemen. Ray was crushed and angry. But he kept his composure and played through the agony. Later, the police were found not guilty much to Ray's chagrin. Still, Ray led the Steeler defense to a Super Bowl appearance.

The bad luck hit again. The following season, Ray blew out his rotator cuff and missed the entire season. I hung in there with Ray who was exhausted from all the trials he has endured in his life. Ray did a great job of rehabbing, and amazingly I was able to land a multimillion dollar free agent contract for Ray with the Carolina Panthers. Talk about being under fire and coming through like a champ. We did it together.

Talk about winning and overcoming adversity, my first client Robert Massey went from a small and unknown school like North Carolina Central University all the way to the Pro Bowl in Hawaii. That's right, after Massey's first contract expired, he wanted out of New Orleans and to be traded. I got him traded to the Phoenix Cardinals, and in that first year with the team, he made it to the Pro Bowl.

It was a long, hard road that Massey traveled, but, he made it. Massey was one of the few players in NFL History to play Division II college ball and make it to the Pro Bowl. What a thrill for me that my first client, who gave me my first shot, made it to the Pro Bowl. Massey's confidence and belief in me did not go in vain. I, too, have overcome a lot of adversity and come a long way. I went from a young Dolphin fan to a true power broker in the NFL. In my own way, I have also gone to the Pro Bowl.

18

Me and Jerry Maguire

"ACTION!" THE DIRECTOR, CAMERON CROWE, YELLS.

I'm on the set of *Jerry Maguire* at the Sony Studios in Hollywood. This is Tom Cruise's opening scene. The lights are bright, the motion picture cameras are rolling.

In the scene, I'm on my cellular phone negotiating with an NFL team, and I say demonstratively, "I want a two million dollar signing bonus."

In comes TOM CRUISE. He walks straight toward me. Having overheard my conversation, he leans over toward me and says impolitely, "Ask for five million to sign. And by the way, stop trying to look like me."

I snap back sarcastically, "In your dreams, Jerry Maguire."

No, in my dreams. There I was, filming a scene with Tom Cruise. As an agent, I'd been around superstars before, but I was still taken aback by the fact that there I was, making a MOVIE with Tom Cruise. And it got better. In between shoots, he was asking me every question in the world: What would you say to a general manager of a team in this situation? What would you say to a player in this situation? What do you wear? Why types of phones and pagers do you use? How do you hang out with your clients? What do you do when they get in trouble? How would you handle this? How would you handle that? What's it like when this happens? What are you thinking here? What would you do? Would you yell and argue or be calm and cool? He talked football with me in between every take. He wanted to know the real scoop about what goes on behind closed doors in the NFL and with an agent. He wanted to be as genuine and authentic as possible. He wasn't taking the $25 million they were paying him and running.

He was emulating ME, and in part, incorporating my persona into his character. I felt like a million bucks as I worked with Tom on how to really do it. How to really be a smooth, charismatic, and dynamic agent.

He had no ego and could not have been more genuine and friendly. I couldn't believe this was how Tom Cruise really is? Yes, he was that cool and down to earth. I even joked with him about his role as a crazy greaser in one of my favorite movies, *The Outsiders.*

Doing that scene with Tom Cruise was one of the great moments of my life. Now let me tell you how this all came to be.

It all started for me in the summer of 1993, when my client, Seattle Seahawks wide receiver Brian Blades, called to tell me about a director/writer he had met in Seattle. When he told me the guy he spoke to was Cameron Crowe, my eyes opened wide as I knew this was the real thing. A movie-lover, I was familiar with Cameron and liked his work in such films as *Fast Times at Ridgemont High* with Sean Penn. Cameron Crowe was asking Brian questions about a movie he hoped to write detailing the life of an agent. Crowe wanted to meet with me and Brian to discuss our business. You can imagine my enthusiasm. I was on the phone immediately, talking to Cameron and hitting him hard with the excitement of being an agent in the NFL.

I was thrilled to get the opportunity to talk to Cameron. I wanted to be involved in *Jerry Maguire,* even though I had no idea that it would become such a box office hit. At the time, Cameron didn't know that Tom Cruise was going to be the star. He mentioned at the beginning stages that it was going to co-star Eddie Murphy. Cameron thought the film was going to be more of a comedy than anything else and that it was going to focus more on the player, with the agent being more of a secondary figure. Still, the idea was to focus on the relationship between the two. He wanted to see what the relationship was like between a young agent like myself and a young client like Brian Blades. He couldn't have predicted that Cuba Gooding would win an Oscar. And he had no idea that many of the movie's best lines would immediately become part of our everyday language. For example, Crowe invented the popular phrase, "Show me the money!"

Cameron was fascinated with what I had to say. We talked about everything involving the agent business. He said he would love to base the main agent's character in part on my lifestyle and personality. I explained to him that because I am about the same age as my clients, we are more like friends than your typical professional association between an agent and his client. My relationships with my clients are unique, and yet they became the role model for a movie about an industry that has no one else out there like me.

In a conversation Cameron had with Jason, he told Jason that the movie was "going to be about the World of Drew." I had won him over, and he wanted to take it to the next level.

I flew to the Sony Studios to meet with Cameron and the producers of the film. I was ready and couldn't WAIT to get in there and go for it. In a room filled with ten people, Crowe brought a camera crew in to film me. They rolled the cameras and he told me to do my thing. I did much more than that. I talked, screamed, yelled, punched, kicked, fought, pleaded, and cried into that camera. I made my sales pitch, my recruiting pitch, and my presentation. I opened myself up, poured out my guts, and showed them my mannerisms, my look, my dress, my lifestyle, my around-the-clock work schedule, my relationship with my girlfriend and my relationship with my clients. Cameron was urging me to go on as they shot how I talked and how I yelled. I gave them more than just my stories. I gave them my soul, I gave them Drew Rosenhaus—the real Jerry Maguire.

When I almost collapsed from exhaustion, Crowe couldn't stop complimenting me. Wanting more and more, and fascinated with my relationship with Brian Blades, he actually asked me, after all the work I just did, to go again but this time to recount the sales pitch that I made to Brian that won Brian over. I looked at him like there was nothing he or anyone could say or do to stop me. I sucked it up and went several more minutes going over the presentation, then went through negotiating strategy, going over the X's and O's of the agent business. I gave him everything I had and then much more. I wasn't going to stop. With every ounce and fiber of my being, I sold and sold myself. I wanted Cameron to see the heart and fire that it takes to make a great agent. I wanted his character to have the passion that I had. I wanted him to be dynamic and outrageous. And I wanted Cameron to be so impressed with my real life personality that he would have to incorporate me in the Maguire character.

Acting like they had just climaxed from great sex, they finally stopped me. They had everything they wanted and loved it. He said I was the prototype agent for the movie business: young, handsome, controversial, daring, energetic, outgoing, and aggressive.

Actor Ethan Hawke was there, interviewing for the role of Bob Sugar, the rival agent, watching me work. When I was done, he was so impressed he said, "My agent could learn a few things from you. It's too bad you don't represent actors."

I went home knowing that I gave it my best. Now it was up to them to put me in the movie and use more of my knowhow as a consultant. My fingers were crossed.

Cameron and his staff called me repeatedly over the next year, asking me questions about certain situations: How would you do this, how would you do that, what would you do in this circumstance, what would an agent say, what would a player do, what would a player say, what would an agent wear, where would he be, what type of flight would he take, what kind of phone would he use, what kind of computer, what kind of food would he eat. No one from the world of Hollywood knew anything about what the sports agent business was really like. So I educated them about it.

I was rewarded for all my contributions to the film in several ways. I was paid a few thousand dollars for my efforts. I would be acknowledged in the credits of the movie. The studio agreed to publicize my contributions as a consultant to the film. And, best of all, they agreed to fly me to Hollywood to take part in two of the actual scenes of the movie with Tom Cruise. Yes!!!

Finally, the day I was waiting for arrived and they flew me in for my first scene. I loved every minute of it—everything was, of course, first class. They enrolled me in the Screen Actors Guild so I could have a couple of lines with Tom Cruise. I had my own trailer, makeup artist, and hair stylist. I didn't need any of it. I came prepared and was dressed in my navy blue Hugo Boss pin-striped suit, my Versace tie, and trademark black shark skin boots. The wardrobe lady came to look at my clothes, and she was so happy with what I was wearing that she preferred my clothes over what she had for me. What would you expect? I am the real deal.

Dressed for success, it was time to go to work. As I walked onto the set, Tom Cruise recognized me instantly. He came over and introduced himself for the first time. He acted like he knew me for years after all of the film of me he had studied. He was incredibly gracious and warm. He thanked me for my contributions and said he was glad I was in the film. He joked, "Just don't steal the show."

I asked him if he was ready to match up against me in our confrontational movie scene. Transcending into Jerry Maguire, he gave me that smile of confidence that women swoon over. The cinematographer kept saying to me, "Hey the real Jerry Maguire, stand over here . . . do this . . . do that." The crew was excited to be working with me.

On the set were several NFL people—Wayne Fontes, Mike White, Jeff Lurie, Jim Irsay, and Rich Kotite. In the scene, Tom makes his opening in a hotel lobby at the NFL Owners Meetings. He greets the various football coaches and owners and then is supposed to make his way toward me, where we go after each other.

I take my position, and Cameron Crowe yells, "Action." I get on my phone and demand, "I want two million on the signing bonus."

As Cruise approaches, I am looking mean and very serious. I am focused and intense as I get ready to rip his head off. Tom comes toward me looking just as serious if not more, as the intensity between the two of us is overwhelming. Leaning toward me, he playfully punches me in the chest and shouts, "Hey, shmuck, stop trying to steal my clients."

I broke out in laughter. The whole cast also broke out in laughter. Tom couldn't help himself and would not stop laughing. He was having some fun with me on the set. But being the consummate professional, he redid the scene and wrapped it up in only two or three takes. I was having the time of my life. I could have shot that scene all day.

The day before I had been invited to watch the "show me the money" scene as a consultant. I also was asked to examine the various background sets for authenticity. I checked out Jerry Maguire's office and gave them my approval. During the course of the year, I had sent them all kinds of paraphernalia and stuff to set up Maguire's office. It was cool to watch the producers transform a movie studio into a real-life sports agent's office and home. Everything was very realistic about the sets.

While at the set I hung out with actor Jay Mohr, who played Bob Sugar—the rival agent bad guy, and actor Donal Logue who played Sugar's assistant Rick. The three of us sat in Maguire's office cracking jokes. I talked some more about the real-life NFL, and Jay imitated me and Christopher Walken. Both imitations were the best and funniest I had ever seen. Renee Zellweger joined us shortly afterward in the office.

At the end of the filming, as I left the scene, Jay Mohr led a standing ovation for me with Renee Zellweger joining in. I couldn't believe that I was getting a standing ovation from these talented actors. I was flattered, and it made me feel like my hard work was appreciated. I especially appreciated Renee's flattering remarks. I liked her and would have liked to spend a little more time on the set getting to know her.

The second scene I did was at the Havana Club in Hollywood, a high-class cigar smoking bar. They flew me and Brian Blades in for the bachelor party scene where I was the same competitor agent. In the scene I was at the bar standing behind Donal Logue, smiling, as he says, "Everybody loves you." We worked from 5:00 P.M. to 5:00 A.M. on the bachelor party scene. Tom was busy the entire night and never got off his feet.

And those were my scenes—two perfect scenes for me. I loved it. I loved Hollywood. I stayed in the Beverly Hills Wilshire Hotel which is one of the nicest. I was given a limo with my own chauffeur who took me all around. It was cool being around the studios and seeing movies being filmed at Tri Star and Sony Pictures.

I felt at home. I really fit in with the producers and actors. Normally, I am out of place, sticking out like a sore thumb with the smooth clothes I wear and my slicked back hair. But not in Hollywood. I left there with a feeling that I would be back again someday.

When *Jerry Maguire* finished production, they had the *Jerry Maguire* wrap party on Saturday, July 6, at a club called the Opium Den in Los Angeles. I could hardly enjoy the party because I was on pins and needles over the upcoming July 14 edition of *Sports Illustrated* that was going to feature me.

The following day, on a Sunday, were the finals of Wimbledon. I was anxious because I had been told by the magazine editors that if Malivai Washington won Wimbledon, he would make the cover instead of me. If he lost then I would be on the cover. As a general rule of self-respect, I make it a point to never root for people to fail or take pleasure in their defeats for they are not my victories. But this was a very rare exception.

Washington was to face the unheralded Richard Krajicek in the Finals. This was a big day. If Krajicek wins, than I get on the cover of *Sports Illustrated*—something no other agent had ever done. I suddenly became Krajicek's biggest fan.

Of course I desperately wanted to make the cover. It would be one of my life's greatest achievements. Very few nonathletes in history have been on the cover of *Sports Illustrated*. It would be a dream come true. I needed Krajicek to win. I recall telling Cameron Crowe the scenario and he wished me good luck.

The whole *Sports Illustrated* experience was a saga from start to finish. First, I heard that the magazine was simply doing a story on the power of agents and that I was one of ten guys they were going to feature. Then I was excited to learn that they only wanted to feature three unique agents in the story: Leigh Steinberg, Eugene Parker, and myself. After interviewing the three of us, they decided to focus the story on me. I almost fainted when I heard that *S.I.* was doing a feature story exclusively on me. I never dreamed I had a chance at the cover.

I didn't sleep much that Saturday night before the match. To make matters worse, my Sunday flight was scheduled during the same time the match would be played. I would have to wait five hours, flying from Los Angeles to Miami before I would know who had won the match. It was agonizing. Jason would watch the match for me, and before I left, I ordered him to give me good news when I got off the plane. Jason went to my grandparents' apartment to watch the game as they are big tennis fans. The minute the plane landed, I called Jason and I knew it right away.

"We did it Drew, you got your good news," Jason said. I had made the cover.

It was cool seeing the cover picture the very first time. I felt like a father waiting for a child to be born as I waited by the fax machine to get my first look at the cover and article. Being on the cover of *S.I.* has had a huge impact on my life. Between *Jerry Maguire* and *Sports Illustrated,* my life would never be the same.

For example, just the other night, I was at a party and a TV station came over to interview me. They started off the interview by calling me the "real Jerry Maguire." I have gotten so much hype from the movie it is unbelievable. Since my participation in the film, I have been featured in *Forbes Magazine, Penthouse,* and *Entertainment Weekly,* and I have been on the *Geraldo Rivera Show, Inside Edition, A Current Affair, Good Morning America,* CNN, and *Comedy Central,* to name a few.

As the movie production came to an end, the promotions for the movie began. The producers for *Jerry Maguire* flew back to Hollywood to do a *GQ* magazine photo shoot with Tom Cruise, Cuba Gooding and agent Leigh Steinberg who also was a consultant on the film. I had a nice solo shot in the magazine. It was a good promotion for the movie, and it was really cool being in *GQ* with Tom Cruise. It was in their December edition for the holidays.

After doing the *GQ* shoot, I was psyched up and ready to watch me in action at the World Premiere of *Jerry Maguire.* The premiere was on Friday, December 6, 1996, and was held in New York on a cruise ship.

Dressed in my top suit still wearing my boots, I walked down press row with Tom Cruise and all the celebrities. I brought my girl friend Krissy, who fit right in as a buxom, six foot tall blonde. To say I was excited would be a gross understatement. Watching the movie was like watching my life. It was an exhausting experience as I relived all the highs and lows with *Jerry Maguire* all over again. I said to Krissy several times during the movie, "Hey that's me!" or "they took that from me."

When the movie ended, I was very pleased with the way it captured me and my business. When Cameron Crowe came up to thank me for my help as a consultant on the film, I thanked him for the opportunity to be involved in such a great movie.

As for Tom Cruise, many critics believed the movie was excellent and some of his best work. He was sure to be nominated for an Academy Award for Best Actor. When he saw me, he walked right up and thanked me, telling me that it was a pleasure dealing with me. We had become friends. A class act, Tom sent me a photo of our opening scene. On the picture, he wrote, "Stop! I said stop trying to look like me." and signed it. That picture stands tall on my office wall. I take a lot of pride in that and I thank Tom for doing right by me.

The best part of my *Jerry Maguire* experience was dealing with actors Tom Cruise, Cuba Gooding Jr., Jay Mohr, Donal Logue, and Renee Zellweger.

Cuba was also a super guy. He had tremendous passion for his role and really transformed himself into the player Rod Tidwell. What strikes me about him is that he always looks you in your eye and raises his chin when you speak with him. He is a very genuine person.

Jay and Donal are real-life comedians and were a lot of fun. I remembered Logue as the crazy cab driver who made some appearances on MTV. I got a kick out of his work. And it was great the way they continually told jokes and poked fun at me. Mohr was a classic. He has a great sense of humor and is very likable. These two guys really studied my character and seemed to really enjoy my personality. After watching me so much on film, they were giddy to talk with me and see what I was like in person. It was flattering that such talented, young actors took such a strong interest in me. As a matter of fact, Mohr was quoted in the *Fort Lauderdale Sentinel,* saying, "I looked at a lot of video tape of agents talking about their work, how they do what they do, and the guy that kept sticking in my mind was Rosenhaus. He went on for hours. I brought my manager into the room and said, 'You've got to see this guy. He's an animal.' "

I had a great time hanging out with Mohr and Logue. We spent hours making fun of each other and taking shots. I was glad to see that I could hang in there with the big timers when it came to verbal jousts. You know you're good when you can make two comedians laugh constantly. I'm glad to say I developed a friendship with Mohr and we keep in touch. In fact he left a message recently congratulating me on a player signing that he read about in the newspaper.

Last but not least I enjoyed working with and getting to

know Renee. She is as sweet and pretty in person as she was in the movie. She does not put up a front and was very likeable. I spoke with her at great length. Her character was very realistic and is just about the only type of woman who could put up with being married to a young, successful sports agent. I had a good time hanging out with her at the movie wrap party.

But most of my role with the movie was working several years with Cameron Crowe and his staff. I told Cameron stories about my first client, Robert Massey, and how he stuck with me when I no longer had the backing of a big agent firm—exactly as Cuba Gooding's character did when Jerry Maguire was fired by his firm. I told Cameron about risky negotiations, where Leon Searcy chose to play out his contract, risk injury, and was fortunately rewarded with a monster deal. I told him about Randal Hill's loyalty to me when he was traded from the Dolphins to the Arizona Cardinals.

One of the things that I really liked about *Jerry Maguire* was that it captured the passion and the spirit that it takes to be successful in this business. My brother Jason and I have a real passion and a love for what we do. This is not just a job, it's a way of life. And it was a way of life for Jerry Maguire. In his work he invested his soul in his clients, it was his life blood, it was everything to him. It's precisely the same with us.

In Jerry Maguire, you saw a guy who loved his clients, went the extra yard for them, was conscientious, did whatever he could to help them. With Rod Tidwell—the fictional wide receiver who was the only client to stick with Jerry Maguire—you saw how much Rod appreciated Jerry's contributions. Not only did he feel that Jerry contributed to him by negotiating a whopping contract, but he appreciated the help off the field with his family, with his personal life. He appreciated that Jerry helped him become the best player he could be by giving him advice about playing the game with his heart, not his head, and playing for the love of the game, playing the game like a kid, not a businessman. In this movie, the agent helped Rod play better and have a successful season. That's not fiction.

But to do that, Jerry Maguire had to be strong enough to tell his only remaining client some of the negative things that Rod was doing. That's an important role for an agent to play. As an agent you absolutely, positively have to tell a client the truth, not necessarily what the client wants to hear. You have to tell the client what's best for him. You have to be brutally honest. It may get you fired, it may get you canned, it may get the client to hate you, but you owe it to the client to tell him what's best for him, not what's best for you. Jerry Maguire gave his client good advice and they both won as a result. You must always be truthful with your client. Even if the truth hurts. Believe me, if you don't, it will hurt a lot more in the end.

In the movie, you also got a very true picture of the competition, the fierce battling, that exists between agents. It was very realistic to see the other agents like Bob Sugar try to undercut and backstab Jerry Maguire. There are rules that agents follow when it comes to beating other competitors. Agents are hurting one another everyday in this business.

There is a lot of animosity and personal vendettas. It is sad to see how pathetic agents can act in the throes of competition and recruiting. The scenes where Sugar is bad-mouthing and stealing clients away from Maguire happen every day in the agent business. There was no exaggeration of this aspect.

In the movie you saw how ruthless the business can be. But you also saw how loyalty can overcome that ruthlessness. You saw the beauty of a relationship, a bond made with Rod Tidwell. That was my favorite part of the movie— seeing the camaraderie, the loyalty, the character, the relationship that Maguire had with Tidwell. It was a great thing to see two people connect. It didn't matter what color they were, how rich, what their philosophies were in life, those guys were in it together. Those guys were a team. They were a partnership. When you really have it, that loyalty is the most rewarding part of this business.

Good agents want to help their clients excel, help them

succeed, help them make money, help them invest their money, and set them up for life. You want to watch their families feel secure. That's what makes me tick when it comes to this business. And that's what made Jerry Maguire tick, too.

There was a lot of reality in the movie when it showed the constant roller coaster Jerry Maguire was on. This isn't always the glamorous business everyone always imagines. Believe me, an agent has to pay his dues. It is filled with dramatic highs and crushing lows. In *Jerry Maguire,* you saw an agent who was on the verge of signing the number one pick of the draft, Frank Cushman. He was on top of the world when he believed he had the number one pick signed. That's what this business can do for you, it puts you on top of the world. For that moment, you are the man.

Then, in the blink of an eye, the player signed with your most hated rival. Do you know how hard it is to get the number one pick of the draft? It's an unbelievable accomplishment. Maguire had that guy and lost him. Why did he lose him? Because the number one pick was jealous of the amount of attention Jerry was paying to Rod Tidwell. I'm here to tell you how true that is. All of us, Leigh Steinberg, Marvin Demoff, David Falk, and me, the top agents in this sport, have lost clients. When that happens, you don't feel like the man anymore, you feel like you have hit rock bottom. You could have sixty great players, and when you have one guy for whom things don't turn out, you could go right to the bottom. It is painful to lose a client because no matter what you have accomplished or who you have signed in the past, this business is about what you have done lately.

But you can't take time to feel sorry for yourself. You've got to figure out what happened and make sure it doesn't happen again. Success in this business comes only when you understand that adversity makes the strong stronger and the weak weaker. You must keep everything in perspective. So many guys have come and gone. I've seen so many agents represent a guy and disappear. They move on to something else because they can't handle the battle and the extreme pressure. But that's what life is all about. Life is a struggle. So many of my colleagues can't hack it, I've seen them quit.

I've seen them fall apart in the face of adversity. It isn't happening with me. No matter what adversity I go through you'll never see me quit. I hate to lose. But you will never see me dwell on defeat. I refuse to let a negative get me down for too long. I will bounce right back even stronger than I was before. I have learned to roll with the punches and continue to fight. Like I once heard Don Shula say, "I don't get ulcers, I give them." Life is full of constant challenges and there is no room or time to be depressed. I look at each day as a new opportunity.

It was great that they showed Jerry Maguire and Rod Tidwell making the right decision on his contract negotiations. I just hope the public understood what a gamble that was. The story would have been much different—and probably less successful at the box office—had they gambled and lost. But that does happen all the time in the NFL. I hope the public now realizes what players, agents, and teams go through in the NFL. When you read in the transaction section that a player has been cut or a team executive has been fired, understand that this is not just a statistic. There are human beings, people with families, involved.

There are more than just games being played. There are more than just wins and losses. There are lives on the line. Children's futures are at stake. Generations may depend on whether a player gets a contract or not. I deal with these pressures every day. I realize that if I don't get a player a contract, then his kids may not get the chance to go to college. That is why I take my job so seriously and work as hard as I do. Usually, when a team is trying to drive you into signing a unsatisfactory deal, they put your client down— just as they did in the movie when the Cardinals told Jerry Maguire that Rod Tidwell was undersized as a receiver. They're obviously trying to make you feel as if you need to take whatever they give.

That's another trick you hear every day in this job. The team negotiator often talks your player down so badly, it makes you wonder why they want the guy. You just have to realize that is part of the negotiating game. As agents we do the same thing, only it's in the other direction. We really pump the players up. I often try to make my players out to be like Superman. If you hear me talk to a team describing my player, you would think I am representing a god. The team talks the player down, while the agent hypes the player up. Eventually the team and agent will find the common ground and get the deal done where it should be. No player is ever as bad as the team makes him out to be or as good as his agent swears he is. The hardest part is when the player really isn't very good, and the agent has to get on his hands and knees to beg the team to sign him. Sometimes this business can be humiliating. It can make a prideful man lose his ego. I have often had to take a lot of crap from a team just to get them to sign one of my guys. Like Jerry Maguire said, this can be a pride-swallowing business.

The movie was a two-hour lesson on the ups and downs of this business. I felt as if I was there in each scene. I felt like I was there with Jerry at the beginning when his player was arrested. I felt like I was there with him when he had a player that had a problem with drugs. I have been there in real life. I felt like I was there when he had a player land in a hospital bed, with his career in jeopardy. I felt like I was there with him when he lost his girlfriend because of his commitment to his profession. I felt like I was there with him when he lost a lot of his clients. I felt like I was there with him when he signed that top guy, I know that feeling. I've been there. I was there in his stories about working with your client to win the big contract. I've been at that fax machine and gotten both types of offers, the lousy ones and the good ones. I've been there on draft day and I've left the draft feeling great. I've left others not feeling so great. I've had the feeling of having my client picked early. I've also had the feeling of waiting what seemed like an eternity for a guy to get picked. I felt like I was there with him on his many road trips to visit his clients, and when he had to take a lot of crap from the team executive. You get the idea. I could go on and on.

Jerry Maguire was especially good for the business because it cast our profession in a whole different light. Instead of being the money-grubbing slimeballs who are more concerned about ruining teams than we are about improving the game, the movie showed we are human, full of emotion, suffering through good times and bad, but still in love with what we do. Agents were despised by the public, loathed by the teams, and downplayed in the media.

But with Tom Cruise playing a good-guy agent, our image has improved dramatically. The perception of my life has changed a lot since the movie. Instead of people looking at me as a shady character, I now have a good guy identity. People look at me and say, "There's Jerry Maguire," or "Show me the money," instead of what they used to say: "Look, it's that agent guy." People used to wonder what I would do as an agent. The sports agent business was a mysterious profession. Now, everybody in the world knows what I do—I do what Tom Cruise did in the movie. People can identify my traits and characteristics with the Jerry Maguire character. People no longer view me strictly as "The Shark." Ever since the movie, hardly a day has gone by where somebody hasn't said to me "Show me the money!" or "Hey, it's Tom Cruise," or "Did they make the movie about you?" People constantly associate me with Cruise/Maguire. It was the best thing that ever happened to me. I can't keep the women off me. They love my connection with the movie. The movie has also helped my recruiting, as many players know that I contributed to the movie and are very impressed.

The movie's success has prompted a flood of new agents to climb into the business. People were clueless about what we do, then *Jerry Maguire* came along and made every agent look good. All of a sudden now agents are Tom Cruise. It glamorized the profession. There was fierce competition in this business before the movie came out. Can you imagine the competition now? Everybody wants to be an agent. Even Johnnie Cochran, O. J. Simpson's Defense Attorney, has recently become a sports agent. In fact, so many people wanted to be an agent a year ago—remember, this was before the movie debuted—that when I held a seminar on the business, dozens of people signed up. It was a big success. If I were to hold that seminar again today, I'd probably have five times that amount because of the popularity of *Jerry Maguire,* not to mention that *Arliss,* the HBO comedy series starring Robert Wuhl, is a great show and a big hit.

Today, everywhere I go, everybody wants to know more about agents. Everybody wants to know more about *Jerry Maguire.* To all these new agents that have joined our business, I'm glad you're here. That's more agents for me to beat up on. More competition for me to crush. Let me make something clear, I don't wish these guys ill-will. There's not one agent out there that I personally despise or would like to see fail. I don't wish for these guys to lose, but I like to win. It's nothing personal.

It's a pleasure to compete and beat your competition. It is my high. Just remember that *Jerry Maguire* only glossed over the real challenges of our job. I've got a challenge every single day: a negotiation, helping a player invest his money, getting marketing deals, making a decision on whether a client will win or lose in free agency, a player in trouble off the field, helping a player with his family life, helping a guy get ready for the draft, dealing with the draft, dealing with rookies. Man, this isn't easy. You heard of the city that never sleeps, well, this is the job that never sleeps. Now you know why we picked this book's title, *A Shark Never Sleeps.*

At this stage, I'm told there is not a sequel in the works. But if there is going to be, I'm sure it will show Jerry Maguire building from his one comeback client to rival the folks who once spurned him. He'll get those first-round picks and he'll keep them this time. To get to the top, he's going to have to be tough, and he's going to have to beat a bunch of his competitor agents to the punch. Sound familiar? Maybe one day they'll even make a movie about my life story. Stranger things have happened.

Epilogue

To me, a mission statement asks two questions, "Who am I?" and "Where do I go from here?"

Here's my mission statement: First, I'll tell you who I am. As a kid I loved the NFL more than anything. From the days I would take my younger brother out of his crib and have him watch football with me, I formed a bond with Jason that has lasted a lifetime and is stronger than steel. My childhood heroes were the comic-book characters Batman and Conan the Barbarian. I spent countless hours studying for school and training in karate trying to emulate them. I forged a friendship with the Dolphin and University of Miami football players that I admired.

I joined the sports agent profession at an age when most of my competitors were old enough to be my father. I left a powerful sports agency firm to go out on my own with only one client. I took on the toughest negotiator in the NFL for that one client while moonlighting as a Duke Law student. After graduating from law school I lived at home with my parents and worked out of my mom's interior design office while trying to sign big-time clients and negotiate multimillion-dollar contracts.

I survived the trade of one of my top clients. I helped

dozens of clients sign mega contracts and find long-term financial security. I overcame the setback of being dismissed by my superstar client. I dominated the local football teams that I grew up with. I represented the top players in the country and signed them to record-breaking deals. I stood by my clients during times of great adversity and helped them to overcome.

I am the only sports agent in history to be on the cover of *Sports Illustrated.* I worked with Tom Cruise to help make *Jerry Maguire* a smashing success. I was featured in *GQ* and *Forbes,* on ESPN, CNN, ABC and several other major media sources. I have become a celebrity in my home town. I date some of the most beautiful women around. I represented several players that I idolized as a youth. I worked hard and paid my dues. For that I acquired power, fame, and fortune.

Nevertheless, I am still genuine. I still watch the players practice, read the daily sports pages, all of the football magazines, and surf the net for football news. I still love watching the NFL games with Jason and my dad. I am still a little kid at heart. I haven't changed. Jason and I are a team, Batman and Robin, just as we were as kids.

This past off-season, I called Miami Dolphins special teams coach Mike Westhoff to arrange a workout for my client, kicker Olindo Mare.

The workout was held at a local Fort Lauderdale high school football field. As Olindo was kicking some field goals and kickoffs, we were shorthanded as there was no one else to catch the balls and throw them back. Dressed in our suits, suspenders, ties, and boots, we rolled our sleeves up and fielded the kicks. When Olindo kicked a couple over the fence, we jumped the fence and sliced our hands on the rusted barbs. We had fun. Jason even joked with Coach Westhoff about getting a tryout for us as return guys. Westhoff responded, "You guys dropped a few, but I liked the effort."

But this isn't effort to us. That was just another day. Jason and I are constantly working out with and playing around with our clients. Whether it is trying to tackle running back Troy Davis in the sand, or playing catch with Warren Sapp, or trying to wrestle big 315-lb. Tim Bowens, this is what I call fun. I take pride in my skills as a sandlot football player.

One time before training camp started I held my own "Camp Rosenhaus." With wide receivers Brett Perriman and Randal Hill, and cornerbacks J.B. Brown and Robert Massey, Jason and I tried our hand at quarterback and played a couple of games. These guys are friends to me, not just clients, which makes me naturally want to see them succeed.

Working as a team with my clients is what I love about this business. When you see one of my clients score a touchdown or make a great play, I will be there watching and cheering. For when they win, I win; and when they lose, I lose. We are in this together. They are my family.

As for where I go from here? I thought about that as I put Don Shula's induction into the Pro Football Hall of Fame this year into perspective. I remember vividly growing up and idolizing Shula as the head coach of the Dolphins. His unprecedented success in making the Miami Dolphins into champions was a big part of my maturation into a Dolphin fan and evolution into becoming an agent. It was a dream come true to meet with Shula, earn his respect as a business associate, and join him as a powerful figure in the NFL. Now, one thing I'd like to do would be to join him again, this time as the first agent to be inducted in the Pro Football Hall of Fame.

As far as where I go from here on a day-to-day basis, every day I fight to improve my life, my family's life, and the lives of my clients. I must always rise to the occasion and be ready at any time. You never know when opportunity knocks and where danger lurks. That is why the Shark never sleeps.

This isn't a job, it is a way of life. I am having fun and doing well. But not well enough. I am on a mission to be the best ever. This Shark is always hungry, and I want much more. I am determined to get the best contracts, sign the top players, and make the NFL even better. I want the players to love me, the teams to respect me, and my competitors to envy me. I want the fans to be happy. I want my clients to be good role models. I want professional sports to thrive. And that's just for starters.

I will not stop until I get there. There will be obstacles and setbacks. But in the end I will still be standing. In the end, I will be the ultimate winner.

This is why I am called the Shark. And this is why I am much more. But whatever I am, it is the man I wanted to become when I was a little boy thinking about my future. I am not just another shark in a suit. The players who make it to the NFL have endured so much to get there and they entrust their futures and the fate of their families to my care. To them, the Shark is a friend, a protector who guides them through the rough seas. And believe me, the seas get rough.

One minute you're on a pleasure cruise to fantasy island, the next minute you're caught in a torrential storm in the Bermuda triangle. Things can change at any moment. For instance, on a Thursday afternoon, July 17, 1997, I was out at Dolphin practice watching training camp with Jason, my father, Robert, and my cousins, Jordan and Brett Rosenhaus. We all felt like a million bucks.

Jason and I had gotten Yatil Green's contract done early in June. We set a trend in getting the guaranteed money up front that few could follow. In fact, Yatil's contract turned out to be one of the best in the round as he got more signing-bonus money and more money overall than his hometown buddy, Reinard Wilson, who was drafted ahead of him.

As for the Dolphins, they were ecstatic that Yatil was signed so early. They were extremely happy with Yatil's work ethic, his aptitude for picking up the offense, and his dominating play on the field. He was unstoppable. He was taking short passes and outrunning everyone with his speed to sprint sixty yards for a touchdown. At 6'2", and weighing over two hundred pounds, he was breaking tackles and bouncing would-be tacklers off of him. And most of all, it seemed like every time Dan Marino looked Yatil's way, he was running past everyone in the secondary, catching touchdowns. He was everything Jimmy Johnson wanted in a wide receiver. And he was everything I want in a client.

As you could see, we were all smiles as we watched Yatil line up wide with the third-string quarterback taking the snap. Yatil ran a deep route, blowing by the cornerback who was struggling to keep up. Yatil raised his hand for the quarterback to see him wide open for a bomb. The quarterback saw him and threw the deep ball. Unfortunately, the pass got caught up in the wind and was behind Yatil. Yatil slowed down, stopped, spun around, and jumped up for the ball. Yatil leaped high in the air and reached over the cornerback. As Yatil came down on his right leg, his cleat got caught in the turf and he twisted his knee. The right leg collapsed from the torque. Right in front of my very eyes, Yatil was on his back, grabbing his knee, writhing in agony.

In a devastating blow, Yatil had torn his anterior cruciate ligament, his quadriceps muscle and meniscus cartilage in his right knee. Jason and I watched in horror for what seemed to be an eternity as the team doctors and trainers examined Yatil's knee. My heart sank as I watched them cart Yatil off the field. It was just that day that an article appeared in the paper heralding Yatil's impressive start as a pro. I knew that Yatil was seriously hurt the minute I saw Jimmy Johnson's flush red face.

To say that a lot went through my mind at that moment would be a gross understatement. Just the night before, Jason, Yatil and I went to get some dinner at a local restaurant. Fans were coming up to Yatil left and right, asking for autographs. A local superstar who was going to make the difference in the Dolphins' offense this year to take them to the Super Bowl, Yatil was the man in this town. He was on top of the world. It felt great to be his agent. This was my dream come true.

And now here he was, lying on his back with his right knee injured. In the blink of an eye, his season was over before it even started. In an instant, my life had just changed immensely.

Two days later, at 6:30 in the morning, Jason and I were in Yatil's hospital room waiting for the nurse to wheel him in for surgery. We encouraged him to keep his chin up, that he would be back next year better than ever.

Yatil didn't need the encouragement. He was strong and very positive. He wasn't feeling sorry for himself, or asking, "Why did this happen to me?" He was hungry to come back and make his knee stronger than it ever was.

And I wasn't feeling sorry for myself either. Yeah, it hurt. Of course it hurt. But you have to deal with this part of the NFL. The NFL isn't always fair. That is why, in my view, the NFL could stand for the "Not Fair League." There is always going to be adversity, there are always going to be setbacks and disappointments.

Sure, it would have been a lot of fun to watch Yatil play with the Dolphins this year. Sure, I worked extremely hard to make him a Rosenhaus Sports client. Sure, I went through a roller-coaster ride on Draft Day. Sure, it felt great to get Yatil's contract done before the rest of the other first-round picks. Sure, Yatil looked like he was on his way to being AFC Rookie of the Year and the best young receiver in the league.

But that was yesterday. Today, Yatil is on crutches. As for tomorrow, Yatil Green will be back. When Yatil's grandfather, Sam Green, passed away during Yatil's final season with the Hurricanes, Yatil promised him that he would catch a touchdown pass in the NFL. And no matter what it takes, whatever the cost, whatever the pain, however long it takes, Yatil Green will be back for the Miami Dolphins and will catch that touchdown pass. And when you see Yatil Green hold that ball high in the air and point toward the sky, you will know why. When you see the tears in his eyes as he tells his grandfather up above that was for him, you will know why. And when you see me yell in victory and celebrate, you will know why. THIS is the NFL. THIS is what the NFL is all about.

This is what life is all about. Overcoming the sadness and pain, struggling to make it through the lowest valley, and fighting to reach the highest mountaintop. The true measure of a person is how well he handles himself during tough times. The agent profession is not for the meek.

Every year hotshot agents come along and think they can take me on and move me out. And every year I remember something Dan Marino said several years ago when a hotshot rookie made a sarcastic remark about Dan's age. With a face of stone and eyes of fire, Marino turned to the laughing rookie and said, "I was here when you got here, and I'll be here when you're gone."

I never forgot that and neither did any other player who was there in the locker room that day. Especially since that rookie is no longer on the team. And so when I remember all of the newcomer agents who challenged me, I can't help but notice that they are gone too. Whether I had something to do with that, who can say?

What I can say is that this was a lesson they learned the hard way. But this is a lesson all agents learn. All agents will face setbacks and have their share of disappointments. I have had my share and will continue to have my share, but I will grow stronger and continue to thrive in this business, because I have been through more victories and adversity in this business than any of them ever will.

Yes, I have lost some heartbreaking battles. But I have won a lot more than I lost. I help my clients and my friends live out their dreams, and in doing so, I am living mine out as well. I am full of enthusiasm for my work. I wake up every day looking forward to new challenges. Every day something happens in this business, and I am ready to face it head on to make it work out for the best.

The action is so fast-paced and high-staked, I ask you, who has time to sleep? I recently got a call from New York Jets Head Coach Bill Parcells, the "Big Tuna," at 7:00 A.M. When I answered the phone, saying, "Rosenhaus Sports," sharp and alert, Parcells was surprised that I was already working at that hour.

I said, "Coach I have been working since 6:00 A.M."

He asked what time I went to sleep, and I said 2:00 A.M. He responded "Drew, you're the eager beaver. That is why you are so successful, you're always working and never sleep."

241

I told the "Big Tuna" that it was easy for me to work hard since I love what I do. Dealing with warriors like Bill Parcells and Jimmy Johnson is the best. But if you can't match up and earn their respect, the "Big Tuna" will get you canned.

In this NFL business, the competition is fierce, the negotiations can be strenuous, the fans are unforgiving, and the agent is always to blame. But none of that matters to me. What matters to me is that feeling I get when my client hugs me out of gratitude for negotiating the multimillion-dollar contract that gives him financial security for life. That is why I am in this business. I swear it.

So bring on all those who challenge me, for I refuse to be beaten. I love to compete. I love the struggle. I love to battle back from adversity. I love to dream. And I love to win. This is who I am. This is what I do.

As for what I will do and what will happen in the future, I know only one thing for sure: you will see more of Drew Rosenhaus. A lot more. So be advised, if you are my opponent or rival, you better beware of the Shark when you venture out into my waters.